ILLUSTRATION INDEX

Third Edition

by

ROGER C. GREER

The Scarecrow Press, Inc.
Metuchen, N.J.   1973

Covers July 1963 through Dec. 1971

Library of Congress Cataloging in Publication Data

Greer, Roger C   1928-
   Illustration index.

   Previous editions by L. E. Vance and E. M. Tracey.
   1. Pictures--Indexes.   I. Vance, Lucile E.
Illustration index.   II. Title.
N7525.G72 1973   011   72-10918
ISBN 0-8108-0568-5

Copyright 1973 by Roger C. Greer

PREFACE
to the Third Edition

The third edition of the Illustration Index continues the general scope and pattern of indexing of the first and second editions.
Covering the period from July 1, 1963 through December 31, 1971,
it is expanded and updated to incorporate new subject trends, new
fields of endeavor, historical events, activities and products of
man's unceasing imagination and energy.

According to the pattern established by Lucile E. Vance in
compiling the first edition of the Index (1957) and its Supplement
(1961), the present work was originally intended to be a supplement
to the second edition (1966) of the Index. The second edition, ex-
tending coverage through June 1963, was compiled jointly by Lucile
E. Vance and Esther M. Tracey. Although Miss Tracey's name
was new to the title page of the Index, she was not a newcomer to
the project. As they indicated in the preface to the second edition,
both compilers were, staff members of the Grand Rapids, Michigan
Public Library "... when the plan for the first Illustration Index
was launched."

Following publication of the second edition in 1966, Miss
Tracey began collecting entries for a supplement. Her work is
represented by about half of the entries in the present edition. In
the fall of 1968, Miss Tracey decided to ask the Scarecrow
Press to invite someone to take over her work and complete
the project. I accepted the invitation. This third edition, then,
is the result of merging entries compiled by Miss Tracey and
by me. Our work was done independently in time and place. As
time passed and entries accumulated, the need for a supplement
appeared less urgent than the need for an entirely new publication.
Therefore, it should be understood that the present work does not
follow the procedure of the second edition--that is, of incorporating

iii

the entries of the previous edition. On the contrary, this edition should be used as a companion volume, for it covers only the years subsequent to 1963.

The Index is intended to serve the needs of library users of all types of libraries--school, public, academic, and special. The needs of a variety of library users from the elementary school child to the university professor, hobbyist to consumer, sportsman to fashion designer, or teacher to traveler have been the bases for inclusion of material. Nevertheless, the specific periodicals indexed [listed following the preface] have been selected partly on the basis of their availability in the average small and medium-sized public library and school media center. In addition, there was an attempt to continue coverage of those publications which were included in the earlier editions of the Index. It will be noted that Theater Arts has not been included because it ceased publication very shortly after the beginning of the period covered in this edition. No comparable periodical was available to include in its place. However, we feel that material relating to the theater--costume, stage settings, etc.--is well represented by selections from Life, National Geographic, and other periodicals.

Look magazine terminated in October 1971. Because of its continued availability in back files of libraries, it has been indexed through the last issue. Ebony has been added to the list of periodicals indexed for this edition. As with the others, coverage begins with the July 1963 issue. Ideals magazine is excluded from this edition because back files of this publication are not often available to the Index user.

The scope of the present work has remained as consistent as possible with the first and second editions. Therefore, the following subjects are excluded: furniture, nature subjects, animals, paintings, and individual personalities. In all of these instances, an illustration is included if the item portrays a historical object or event, sporting activities, costumes, or topics of general interest. Special emphasis has been given, as usual, to costumes; fashion designs; theatrical stage settings; matter illustrative of various sports and sporting activities--games, teams, players,

iv

and equipment. Topics of interest to hobbyists, especially collec-
tors, and projects of interest to teachers such as puppetry, macrame, papier maché creations, and other activities for children
have also been stressed. Scientific subjects such as heart transplants, undersea and space exploration, and the new technological
creations in the automobile and aircraft industries are generously
represented.

Material depicting the history and cultures of various peoples
and countries of the world has received continued emphasis. References are given for geographical identifications--rivers, lakes,
oceans, islands, mountains. Similarly, political identifications such
as countries, states, provinces, cities and communities are included as are cultural identifications such as monuments, buildings,
bridges, canals, waterways, etc.

The majority of the illustrations referred to are photographs.
If the illustration is not a photograph, it is identified as one of the
following: chart, drawing, diagram, painting, lithograph, sketch,
etching, or watercolor. Color illustrations are identified by "(col)."
Maps are found under the heading "Map, Decorative" as in earlier
editions. In many instances, the practice of including descriptive
information has been continued. Whenever possible, this descriptive
information employs the same terminology as that used in the con-
text of the illustration.

The following represents examples of entries and their arrangement within a particular subject category.

UNDERSEA EXPLORATION
    Look 32: 20-24 (col), 25
    Mar 5 '68
UNDERSEA EXPLORATION--
    DEEPSTAR--ATLANTIC
    Nat Geog. 139: 110-129 (col)
    Jan '71
UNDERSEA EXPLORATION--
    OCEANIC FOUNDATION--
    HAWAII
    Life 68: 70-73 (col) Mar 6
    '70

UNDERSEA EXPLORATION--
    TEKTITE II--GREAT LAME-
    SHUR BAY
    Nat Geog 140: 257-289 (col)
    290-295 (drawings) Aug '71
UNDERSEA LIFE
    Life 65: 69, 72-73 (col), 93
    Oct 4 '68
UNDERSEA LIVING--5 FEMALE
    DIVERS
    Life 69: 30-31 (col) July 17
    '70

In addition to the descriptive information mentioned above, each
entry contains: abbreviated title of the periodical, volume number,

pagination, date, and year. For illustrations appearing in books, references include the abbreviated title of the book and the page or pages. Arrangement of entries under a particular subject category are in chronological order.

Various sources have been used as guides for the subject headings developed in this edition. The more prominent among these sources in addition to the second edition of the Illustration Index are: Sears List of Subject Headings, 9th ed., H. W. Wilson Company, 1965; Subject Headings Used in the Dictionary Catalogs of the Library of Congress, 7th ed., Library of Congress, Washington, D. C., 1966 and Supplements. In addition, I have had to adapt and invent subject headings as well as "see" and "see also" references. Many users of earlier editions suggested that more "see" and "see also" references be included; I have made an effort to do so.

I wish to express appreciation for the resources and assistance provided by the library staffs of the Syracuse University Library, Syracuse Public Library, and the Onondaga Free Library of Onondaga Hill, New York. Although many people have contributed to the compilation of the present edition, it would not exist except for the fundamental assistance in indexing, filing, typing, organizing, and editing provided by my secretary, Ann Douglass. No word of thanks can adequately describe the debt that is owed to her.

Roger C. Greer

July, 1972
Syracuse, New York

BOOKS AND PERIODICALS INDEXED

American Heritage. v. 14-22, July 1963-December 1971

Ebony. v. 19-27, July 1963-December 1971

Grade Teacher. v. 80-89, July 1963-December 1971

Hobbies. v. 68-76, July 1963-December 1971

Holiday. v. 34-50, July 1963-December 1971

Instructor. v. 72-81, July 1963-December 1971

Life. v. 55-71, July 1963-December 1971

Look. v. 27-35, July 1963-October 1971

National Geographic Magazine. v. 124-140, July 1963-December 1971

National Geographic Society. American's Wonderlands: The Scenic National Parks and Monuments of the United States, new enlarged edition, 1966.

School Arts. v. 62-71, July 1963-December 1971

Sports Illustrated. v. 19-35, July 1963-December 1971

Travel. v. 120-136, July 1963-December 1971

Von Braun, Wernher, and Frederick Ordway. History of Rocketry and Space Travel. New York: Crowell, 1966

ILLUSTRATION INDEX

A-1 (artificial satellites). See
  ARTIFICIAL SATELLITES--
  FRANCE--A-1
ABBEYS. See also MONAS-
  TERIES and names of indi-
  vidual abbeys, e. g. WEST-
  MINSTER ABBEY
ABBEYS--TORRE--TORQUAY,
  ENGLAND
  Nat Geog 124: 252 (col) Aug
  '63
ABIDJAN (night scene)
  Nat Geog 130: 156-7 (col)
  Aug '66
ABORIGINES--AUSTRALIA. See
  AUSTRALIA--NATIVE RACES
  --ABORIGINES
ABU SIMBEL, TEMPLES OF
  Nat Geog 127: 630-5 (col) May
  '65
  Nat Geog 129: 694-741 (col)
  May '66
ACADIA NATIONAL PARK
  America's Wonderlands, p.
  484-9 (col)
ACADIANS IN LOUISIANA
  Nat Geog 129: 352-90 (col)
  Mar '66
ACAPULCO, MEXICO
  Nat Geog 126: 848-77 (col)
  Dec '64
  Holiday 44: 69-73 (col) July
  '68
ACCORDIONS
  Nat Geog 129: 883 (col) June
  '66
ACROBATS
  Nat Geog 127: 294-5 (col)
  Mar '65
ACROPOLIS--ATHENS, GREECE
  Nat Geog 124: 100-2, 114-15
  (col) July '63
ACROPOLIS--PROPYLAEA--
  ATHENS, GREECE

Nat Geog 124: 100-1, 114,
  117 (col) July '63
ACUPUNCTURE
  Life 71: 32-35 Aug 13 '71
ADAMS HOUSE--QUINCY, MASS.
  Nat Geog 126: 660 (col) Nov
  '64
ADDIS ABABA
  Nat Geog 127: 572-3 (col)
  Apr '65
AEOLUS (rocket). See ROCK-
  ETS, SOUNDING--AUSTRALIA
  --AEOLUS
AEROBEE (rocket). See ROCK-
  ETS, SOUNDING--U. S. --
  AEROBEE
AFGHANISTAN
  Life 59: 98A Dec 10 '65
  Nat Geog 134: 298-345 (col)
  Sept '68
  Travel 136: 40-45 (col) Nov
  '71
AFRICA--NATIVE RACES--
  BANTU
  Nat Geog 124: 277 (col) Aug
  '63
AFRICA--NATIVE RACES--
  KIKUYU
  Nat Geog 127: 198-9 Feb '65
AFRICA--NATIVE RACES--
  MASSAI
  Life 57: front cover, 76-8
  July 17 '64
  Nat Geog 127: 216-17, 219
  (col) Feb '65
  Nat Geog 130: 704-5 (col)
  Nov '66
AFRICA HALL--ADDIS ABABA
  Nat Geog 127: 574-5 (col)
  Apr '65
AFRICAN TRIBES--ZULU
  Nat Geog 140: 738-775 (col)
  Dec '71
AGA KHAN III--MAUSOLEUM--

9

ASWAN, EGYPT
Nat Geog 127: 617 (col) May
'65
AGED--HOUSING--LEISURE
WORLD (near Los Angeles)
--CALIF.
Life 55: 93-100 Nov 8 '63
AGENA (rocket). See ROCK-
ETS--CARRIERS--U. S. --
AGENA B; AGENA D
AIR BASES--DA NANG, VIET-
NAM (Republic)
Nat Geog 128: 306-7 (col)
Sept '65
AIR POLLUTION
Life 66: 38-50 (col) Feb 7
'69
Life 70: 61, 62-63 (col), 64
(map) Apr 16 '71
AIRBOATS
Nat Geog 124: 898 (col) Dec
'63
AIRCRAFT CARRIERS--U. S. --
CONSTELLATION
Life 57: 31 Aug 21 '64
AIRCRAFT CARRIERS--U. S. --
MIDWAY
Nat Geog 127: 179 (col) Feb
'65
AIRCRAFT CARRIERS, ATOMIC
POWERED--U. S. --ENTER-
PRISE
Nat Geog 127: 146-7, 153-5,
166 (col) Feb '65
AIRLINE STEWARDESSES
Ebony 20: 81-2, 84-6 Nov '64
AIRPLANE COLLISIONS. See
AVIATION--ACCIDENTS
AIRPLANE FLIGHTS--AMELIA
EARHART
Landing at Londonderry,
Northern Ireland, May 21,
1932 (first woman to fly
alone across the Atlantic)
Nat Geog 124: 570-1 Oct '63
AIRPLANE FLIGHTS--WRIGHT
BROTHERS FIRST, 1903
Nat Geog 128: 538 Oct '65
AIRPLANES, AMBULANCE
Nat Geog 129: 243 (col) Feb
'66
AIRPLANES--CESSNA 180
Nat Geog 128: 680 (col) Nov
'65

AIRPLANES--DC-3
Nat Geog 130: 184 (col) Aug
'66
AIRPLANES--DC-8
Nat Geog 129: 606-7 (col)
May '66
AIRPLANES--DC-9
Nat Geog 129: 607 (col) May
'66
AIRPLANES--HELIO COURIER
Nat Geog 126: 270 (col) Aug
'64
AIRPLANES, JET PROPELLED
--BOEING 707
Life 59: 20-24, 26-27 (col)
July 9 '65
AIRPLANES, JET PROPELLED
--BOEING 747
Holiday 46: 28-30, 32-35
(col) July '69
Ebony 25: 54-6 Sept '70
AIRPLANES, MILITARY (used
by belligerents in World War
I)
Life 56: 84 Mar 20 '64
AIRPLANES, MILITARY CARGO.
See AIRPLANES, MILITARY
TRANSPORT
AIRPLANES, MILITARY--ENG-
LAND--BEAUFIGHTER MK-1
(used in World War II)
Hist of Rocketry and Space
Travel, p. 91
AIRPLANES, MILITARY--ENG-
LAND--DE HAVILLAND
FIGHTER (used in World
War I)
Life 56: 68 Mar 20 '64
AIRPLANES, MILITARY--ENG-
LAND--DE HAVILLAND
PILOTLESS PLANE, 1917
Hist of Rocketry and Space
Travel, p. 38
AIRPLANES, MILITARY--ENG-
LAND--F. E. 2b NIGHT
BOMBER (used in World War
I)
Life 56: 68 Mar 20 '64
AIRPLANES, MILITARY--ENG-
LAND--MARTINSYDE FIGHT-
ER (used in World War I)
Life 56: 63 (col) Mar 20
'64

AIRPLANES, MILITARY--ENG-
LAND--R. E. 8 RECONNAIS-
SANCE PLANE (used in World
War I)
Life 56: 69 Mar 20 '64
AIRPLANES, MILITARY--ENG-
LAND--S. E. 5a FIGHTER
(used in World War I)
Life 56: 68-9 Mar 20 '64
AIRPLANES, MILITARY--ENG-
LAND--SEA VIXEN Mk-2
Hist of Rocketry and Space
Travel, p. 144
AIRPLANES, MILITARY--ENG-
LAND--SOPWITH CAMEL,
1918
Life 56: 71-2 Mar 20 '64
AIRPLANES, MILITARY--ENG-
LAND--VULCAN Mk-2
BOMBER
Hist of Rocketry and Space
Travel, p. 143
AIRPLANES, MILITARY--
FRANCE--NIEUPORT FIGHT-
ER (used in World War I)
Life 56: 68-9 Mar 20 '64
AIRPLANES, MILITARY--
FRANCE--SPAD FIGHTER
(used in World War I)
Life 56: 64 (col) Mar 20 '64
AIRPLANES, MILITARY--
FRANCE--VOISIN BOMBER
(used in World War I)
Life 56: 64-5 (col) Mar 20
'64
AIRPLANES, MILITARY--
GERMANY--ALBATROSS
(used in World War I)
Life 56: 62-3 (col) Mar 20
'64
AIRPLANES, MILITARY--
GERMANY--AVIATIK OB-
SERVATION PLANE (used in
World War I)
Life 56: 64 (col) Mar 20 '64
AIRPLANES, MILITARY--
GERMANY--FOKKER TRI-
PLANE (used in World War I)
Life 56: 75 (col) Mar 20 '64
AIRPLANES, MILITARY--RUS-
SIA--BADGER PHOTO-RECON-
NAISSANCE PLANE
Nat Geog 127: 180-1 Feb '65

AIRPLANES, MILITARY TRANS-
PORT--U. S. --BOEING STRAT-
OCRUISER ("Pregnant Guppy")
Life 55: 34A July 5 '63
AIRPLANES, MILITARY TRANS-
PORT--U. S. --C-123
Nat Geog 127: 52-3 (col) Jan
'65
Nat Geog 128: 298-9 (col)
Sept '65
AIRPLANES, MILITARY TRANS-
PORT--U. S. --C-130
Life 70: 40-41 May 21 '71
AIRPLANES, MILITARY TRANS-
PORT--U. S. --KC-135 (jet
tanker)
Nat Geog 128: 340, 342 (col)
Sept '65
AIRPLANES, MILITARY--U. S. --
A-4C SKYHAWK
Nat Geog 127: 160-1, 166 (col)
Feb '65
AIRPLANES, MILITARY--U. S. --
AIR FORCE
Nat Geog 128: 327-9 (col)
Sept '65
AIRPLANES--MILITARY--U. S. --
AIR FORCE ONE
Look 28: front cover, 86-7
(col), 88-92, 94-5 June
2 '64
AIRPLANES, MILITARY--U. S. --
A-11
Life 56: 26-7 Mar 13 '64
AIRPLANES, MILITARY--U. S. --
A-3D SKYWARRIOR
Nat Geog 127: 162 (col) Feb
'65
AIRPLANES, MILITARY--U. S. --
B-17
Life 57: 107-9 Nov 20 '64
Nat Geog 128: 295, 297 Sept
'65
AIRPLANES, MILITARY--U. S. --
B-52
Nat Geog 128: 316-17 (col)
Sept '65
Life 59: 36-41 (col) Nov 12
'65
AIRPLANES, MILITARY--U. S. --
B-70; XB-70A
Life 57: 129-30 Oct 2 '64
AIRPLANES, MILITARY--U. S. --

Am Heritage 21: 64-65 June '70

AIRPLANES IN INSECT CONTROL--CROP SPRAYING
Nat Geog 129: 620-1 (col) May '66

AIRPORTS--DULLES INTERNATIONAL--WASHINGTON, D. C.
Nat Geog 126: 774-5 (col) Dec '64

AIRPORTS--JOHN F. KENNEDY INTERNATIONAL--T. W. A. FLIGHT CENTER--NEW YORK
Nat Geog 126: 104-5 (col) July '64

AIRPORTS--O'HARE INTERNATIONAL--CHICAGO
Life 70: 56-66 Jan 8 '71

AIRPORTS--LOOTING
Life 70: 16-17 (col), 18-19, 23 (col) Feb 12 '71

AIRPORTS--UNITED STATES
Holiday 46: 48-51 (col) July '69

AIRSHIPS, 1909
Life 55: 76 (col) Nov 22 '63

AIRSHIPS--DIRIGIBLES--ENGLAND (used in World War I)
Life 56: 70-1 Mar 20 '64

AIRSHIPS--ZEPPELINS--GERMANY (used in World War I)
Life 56: 66 (col) Mar 20 '64

ALASKA
Nat Geog 127: 776-819 (col) June '65

ALASKA--MATANUSKA VALLEY
Nat Geog 127: 810-11 (col) June '65

ALEXANDER THE GREAT (drawings and photographs retracing his steps through history)
Nat Geog 133: 1-65 (col) Jan '68

ALEXANDRIA, EGYPT
Holiday 39: 68-77 (col) Feb '66

ALHAMBRA--COURT OF THE LIONS--GRANADA, SPAIN
Nat Geog 127: 306 (col) Mar '65

ALHAMBRA--GRANADA, SPAIN
Travel 132: 32, 34 Nov '69

ALICE SPRINGS, AUSTRALIA
Nat Geog 129: 230-57 (col) Feb '66

ALPS
Nat Geog 128: 350-95 (col) Sept '65

AMERICA--THE WEST (as depicted by Japanese artists in 1860's)
Am Heritage 14: 16-17 (col), 18, 19-30 (col) Aug '63

AMERICAN ARCHITECTURE. See ARCHITECTURE, AMERICAN--19TH CENT.

AMERICAN LEGION
Life 69: 28-29 (col), 30-31 Sept 11 '70

AMISH MENNONITES. See MENNONITES

AMMAN, JORDAN
Nat Geog 126: 788-9, 792-3 (col) Dec '64
Nat Geog 128: 273 (col) Aug '65

AMPHICARS. See AUTOMOBILES, AMPHIBIOUS

AMPHITHEATERS, ROMAN--ARLES, FRANCE
Nat Geog 126: 164-5 (col) Aug '64

AMPHORAE
Nat Geog 124: 141, 143, 148 (col) July '63

AMSTERDAM
Holiday 40: 83-85, 87-89 (col) Dec '66

AMUSEMENT PARKS--TIVOLI GARDENS--COPENHAGEN
Nat Geog 125: 288-9 (col) Feb '64

ANASAZI INDIANS. See INDIANS OF NORTH AMERICA --ANASAZI

ANCHORAGE, ALASKA (night scene)
Nat Geog 127: 808-9 (col) June '65

ANDALUSIA, SPAIN
Travel 134: 54-55 Oct '70

ANGEL ARCH--CANYONLANDS
America's Wonderlands, p. 228-9 (col)

ANGEL FALLS--VENEZUELA

Life 59: 80-82 (col) Oct 15
'65

ANGKOR WAT--CAMBODIA
Nat Geog 126: 528-9 (col)
Oct '64
Nat Geog 129: 266 (col) Feb
'66
Life 68: 50-57 (col) June 5
'70

ANGUILLA (island). See LEE-
WARD ISLANDS

ANIMAL SCULPTURE (papier-
mache)
Sch Arts 71: 22-23 Oct '71

ANNAPOLIS, MD.
Holiday 42: 68-73 (col) Oct '67

ANTARCTICA
Nat Geog 134: 568-592 (col)
Oct '68
Travel 136: 43 (col) Sept '71
Nat Geog 140: 623-655 (col)
Nov '71

ANTENNAS--BIG HORN--AND-
OVER, ME. (transmits and
receives signals from Early
Bird satellite)
Hist of Rocketry and Space
Travel, p. 186

ANTENNAS--GOLDSTONE,
CALIF. (for tracking space
vehicles)
Nat Geog 126: 695 (col) Nov
'64

ANTI-MISSILE MISSILES. See
GUIDED MISSILES

ANTI-SUBMARINE WARFARE.
See SUBMARINE WARFARE

ANTI-AIRCRAFT MISSILES.
See GUIDED MISSILES

ANTIGUA (island). See LEE-
WARD ISLANDS

ANTIQUITIES. See Name of
Country with Subdivision
Antiquities, e.g. TURKEY--
ANTIQUITIES

APACHE INDIANS. See INDI-
ANS OF NORTH AMERICA--
APACHE

APARTMENT HOUSES--CHICAGO
--MARINA CITY
Life 55: 78 July 19 '63

APARTMENT HOUSES--ENG-
LAND

Nat Geog 129: 760-1 (col)
June '66

APARTMENT HOUSES--IVORY
COAST
Nat Geog 130: 156-7 (col)
Aug '66

APARTMENT HOUSES--JAPAN
Nat Geog 126: 470-1 (col)
Oct '64

APARTMENT HOUSES--MARINA
CITY, CHICAGO
Look 28: 53-55 (col), 67-68
Jan 14 '64
Ebony 20: 106-8, 113 Nov '64
Ebony 20: 97 Aug '65

APARTMENT HOUSES--PORTU-
GAL
Nat Geog 128: 454-5 (col)
Oct '65

APARTMENT HOUSES--RU-
MANIA
Nat Geog 128: 72-3 (col)
July '65

APARTMENT HOUSES--RUSSIA
Life 55: 34-5 Sept 13 '63
Nat Geog 129: 332-3 (col)
Mar '66

APARTMENT HOUSES--SINGA-
PORE
Nat Geog 130: 294 (col) Aug
'66

APARTMENT HOUSES--U.S.
Look 28: 93-98 July 28 '64

APHRODISIAS--ANATOLIAN UP-
LANDS OF TURKEY
Nat Geog 132: 280-293 (col)
Aug '67

APPALACHIA--1914
Am Heritage 20: 26-28, 30,
32-41 Feb '69

APPALACHIAN REGION--POV-
ERTY AREA
Life 56: 54-65 Jan 31 '64

AQUANAUTS
Life 57: 75-7 (col) Sept 4 '64
Nat Geog 129: 498-537 (col)
Apr '66
Nat Geog 130: 421 (col) Sept
'66

AQUANAUTS, ANTARCTIC
Nat Geog 129: 56, 58 (col)
Jan '66

AQUARIAN ALPHAPHONE

Life 69: 60-61 Aug 21 '70
AQUARIUMS--SEATTLE
Nat Geog 129: 427 (col) Mar
'66
AQUEDUCTS--FRANCE
Nat Geog 126: 158-9 (col)
Aug '64
AQUEDUCTS--SPAIN, 1790
Nat Geog 127: 338-9 (col)
Mar '65
ARAN ISLANDS--IRELAND
Nat Geog 139: 544-573 (col)
Apr '71
ARCHEOLOGISTS WORKING
UNDERSEA
Nat Geog 124: 140-1 (col)
July '63
ARCHEOLOGY. See FOSSILS;
MAN, PREHISTORIC; MUM-
MIES
ARCHEOLOGY, SUBMARINE.
See BURIED TREASURE
ARCHITECTURE. See also
APARTMENT HOUSES;
CHURCHES; COURTHOUSES;
HOUSES; etc.
ARCHITECTURE, AMERICAN--
19TH CENTURY (cast iron
buildings in New York City)
Life 69: 56-61 Aug 14 '70
ARCHITECTURE, DOMESTIC--
CALIFORNIA
Nat Geog 129: 630-1, 653
(col) May '66
ARCHITECTURE, GOTHIC--
U.S.--17TH AND 18TH CENT.
(works of A.J. Davis)
Am Heritage 22: 28-47 (col)
Oct '71
ARCHITECTURE, MODERN
Life 58: 94-97 (col) Feb 26
'65
Ebony 26: 33-5 (col), 36 June
'71
Life 71: 8 (col) July 23 '71
ARCHITECTURE, MODERN
(American Republic Insurance
Company, Des Moines, Iowa)
Life 60: 54-57 (col) Apr 29
'66
ARCHITECTURE, MODERN (CBS
Building in N.Y.C.)

Life 60: 50-53 (col) Apr 29
'66
ARCHITECTURE, MODERN--
LABORATORIES
Life 70: 74-76 (col), 77, 78-
79 (col) Apr 16 '71
ARCHITECTURE, MODERN--
SKI CHALET
Life 64: 52-55 (col) Mar 22
'68
ARCHITECTURE, MODERN--
20TH CENT. (by Le Corbus-
ier)
Life 59: 118-21, 123 (col),
124 Sept 24 '65
ARCHITECTURE, MOORISH--
PORTUGAL
Nat Geog 128: 498 (col) Oct
'65
ARCTIC REGION
Life 66: 66B (col), 66C-66D
Apr 25 '69
Nat Geog 140: 484-519 (col)
Oct '71
ARCTIC REGION--STAIB EX-
PEDITION, 1964
Nat Geog 127: 254-81 (col)
Feb '65
ARCTIC RESEARCH LABORA-
TORY--BARROW, ALASKA
Nat Geog 128: 682-3 (col)
Nov '65
ARCTIC RESEARCH LABORA-
TORY--ICE STATION NO. 2
(Arlis II)
Nat Geog 128: 670-91 (col)
Nov '65
ARENAS. See Names of Cities
with Subdivision Arena, e.g.
PITTSBURGH--ARENA; etc.
ARGENTINA
Travel 126: 51-54 (col) Dec
'66
ARIEL (artificial satellite).
See ARTIFICIAL SATELLITES
--ENGLAND--ARIEL
ARLINGTON, VA.--ARLINGTON
NATIONAL CEMETERY
Look 28: 81-3 (col) Nov 17
'64
ARMOR. See also SHIELDS
ARMOR, MEDIEVAL, 11TH

CENT. (Bayeux Tapestry)
Nat Geog 130: 206-51 (col)
Aug '66
ARMOR, 16TH CENT.
Nat Geog 130: 819 (col) Dec
'66
ARMSTRONG, LOUIS--FUNER-
AL RITES
Ebony 26: 31 (col), 32, 33
(col), 34, 36 Sept '71
ARQUEBUSES--SPAIN, 1565
Nat Geog 129: 212-13 (col)
Feb '66
ARRAN (island)
Nat Geog 128: 80-99 (col)
July '65
ART, CHILDREN'S
Grade Teach 84: 84-87 May-
June '67
Grade Teach 85: 120-121,
202-203 Sept '67
Life 67: 62-65 Dec 19 '69
Life 69: 80-83 (col) Nov 13
'70
ART, CHILDREN'S (mentally
retarded and blind children)
Sch Arts 63: 4-20, 30-34
Jan '64
ART, CHILDREN'S--RUSSIA
AND AMERICA
Life 71: 76-79 (col) Oct
15 '71
ART, CHILDREN'S--SCHOOL
PROJECTS
Sch Arts 70: 14-18, 21-42
May '71
Sch Arts 71: 18-27 Sept '71
ART COLLECTIONS--LEHMAN
Life 70: 40-47 (col) Jan 29
'71
ART, COMPUTER
Life 65: 52-54, 56 (col), 58
Nov 8 '68
ART, OP
Holiday 38: 66-69 (col) Nov
'65
ART FORMS
Life 70: 66-69 (col) June 25
'71
Look 35: 50-51 (col) Aug 10
'71
ART GALLERY--NATIONAL
GALLERY OF ART--WASH-

INGTON, D. C.
Nat Geog 131: 350-371 (col)
Mar '67
ART SHOW--ARCHITECTURAL
LEAGUE OF NEW YORK
Life 67: 81-82 Dec 12 '69
ART STUDIOS
Life 68: 62-65 (col) Mar 27
'70
ARTIFICIAL ISLANDS--TEXAS
TOWERS
Life 55: 7 July 26 '63
ARTIFICIAL SATELLITES--
ASTRONOMICAL APPLICA-
TIONS--ORBITING SOLAR
OBSERVATORY (NASA Satel-
lite launched Feb. 1965)
Nat Geog 128: 740 (col) Nov
'65
ARTIFICIAL SATELLITES--
ENGLAND--ARIEL 1, 1962
Hist of Rocketry and Space
Travel, p. 190
ARTIFICIAL SATELLITES--
FRANCE--A-1, 1965
Hist of Rocketry and Space
Travel, p. 190
ARTIFICIAL SATELLITES--
FRANCE--D-1, 1966
Hist of Rocketry and Space
Travel, p. 190
ARTIFICIAL SATELLITES--
ITALY--SAN MARCO 1, 1964
Hist of Rocketry and Space
Travel, p. 190
ARTIFICIAL SATELLITES--
RECOVERY. See SPACE
VEHICLES--RECOVERY
ARTIFICIAL SATELLITES--
RUSSIA--MOLNIYA (drawing)
Hist of Rocketry and Space
Travel, p. 182
ARTIFICIAL SATELLITES--
RUSSIA--PROTON 1 (drawing)
Hist of Rocketry and Space
Travel, p. 182
ARTIFICIAL SATELLITES--
RUSSIA--SPUTNIK 2, 1957
(carried dog in orbit around
the earth)
Hist of Rocketry and Space
Travel, bet. p. 164-5
(col), 180

ARTIFICIAL SATELLITES--RUS-
SIA--SPUTNIK 3, 1958
Hist of Rocketry and Space
Travel, bet. p. 164-5 (col)
ARTIFICIAL SATELLITES--U. S.
--EARLY BIRD 1, 1965
("world's first operational
commercial communications
satellite")
Hist of Rocketry and Space
Travel, p. 186
ARTIFICIAL SATELLITES--U. S.
--EXPLORER 12, 1961
Hist of Rocketry and Space
Travel, bet. p. 164-5 (col)
ARTIFICIAL SATELLITES--U. S.
--PEGASUS 2, 1965
Hist of Rocketry and Space
Travel, p. 188
ARTIFICIAL SATELLITES--U. S.
--TIROS, 1962
Hist of Rocketry and Space
Travel, bet. p. 164-5 (col)
ARTIFICIAL SATELLITES--U. S.
--VANGUARD 3
Hist of Rocketry and Space
Travel, p. 184
ARTISTS, NEGRO. See NEGRO
ARTISTS
ASSEMBLY LINES, AIRPLANE--
CALIFORNIA
Nat Geog 129: 606-7 (col)
May '66
ASSEMBLY LINES, AUTOMO-
BILE--AUSTRALIA
Nat Geog 124: 377 (col)
Sept '63
ASSEMBLY LINES, AUTO-
MOBILE--ISRAEL
Nat Geog 127: 414-15 (col)
Mar '65
ASTROBEE (rocket). See
ROCKETS, SOUNDING--U. S.
--ASTROBEE
ASTRONAUTS. See also
WOMEN AS ASTRONAUTS
ASTRONAUTS--CLOTHING
Life 55: front cover, 7, 30-
8 (col) Sept 27 '63
Nat Geog 125: 358, 368, 380,
384, 390-1 (col) Mar '64
Nat Geog 127: 132-3, 136-7,
140-1 (col) Jan '65

Nat Geog 128: 440-7 (col)
Sept '65
Life 65: 34-37 (col) Aug 9
'68
ASTRONAUTS--FUNERAL RITES
Life 62: front cover, 20-31
(col) Feb 10 '67
Ebony 23: 90-2 Feb '68
ASTRONAUTS, NEGRO. See
NEGRO ASTRONAUTS
ASTRONAUTS--PROJECT APOL-
LO
Life 58: 22-3 (col), 25-7
June 25 '65
Life 62: front cover (col),
18-27 Feb 3 '67
Life 65: 36-8, 39 (col)
Oct 25 '68
Life 65: 26-27 Nov 1 '68
Life 66: 44-51 (col) May 16
'69
Life 67: front cover, 16D, 17
(col), 18, 19-25 (col), 26,
27-9 (col) July 4 '69
Nat Geog 137: 858-861 (col)
June '70
Travel 134: 54 July '70
Life 69: 48, 49-50 (col), 51-
2, 56 July 31 '70
Life 70: 32-3 (col) Feb 19
'71
ASTRONAUTS--PROJECT
GEMINI
Life 55: front cover, 30-8
(col) Sept 27 '63
Nat Geog 125: 372-3 (col)
Mar '64
Nat Geog 127: 122-44 (col)
Jan '65
Life 58: cover, 34-44 (col)
Apr 2 '65
Life 59: 112-113 Nov 5 '65
ASTRONAUTS--PROJECT MER-
CURY
Hist of Rocketry and Space
Travel, p. 209
ASTRONAUTS--RUSSIA
Life 55: 34-34A July 5 '63
Life 58: 41-43 (col), 44
May 14 '65
ASTRONAUTS--TRAINING--
PROJECT GEMINI
Nat Geog 127: 122-44 (col)
Jan '65

AUTOMOBILES, 1957-71
Look 35: 44-45 (col) Sept 21
'71
AUTOMOBILES, 1964
Look 27: 86-98 (col) Oct 22
'63
AUTOMOBILES, 1965
Look 28: 44-57 (col) Oct 6
'64
AUTOMOBILES, 1967
Look 30: 86-99 (col) Oct 18
'66
Ebony 22: 92-4, 96-9 (col)
Jan '67
AUTOMOBILES, 1968
Look 31: 83-95 (col) Oct 17
'67
Ebony 23: 90-4, 96-7 (col)
Jan '68
AUTOMOBILES, 1969
Look 32: 71-84 (col) Oct 15
'68
Holiday 44: 114-119 (col)
Oct '68
Ebony 24: 84-9 (col) Jan '69
AUTOMOBILES, 1970
Look 33: 64-79 (col) Oct 7
'69
Ebony 25: 76-81 (col) Jan
'70
AUTOMOBILES, 1971
Look 34: 64-71 (col), 73,
75-76, 79 Oct 6 '70
Ebony 26: 64-9 (col) Jan '71
AUTOMOBILES, 1972
Look 35: 46-53 (col), 55-57,
60 Sept 21 '71
AUTOMOBILES, 1973
Life 71: 36-39 (col) Aug 13
'71
AUTOMOBILES--ALL TERRAIN
VEHICLE
Holiday 47: 66-67 (col) May
'70
AUTOMOBILES, AMPHIBIOUS--
AMPHICAR--GERMANY (Fed-
eral Republic)
Nat Geog 128: 45 (col) July
'65
AUTOMOBILES, ANTIQUE
Look 30: 43-45 (col) Aug 9
'66
Am Heritage 18: 32, 34-35,

37, 39 Apr '67
Sports Illus 30: 45-46 (col)
Feb 10 '69
Sports Illus 34: 22-25 May
10 '71
AUTOMOBILES, ANTIQUE
(Clarence P. Hornung's Gal-
lery of the American Auto-
mobile) (color plates)
Am Heritage 17: 65-79 (col)
Dec '65
AUTOMOBILES--ANTIQUE
ROLLS-ROYCES
Life 66: 58-63 (col), 65 June
27 '69
AUTOMOBILES--"BATMOBILE"
Ebony 21: 40 Apr '66
AUTOMOBILES--BUICK--WILD-
CAT, 1965
Life 57: 115 (col) Oct 16 '64
AUTOMOBILES--CADILLAC--
FLEETWOOD, 1965
Life 57: 118 (col) Oct 16 '64
AUTOMOBILES--CHEVROLET--
CORVAIR, 1965
Life 57: 119 (col) Oct 16 '64
AUTOMOBILES--CHEVROLET--
IMPALA, 1965
Life 57: 118 (col) Oct 16 '64
AUTOMOBILES--CHRYSLER--
NEWPORT, 1965
Life 57: 120 (col) Oct 16 '64
AUTOMOBILES--DODGE--
POLARA, 1965
Life 57: 120 (col) Oct 16 '64
AUTOMOBILES--FORD, 1896
(Henry Ford in his first
model)
Nat Geog 128: 538 Oct '65
AUTOMOBILES--FORD, 1908
Look 29: 20 Jan 12 '65
AUTOMOBILES--FORD, 1912
Ebony 18: 212 Sept '63
AUTOMOBILES--FORD--MODEL
T
Nat Geog 124: 179 (col) Aug
'63
AUTOMOBILES--FORD--MUS-
TANG, 1964
Life 56: 51-2 (col) Apr 17
'64
AUTOMOBILES, FOREIGN
(sports cars)

Look 34: 30-37 (col), 39
    Apr 7 '70
AUTOMOBILES, FOREIGN--
    ENGLAND, 1910
    Life 55: 84 Nov 22 '63
AUTOMOBILES, FOREIGN--
    LAND ROVER--ENGLAND
    Nat Geog 127: 230 (col) Feb
    '65; 553 (col) Apr '65
    Nat Geog 128: 255 (col)
    Aug '65
AUTOMOBILES, FOREIGN--
    MERCEDES, 1903 (chain-
    driven)
    Life 55: 57 July 26 '63
AUTOMOBILES, FOREIGN--
    OPEL-RAK 1--GERMANY,
    1928 (rocket powered)
    Hist of Rocketry and Space
    Travel, p. 65
AUTOMOBILES, FOREIGN--
    RENAULT LANDAULETTE,
    1903
    Nat Geog 129: 773 (col)
    June '66
AUTOMOBILES, FOREIGN--
    SEAT 600--SPAIN
    Nat Geog 127: 299 (col)
    Mar '65
AUTOMOBILES, LUXURY
    Holiday 48: 56-58 (col) July-
    Aug '70
AUTOMOBILES--MERCURY--
    MONTEREY, 1965
    Life 57: 122 (col) Oct 16
    '64
AUTOMOBILES--PONTIAC--
    BROUGHAM, 1965
    Life 57: 119 (col) Oct 16 '64
AUTOMOBILES--RACING CARS
    Life 58: 92-94 Apr 30 '65
    Sports Illus 25: 35-38 (col),
    40 Aug 8 '66
    Holiday 45: 72-75 (col) Feb
    '69
    Life 68: 70-73 (col) May 22
    '70
AUTOMOBILES--RACING CARS
    --ITALY
    Sports Illus 35: 25-28 (col)
    Aug 30 '71
AUTOMOBILES--RACING CARS
    --LOTUS FORD

Life 59: 72-76 (col) July 16
    '65
AUTOMOBILES--RACING CARS
    --PORSCHE
    Sports Illus 32: 21-22 (col)
    Feb 9 '70
AUTOMOBILES, RACING--
    GRAND PRIX--DIEPPE,
    FRANCE, 1912
    Life 55: 66-7 Nov 29 '63
AUTOMOBILES--RAMBLER--
    CLASSIC, 1965
    Life 57: 117 (col) 16 '64
AVALANCHES--ALPS
    Life 58: 38B May 28 '65
AVIATION--ACCIDENTS
    Life 59: 33 Dec 17 '65
    Life 60: 36-36C, 38-39 (col)
    Mar 18 '66
    Life 60: 28-33 (col) June 24
    '66
    Life 65: 43 (col) Aug 9 '68
AVIATION--ACCIDENTS--COL-
    LISION OF U.S. AIR FORCE
    AIRPLANES IN MID-AIR,
    1964
    Life 57: 32-3 July 10 '64
AVIATION--ACCIDENTS--
    CRASH OF DC-7 (F.A.A.
    planned safety test)
    Life 56: 123-8 (col) June 12
    '64
AXE BLADES, IRON
    Nat Geog 124: 415 (col) Sept
    '63
AXE BLADES, MEDIEVAL
    Nat Geog 130: 250 Aug '66
AXES, BATTLE--VIKINGS
    Nat Geog 126: 714 (col)
    Nov '64
AXES, HANDLELESS--STONE
    AGE--AFRICA
    Nat Geog 127: 203 (col)
    Feb '65
AXES, ICE--MOUNTAIN
    CLIMBERS'
    Life 55: 72 (col) Sept 20 '63
    Nat Geog 124: 479-81, 485,
    500 (col) Oct '63
AYMARA INDIANS. See INDI-
    ANS OF SOUTH AMERICA--
    BOLIVIA--AYMARA

B

BAALBEK, LEBANON (Roman
    temple ruins)
    Nat Geog 128: 264-5 (col)
        Aug '65
BADLANDS NATIONAL MONU-
    MENT--S. DAKOTA
    America's Wonderlands, p.
        156-7 (col)
BAGGAGE
    Holiday 38: 131, 133 (col),
        134, 135-136 (col) Dec '65
BAGPIPERS--BELFAST
    Nat Geog 126: 236 (col) Aug
        '64
BAGPIPERS--CANADA
    Nat Geog 130: 376 (col)
        Sept '66
BAHAMA ISLANDS
    Holiday 36: 60 (map), 61,
        64-65, 68-69, 72-73 (col)
        Dec '64
    Nat Geog 131: 218-267 (col)
        Feb '67
BAHIA, BRAZIL
    Holiday 48: 62-65 (col) Sept-
        Oct '70
BAJA, CALIFORNIA
    Look 34: 38-42 (col), 43-44
        Sept 8 '70
    Holiday 48: 48-51 (col) Nov
        '70
BALI ISLAND
    Nat Geog 124: 436-58 (col)
        Sept '63
    Holiday 42: 48-53 (col) July
        '67
    Life 66: 42-55 (col) Jan 31
        '69
    Travel 132: 42 (col), 44 (col-
        map), 45 Oct '69
    Nat Geog 136: 656-697 (col)
        Nov '69
BALLET, ENGLAND'S ROYAL
    Life 70: 54-57 (col) Feb 12
        '71
BALLET--HARKNESS BALLET
    Nat Geog 130: 633 (col)
        Nov '66
BALLET, LENINGRAD KIROV
    Life 70: 38-43 Jan 22 '71
BALLET--NEW YORK CITY

    Holiday 45: 54-57 (col) Mar
        '69
BALLET--NEW YORK CITY
    (in "Dances at a Gathering")
    Life 67: 42-51 (col) Oct 3
        '69
BALLET, NEW YORK CITY
    (under Balanchine)
    Life 58: 94B-98, 100, 102,
        105 June 11 '65
BALLET--ROYAL BALLET--
    CAMBODIA
    Nat Geog 126: 530-1 (col)
        Oct '64
BALLET DANCERS. See
    DANCERS, BALLET
BALLETS--"SCHEHERAZADE"
    (danced by Nijinsky and Kar-
    savina)
    Life 55: 83 Nov 22 '63
BALLETS--"SWAN LAKE"
    Nat Geog 129: 334-5 (col)
        Mar '66
BALLETS--"THE FIREBIRD"
    Life 69: 32-37 (col) July 31 '70
BALLETS--"THE NUTCRACKER
    SUITE"
    Life 57: 44 (col) Oct 16 '64
    Nat Geog 124: 383 (col) Sept '63
BALLOON ASCENSIONS--"EAGLE,"
    1897
    Life 68: 63-64 Apr 3 '70
BALLOON ASCENSIONS--HOT-
    AIR BALLOONS
    Nat Geog 129: 392-407 (col)
        Mar '66
BALLOON ASCENSIONS--"THE
    FREE LIFE"
    Life 69: 38-40 (col) Oct 23 '70
BALLOON GONDOLAS
    Nat Geog 129: 398, 401, 405
        (col) Mar '66
BALLOONS, HOT-AIR
    Nat Geog 129: 392-407 (col)
        Mar '66
BALLOON RACING
    Life 58: 49-52, 55-56, 58
        June 4 '65
BALLOON RACING--HOT-AIR
    BALLOONS
    Nat Geog 129: 392-407 (col)
        Mar '66
BALLOONS

Ebony 22: 44-5 Mar '67
Travel 127: 60, 62 Apr '67
Life 65: 76-80 Sept 6 '68
Life 69: 62-65 (col) Aug 21 '70
BALLOONS, RESEARCH--VEE-
BALLOON
Life 55: 34A July 5 '63
BALLOONS, WEATHER
Nat Geog 128: 418, 427 (col)
Sept '65
BALLUTES. See SPACE VE-
HICLES--SAFETY DEVICES
AND MEASURES--BALLUTES
BALTIMORE--MONUMENTS--
WASHINGTON
Nat Geog 126: 398 (col) Sept
'64
BANDELIER NATIONAL MONU-
MENT--N. MEXICO
America's Wonderlands, p.
314 (col), 315
BANFF, ALBERTA
Nat Geog 130: 368-9 (col)
Sept '66
BANGKOK, THAILAND
Holiday 47: 38-41 (col) Feb
'70
BANKERS' BUILDING--LOS
ANGELES
Ebony 20: 120 June '65
BANKS ISLAND
Nat Geog 125: 702-35 (col)
May '64
BANTUS. See AFRICA--NA-
TIVE RACES--BANTU
BAR HARBOR--MAINE
Holiday 38: 46-53 (col) July
'65
BARBADOS ISLANDS--CARIB-
BEAN
Holiday 35: 72-77 (col) Feb
'64
Travel 136: 70-3 July '71
BARBER SHOPS, OUTDOOR--
EGYPT
Nat Geog 127: 594 (col) May
'65
BARBERS
Life 56: 108 Feb 21 '64
BARCELONA
Nat Geog 127: 298-9 (col)
Mar '65
BARCOS. See BOATS--BARCOS

BARGES, CANAL--NETHERLANDS
Nat Geog 126: 182-3 (col)
Aug '64
BARGES, LANDING--SABLE
ISLAND
Nat Geog 128: 420 (col) Sept
'65
BARGES, MULE-DRAWN--
CHESAPEAKE AND OHIO
CANAL
Nat Geog 126: 756 (col) Dec
'64
BARN-RAISING
Nat Geog 128: 238-9 (col)
Aug '65
BASEBALL--ALL STARS 1964
Look 28: 59, 61-63 Oct 20
'64
BASEBALL CLUBS--LOS AN-
GELES DODGERS
Life 55: 106B-107, 111 Oct
4 '63
Life 56: 88A-90 Mar 20 '64
BASEBALL CLUBS--NEW YORK
YANKEES
Life 55: 108-10, 112 Oct 4
'63
BASEBALL--PITCHERS
Sports Illus 22: 49-52 (col)
May 10 '65
BASEBALL--SPRING TRAINING
Sports Illus 32: 24-28 (col)
Mar 2 '70
BASEBALL STARS
Ebony 18: 102-4, 106, 108,
110 Oct '63
Look 27: 51, 53-54 Dec 31
'63
Look 28: 68-73 Apr 7 '64
Look 28: 38, 40-41 June 2
'64
Ebony 19: 153-4, 157-8,
160, 162, 164 June '64
Look 28: 97-100, 102 July
14 '64
Ebony 19: 36-8, 40, 42 Aug
'64
Ebony 19: 39, 41-42, 44,
46 Oct '64
Look 29: 70-74 Feb 23 '65
Ebony 20: 153-8, 160, 162
June '65
Look 29: 99-100, 103 June
15 '65

Life 59: cover (col), 46-53
  July 30 '65
Ebony 20: 73-4, 76 Sept '65
Life 59: 26-33 Oct 1 '65
Ebony 21: 39 Jan '66
Ebony 21: 120-2, 124, 126,
  128, 130 June '66
Sports Illus 25: 27-30 (col)
  July 11 '66
Ebony 21: 88-90, 92, 94,
  Sept '66
Ebony 22: 128-30, 132, 134,
  136-8 June '67
Ebony 22: 50-2, 54-6 July '67
Ebony 22: 38-40 Sept '67
Ebony 22: 100-2, 104, 106,
  108 Oct '67
Ebony 23: 143-8, 150, 152,
  154-5 June '68
Ebony 23: 103-6, 108 Sept '68
Ebony 24: 136-40, 142-6
  June '69
Ebony 24: 92-4, 96, 98-100
  Oct '69
Ebony 25: 111 Mar '70
Sports Illus 32: 53-6, 57-9, 65-
  9, 71-2 (col) Apr 13 '70
Sports Illus 32: 25-26 (col)
  Apr 20 '70
Ebony 25: 128-30 (col), 132,
  134, 136-8, 140-2 June '70
Sports Illus 32: 10-12 (col)
  June 1 '70
Life 68: 36-39 (col), 40 June
  5 '70
Sports Illus 33: 10, 11-12 (col)
  July 27 '70
Ebony 25: 88-90 July '70
Sports Illus 33: 27-35 July 6
  '70
Sports Illus 33: 17-20 (col)
  Sept 28 '70
Ebony 26: 44, 50-2 Jan '71
Ebony 26: 92-4, 96, 99-100,
  102, 104, 106 June '71
Sports Illus 35: 13-16 (col)
  July 5 '71
Ebony 26: 94-5 (col), 96-9
  Sept '71
Ebony 26: 132-4 Oct '71
BASEBALL STARS--THE
  "GREATS"
Look 28: 30, 32 Dec 29 '64

BASEBALL TEAMS--BALTI-
  MORE ORIOLES
  Look 29: 85-88, 91 May 18
    '65
BASEBALL TEAMS--CINCIN-
  NATI REDS
  Look 27: 66-69 Aug 27 '63
BASEBALL TEAMS--MINNE-
  SOTA TWINS
  Look 29: 83, 85, 87 June 1
    '65
BASEBALL TEAMS--PHILA-
  DELPHIA PHILLIES
  Look 28: 87-92 Aug 25 '64
BASEBALL TEAMS--YANKEES
  Look 27: 79-82, 85 July 16
    '63
BASKET MAKING
  Hobbies 73: 118, 120 May '68
  Hobbies 76: 146-7 Dec '71
BASKETBALL--ALL AMERICA,
  1963
  Look 27: 129-130 Dec 17 '63
BASKETBALL--ALL AMERICA,
  1963-64
  Look 28: 80-82 Mar 24 '64
BASKETBALL--ALL AMERICA,
  1964-65
  Look 29: 87-89 Mar 23 '65
BASKETBALL--ALL AMERICA,
  1965-66
  Look 30: 106, 109 Mar 22
    '66
BASKETBALL--ALL AMERICA,
  1966-67
  Look 31: 71-73 Mar 21 '67
BASKETBALL--ALL AMERICA,
  1967-68
  Look 32: 91, 93-94 Mar 19
    '68
BASKETBALL--ALL AMERICA,
  1968-69
  Look 33: 79-80 Apr 1 '69
BASKETBALL--ALL AMERICA,
  1969-70
  Look 34: 53-54 Mar 24 '70
BASKETBALL, COLLEGE--
  STARS
  Sports Illus 33: 33-38 (col)
    Nov 30 '70
BASKETBALL PROS
  Sports Illus 24: 30-31 May
    9 '66

Sports Illus 25: 40-44 (col)
Oct 24 '66
Sports Illus 25: 43-46 (col)
Dec 5 '66
Ebony 22: 40, 42-3 Feb '67
Ebony 23: 64-6, 68, 70, 72-
3 Jan '68
Ebony 23: 124-6, 128, 130
Mar '68
Sports Illus 28: 35-38 (col)
Apr 15 '68
Ebony 24: 44-6, 50, 52, 54
Feb '69
Life 66: 52-52B, 57, 62
May 16 '69
Life 67: 40-43 (col) Nov 14
'69
Ebony 25: 164-5 (col), 166,
168, 171-3 Dec '69
Sports Illus 31: 35-38 (col)
Dec 1 '69
Sports Illus 32: 14-17 Jan 26
'70
Ebony 25: 36-8, 40-2, 44
Feb '70
Sports Illus 32: 8-11 Feb 2
'70
Ebony 25: 120-2 Mar '70
Sports Illus 32: cover (col),
20-22, 25 Mar 9 '70
Sports Illus 32: 23-26 (col)
Mar 16 '70
Life 68: 58-59 May 1 '70
Ebony 25: 49-51, 54, 56
July '70
Ebony 26: 83-6, 88-90, 92-
3 Jan '71
Ebony 26: 38-40, 42 Feb '71
Ebony 26: 60-2, 64-6, 96-8,
100, 102-3 Mar '71
Sports Illus 35: 46, 51-52,
57-58, 67-68, 73 (col)
Nov 29 '71
BASKETBALL PROS--CELTICS
Look 30: 64-66, 69 Feb 8 '66
Ebony 22: 60-1, 64, 66-8
Jan '67
BASKETBALL STARS
Ebony 19: 71-2, 74, 76-8
Jan '64
Ebony 19: 57-8, 60, 62, 64
Aug '64
Ebony 20: 35-6, 38 Feb '65

Look 29: 86-90 Feb 9 '65
Ebony 20: 84-6, 88, 90 Apr
'65
Sports Illus 26: 14-17 Mar
27 '67
Life 62: 82-84, 86, 88 Apr
21 '67
Life 68: 47-50 Mar 13 '70
BASKETS, INDIAN (N. Ameri-
can)
Hobbies 69: 113, 123 May
'64
BASKETS, INDIAN (N. Ameri-
can)--PUEBLOS, 20TH
CENT.
Nat Geog 125: 201-2 (col)
Feb '64
BASKETS--MALAYSIA
Nat Geog 124: 778-9 (col)
Nov '63
BASQUE COUNTRY--PYRENEES
Nat Geog 134: 241-277 (col)
Aug '68
Holiday 44: 74-79 (col) Oct
'68
BASQUES IN THE UNITED
STATES
Nat Geog 129: 870-88 (col)
June '66
BASQUES--SPAIN
Nat Geog 127: 321 (col)
Mar '65
BAT (guided missile). See
GUIDED MISSILES--U.S.--
BAT
BATHING SUITS. See COS-
TUME--BATHING SUITS
BATHYSCAPHE--TRIESTE
Nat Geog 125: 764-5, 768-9,
775-7 (col) June '64
(THE) BATTERY--NEW YORK
CITY
Am Heritage 15: 59 (drawing,
col) Feb '64
BATTLE OF BEECHER ISLAND,
1868
Am Heritage 18: 44 (drawing)
Feb '67
BATTLE OF BULL RUN
Am Heritage 16: 32 (litho-
graph, col) June '65
BATTLE OF BUNKER HILL
(muster roll)

Ebony 19: 46 Feb '64
BATTLE OF BUNKER HILL
(sketch)
Ebony 19: 44 Feb '64
BATTLE OF BUNKER HILL
(drawing)
Am Heritage 19: 10-11 (col)
Oct '68
BATTLE OF CHU LAI
Life 59: 22-27 (col) Sept 3
'65
BATTLEFIELDS--AMERICAN
REVOLUTION--YORKTOWN
SURRENDER BY CORN-
WALLIS (painting)
Nat Geog 126: 652-3 (col)
Nov '64
BATTLEFIELDS--CIVIL WAR
Ebony 18: 144 Sept '63
BATTLEFIELDS--WORLD WAR
I--VERDUN
Life 56: 68-83 (col) June 5
'64
BATTLES. See also WORLD
WAR I--CAMPAIGNS AND
BATTLES; WORLD WAR I--
NAVAL OPERATIONS; WORLD
WAR II--CAMPAIGNS AND
BATTLES; UNITED STATES--
CIVIL WAR--CAMPAIGNS
AND BATTLES; UNITED
STATES--CIVIL WAR--NAVAL
OPERATIONS
BATTLES--HASTINGS, 1066
(painting)
Nat Geog 130: 246-7 (col)
Aug '66
BATTLES--LITTLE BIG HORN
(Custer Massacre, 1876)
Nat Geog 128: 666-7 (col)
Nov '65
Nat Geog 128: 896-7 (col)
Dec '65
BATTLES--TIPPECANOE, 1811
(lithograph)
Nat Geog 127: 96-7 (col) Jan
'65
BATTLES, NAVAL--CONSTEL-
LATION AND L'INSURGENTE,
1799 (engraving)
Nat Geog 126: 662-3 (col)
Nov '64
BAYEUX TAPESTRY

Nat Geog 130: 206-51 (col)
Aug '66
BAZOOKAS--U.S. (used in
World War II)
Hist of Rocketry and Space
Travel, p. 94-5
BAZOOKAS--U.S.--ROBERT
GODDARD's, 1918
Hist of Rocketry and Space
Travel, p. 37
BEACHES. See Names of Cities
with Subdivision Beach, e.g.
CARMEL, CALIF.--BEACH
BEARTOOTH GAME RANGE--
MONTANA
Life 69: 32-33 (col) July 4
'70
BEAUTY CONTESTS--MISS
AMERICA CONTEST, 1940
Life 70: 45-8 Feb 5 '71
BEAUTY CONTESTS--MISS
AMERICA CONTEST, 1964
Ebony 19: 102-4, 106-9
Oct '64
BEAUTY CONTESTS--MISS
AMERICA CONTESTS, 1960-
69
Life 67: 54-5 (col) Dec 26
'69
BEAUTY CONTESTS--MISS
TEEN-AGE AMERICA CON-
TEST, 1963
Life 55: 44B Nov 15 '63
BEAUTY CONTESTS--MISS
UNIVERSE CONTEST
Ebony 23: 36-8 (col), 40-2
Sept '68
BEAUTY SHOPS--KENNETH'S
--NEW YORK
Life 57: 46 (col) Oct 16 '64
BEAVER TRAPS (poplar log
bait)
Nat Geog 124: 432 (col)
Sept '63
BEDOUINS
Nat Geog 125: 98-101 (col)
Jan '64; 402-3 (col) Mar
'64
Nat Geog 128: 276-7, 282
(col) Aug '65
Nat Geog 129: front cover,
18-19, 30-5 (col) Jan
'66

(island)
Nat Geog 129: 793 (col) June
'66
BLUE ANGELS. See UNITED
STATES--NAVY--BLUE
ANGELS
BLUE RIDGE MOUNTAIN
COUNTRY--NORTH CAROL-
INA
America's Wonderlands, p.
462-5 (col)
BOAT RACING--LONG BEACH
TO SAN FRANCISCO
Sports Illus 25: 21-25 (col)
Nov 7 '66
BOATS. See also AIRBOATS;
BARGES; CANOES; FERRIES;
FISHING BOATS; FLATBOATS;
GONDOLAS; HOUSE BOATS;
HYDROFOILS; JUNKS; KAY-
AKS; RAFTS; SAILBOATS;
SAILING VESSELS; SAMPANS;
SCHOONERS; SHIPS; STEAM-
BOATS; STEAMSHIPS; SUB-
MARINE BOATS; WARSHIPS;
YACHTS
BOATS--BALSAS--S. AMERICA
Nat Geog 125: 255 (col) Feb
'64
BOATS--BARCOS DO MAR--
PORTUGAL
Nat Geog 128: 453, 475 (col)
Oct '65
BOATS--BARCOS RABELOS--
PORTUGAL
Nat Geog 128: 488-9 (col)
Oct '65
BOATS--CABALLITOS (made of
totora reeds)--PERU
Nat Geog 125: 236 (col) Feb
'64
BOATS--CORACLES
Nat Geog 127: 751 (col) June
'65
BOATS, EXCURSION. See FER-
RIES
BOATS, LAND (used for racing
on dry sand)
Nat Geog 129: 626-7 (col)
May '66
BOATS, SHRIMP. See FISHING
BOATS, SHRIMP
BOATS, SUBMARINE. See

SUBMARINE BOATS
BODY SURFING. See SURF
RIDING
BOLAS
Nat Geog 127: 220 (col) Feb
'65
BOLIVIA
Nat Geog 129: 153-95 (col)
Feb '66
Travel 126: 51-54 (col) Sept
'66
BOLSHOI BALLET
Nat Geog 129: 334-5 (col)
Mar '66
BOMBINGS
Life 68: 24-26, 32 Mar 27 '70
BOMBINGS--STATE UNIVER-
SITY OF WISCONSIN
Life 69: 38-42 Sept 18 '70
BOOK CHARACTERS--TINKER
BELL--DISNEYLAND
Nat Geog 124: 198 (col) Aug
'63
BOOK DESIGN
Sch Arts 65: 34, 36-37 Jan
'66
BOOKBINDING--SCHOOL PRO-
JECT
Grade Teach 84: 123-125 Sept
'66
BOOTS, SKI
Sports Illus 34: 50 (col), 51
Jan 25 '71
BOSTON, 1860
Life 59: 50 Dec 24 '65
BOSTON--AERIAL VIEW
Life 59: 80-81 (col) Dec 24
'65
BOSTON ATHENAEUM (interior)
Nat Geog 130: 793 (col) Dec
'66
BOSTON--CITY PLANNING--
GOVERNMENT AND PRU-
DENTIAL CENTERS
Life 57: 45 (col) Oct 16 '64
Nat Geog 130: 790-1, 794-5
(col) Dec '66
BOSTON MASSACRE, 1770
(sketch)
Nat Geog 130: 792 (col) Dec
'66
BOSTON--MUSEUM OF FINE
ARTS

Life 68: 36-43 (col), 46 Feb 13 '70
BOSTON--PARKS--BOSTON COMMON, 1848 (lithograph)
Nat Geog 124: 656-7 (col) Nov '63
BOTA, GOAT-SKIN (Basque wine vessel)
Nat Geog 129: 885 (col) June '66
BOW AND ARROW (long arrow)
Nat Geog 125: 736 (col) May '64
BOWLING, LAWN--PLYMOUTH, ENGLAND
Nat Geog 124: 214-15 (col) Aug '63
BOXING--CLAY VS LISTON
Life 56: 34-7 (col) Mar 6 '64
Ebony 19: 77-9 Apr '64
Sports Illus 22: 22A-22D (col), 25 May 10 '65
Sports Illus: 22A-22D (col) 25 June 7 '65
BOXING--CLAY VS PATTERSON
Life 59: 115-116 Nov 19 '65
Sports Illus 23: 20-23, 25 Nov 29 '65
Sports Illus 23: 41-44 (col) Dec 6 '65
BOXING--FRAZIER VS CLAY
Ebony 26: 134-6 (col) Mar '71
Sports Illus 34: 17-20 (col) Mar 15 '71
Life 70: 20-7 (col) Mar 19 '71
Ebony 26: 132-3 (col) May '71
BOXING--LISTON VS PATTERSON
Sports Illus 20: 18-21 Feb 24 '64
THE BRAIN
Life 71: 42-59 (col) Oct 1 '71
Life 71: 42-56 (col) Oct 22 '71
Life 71: 55-64 (col), 66, 74-75 (col) Nov 12 '71
BRAZIL
Life 62: 52-57 (col) Apr 14 '67
Holiday 42: 52-59 (col) Sept '67
Life 71: 26-31 (col) Nov 12 '71
BRAZIL, AMERICANA (colony set up by Negroes in 18th Cent.)
Ebony 22: 89-90, 92, 94 Nov '66
BREAD, BASQUE SHEEP HERDERS'--NEVADA
Nat Geog 129: 874 (col) June '66
BREAD, FRENCH--BRITTANY
Nat Geog 127: 487 (col) Apr '65
THE BREAKERS (home of Cornelius Vanderbilt II)--NEWPORT, R.I.
Life 57: 56-7 (col) Aug 14 '64
BREST, FRANCE
Nat Geog 127: 486-7 (col) Apr '65
BRIDGE OF LIONS--ST. AUGUSTINE
Nat Geog 129: 228-9 (col) Feb '66
BRIDGE OF SIGHS--VENICE
Life 56: 62 (col) Feb 21 '64
BRIDGE-TUNNEL--CHESAPEAKE BAY. See CHESAPEAKE BAY BRIDGE-TUNNEL
BRIDGES--NEW YORK CITY
Look 28: 86-7 (col), 88 Feb 11 '64
BRIGANTINES. See SAILING VESSELS--BRIGANTINES
BRIGHT ANGEL POINT--GRAND CANYON
America's Wonderlands, p. 19 (col)
America's Wonderlands, p. 164-5 (col)
BRIGHT ANGEL TRAIL--GRAND CANYON
America's Wonderlands, p. 171 (col)
BRITANNIA ROYAL NAVAL COLLEGE--DARTMOUTH, ENGLAND
Nat Geog 124: 250-1 (col) Aug '63
BRITTANY
Nat Geog 127: 470-503 (col) Apr '65

BRONC RIDING
  Nat Geog 129: 556 (col) Apr
  '66
BRUSHES. See also HAIR
  BRUSHES
BRUSHES, INDIAN (N. Ameri-
  can)--MESA VERDE NATION-
  AL PARK
  Nat Geog 125: 208 (col) Feb
  '64
BRYCE CANYON NATIONAL
  PARK
  Nat Geog 125: 563 (col) Apr
  '64
BRYCE CANYON--UTAH
  America's Wonderlands, p.
  52-3 (col)
  America's Wonderlands, p.
  198-207 (col)
BUCK ISLAND REEF NATIONAL
  MONUMENT--VIRGIN IS-
  LANDS
  America's Wonderlands, 12
  (col)
BUDDHA--POLONNARUWA
  (ruins)--CEYLON
  Nat Geog 129: 484 (col) Apr
  '66
BUDDHA, RECLINING--CAM-
  BODIA
  Nat Geog 126: 547 (col) Oct
  '64
BUDDHA, RECLINING--
  POLONNARUWA
  Holiday 47: 42-43 (col) Apr
  '70
BUDDHA--XA LOI PAGODA--
  SAIGON
  Nat Geog 127: 866 (col)
  June '65
BUDDHA--YUN KANG CAVES--
  CHINA (People's Republic)
  Nat Geog 130: 470-1 Oct '66
BUDDHIST FUNERAL RITES--
  VIETNAM (Republic)
  Nat Geog 129: 282-3 (col)
  Feb '66
BUDDHIST PRAYER WALLS.
  See PRAYER WALLS, BUD-
  DHIST
BUDDHIST PRAYER WHEELS.

See PRAYER WHEELS, BUD-
  DHIST
BUDDHIST PRIESTS. See
  COSTUME--BUDDHIST
  PRIESTS; COSTUME--
  LAMAS
BUDDHIST SUICIDE--VIETNAM
  (Republic), 1963
  Life 55: 34 (col) Nov 15 '63
BUENOS AIRES
  Nat Geog 132: 662-695 (col)
  Nov '67
BUGGIES, HORSE-DRAWN
  Nat Geog 128: 229, 246-7,
  253 (col) Aug '65
BUILDINGS, LIBRARY. See
  LIBRARY ARCHITECTURE
BUILDINGS, SCHOOL. See
  SCHOOL BUILDINGS
BULLETIN BOARDS--LAN-
  GUAGE ARTS
  Grade Teach 84: 48 May-
  June '67
BULLETS. See CARTRIDGES
BULLFIGHTS. See also MATA-
  DORS
BULLFIGHTS
  Ebony 26: 78-9 (col), 80,
  82, 84 Mar '71
BULLFIGHTS--MEXICO
  Life 55: 92 July 12 '63
BULLFIGHTS--PORTUGAL
  Nat Geog 128: 464-5 (col)
  Oct '65
BULLS, RUNNING OF THE.
  See PAMPLONA, SPAIN--
  RUNNING OF THE BULLS
BUNKER HILL MONUMENT--
  CHARLESTOWN, MASS.
  Ebony 19: 45 Feb '64
  Nat Geog 130: 803 (col)
  Dec '66
BURIAL CHAMBERS, INDIAN
  (N. American)--MESA VERDE
  NATIONAL PARK
  Nat Geog 125: 195 (col) Feb
  '64
BURIED TREASURE--FLORI-
  DA'S EAST COAST (Spanish
  ship sunk, 1715)

Nat Geog 127: 1-37 (col)
Jan '65
BURIED TREASURE--KYRENIA,
CYPRUS SHIP
Nat Geog 137: 840-57 (col)
June '70
BURIED TREASURE--ROUTE OF
CANADIAN VOYAGEURS AND
FUR TRADERS (along Minn. -
Ontario border)
Nat Geog 124: 412-35 (col)
Sept '63
BURIED TREASURE--TURKISH
COAST (Byzantine ship sunk
circa 1300 years ago)
Nat Geog 124: 138-55 (col)
July '63
BUSHMAN, AFRICAN
Life 61: 135-136 (col) Dec 9
'66
BUTTONS, COIN
Hobbies 68: 48 Sept '63

C

CABINS, SKI--VERMONT (Eliot
Noyes, architect)
Look 29: 76-77 (col), 78-79
Feb 23 '65
CABLEWAYS--ALPS
Nat Geog 128: 353 (col) Sept
'65
CABLEWAYS--CABLE CARS--
LISBON, PORTUGAL
Nat Geog 128: 461 (col) Oct
'65
CABLEWAYS--CABLE CARS--
PITTSBURGH
Nat Geog 127: 365 (col) Mar
'65
CABLEWAYS--CABLE CARS--
SAN FRANCISCO
Nat Geog 129: 641 (col)
May '66
CABLEWAYS (near Palm Springs)
--CALIF.
Life 55: 51, 53 Nov 1 '63
CABLEWAYS--JACKSON, WYO.
Nat Geog 128: 890 (col) Dec
'65

CAESAREA
Nat Geog 127: 420-1 (col)
Mar '65
CAIRNS, IRELAND
Look 35: 42-43 (col) Mar
23 '71
CAIRO
Nat Geog 127: 588-9 (col)
May '65
CAJUN COUNTRY--LOUISIANA
Holiday 47: 70-73 (col) May
'70
CAJUNS. See ACADIANS IN
LOUISIANA
CALCULATING MACHINES--
COMPUTERS--WHIRLWIND
Life 57: 115 Sept 25 '64
CALCULATING MACHINES--
20TH CENT.
Nat Geog 138: 594-633 (col)
Nov '70
CALF RIDING--SYDNEY,
AUSTRALIA RODEO
Nat Geog 124: 351 (col)
Sept '63
CALIFORNIA
Nat Geog 129: 596-679 (col)
May '66
CALLIGRAPHY
Sch Arts 70: 34-36 Dec '70
CAMBODIA
Nat Geog 126: 515-51 (col)
Oct '64
Life 68: 36-41 (col) May 8
'70
Life 69: 23-30 (col) July
10 '70
CAMEL RIDERS--JORDAN
Nat Geog 126: 814-15 (col)
Dec '64
CAMERAS, SATELLITE-TRACK-
ING--K-50
Nat Geog 130: 809 (col) Dec
'66
CAMERAS, SOLAR. See
ASTRONOMICAL PHOTOG-
RAPHY--SOLAR CAMERA
CAMPAIGNS, POLITICAL. See
POLITICAL CAMPAIGNS;
PRESIDENTIAL CAMPAIGNS;
PRIMARIES

CAMPERS, AUTOMOBILE. See
  AUTOMOBILE CAMPERS
CAMPERS--MOBILE
  Life 69: 20-23, 24-25 (col),
    26-27 Aug 14 '70
CAMPING EQUIPMENT
  Life 71: 44-46 (col), 49 Sept
    3 '71
CAMPINOS. See COWBOYS--
  PORTUGAL
CAMPS (for young aviators)
  Life 71: 60-63 (col) Aug 27
    '71
CANADA
  Look 31: 20-30 (col) Aug 22
    '67
CANALS--JULIANA--NETHER-
  LANDS
  Nat Geog 126: 179 (col) Aug
    '64
CANALS--SAULT STE. MARIE
  (Soo)
  Nat Geog 124: 94-5 (col)
    July '63
CANALS--SAULT STE. MARIE
  (Soo)--MACARTHUR LOCK
  Nat Geog 126: 568 (col)
    Oct '64
CANARY ISLANDS
  Nat Geog 135: 116-139 (col)
    Jan '69
CANNERIES, CITRUS FRUIT--
  FLORIDA
  Nat Geog 124: 878-9 (col)
    Dec '63
CANNERIES, SALMON--ALASKA
  Nat Geog 127: 789 (col) June
    '65
CANNON--LA SIBILA--CASTIL-
  LO DE SAN MARCOS--ST.
  AUGUSTINE, FLA.
  Nat Geog 129: 196-7 (col)
    Feb '66
CANNON--U. S.--CIVIL WAR
  Nat Geog 124: 1, 24-5, 39,
    46, 50-1 (col) July '63
CANOE RACES--FRANCE
  Sports Illus 32: 27-32 (col)
    June 29 '70
CANOES
  Nat Geog 128: 34-9, 42-3,
    54-5, 62-3, 65, 68-9
    (col) July '65

CANOES, DUGOUT (bucas)--
  PHILIPPINES
  Nat Geog 130: 316-17, 338-9
    (col) Sept '66
CANOES, OUTRIGGER
  Nat Geog 126: 322 (col) Sept
    '64
  Nat Geog 129: 470-1, 476-7
    (col) Apr '66
CANOES--PIROGUES
  Nat Geog 126: 536-7 Oct '64
  Nat Geog 129: 371 (col) Mar
    '66
CANYON, ARAVAIPA--ARIZONA
  Life 69: 28-29 (col) July 4
    '70
CANYON DE CHELLY--ARIZONA
  America's Wonderlands, p.
    320-5 (col)
CANYONS--UTAH
  America's Wonderlands, p.
    222-3 (col)
  Nat Geog 140: 70-91 (col)
    July '71
CANYONS--ZION--UTAH
  Nat Geog 125: 562-3 (col)
    Apr '64
CAPE COD
  Nat Geog 130: 826-9 (col)
    Dec '66
  America's Wonderlands, p.
    56-7 (col)
  America's Wonderlands, p.
    478-83 (col)
CAPE HATTERAS
  America's Wonderlands, p.
    470-5 (col)
CAPERNAUM, ISRAEL
  Nat Geog 128: 856-7 (col)
    Dec '65
CAPITOL--MISSISSIPPI
  Ebony 21: 128 Feb '66
CAPITOL--WASHINGTON, D. C.
  Nat Geog 125: 1-59 (col)
    Jan '64
CAPITOL--WASHINGTON, D. C.
  (designs by Benjamin Latrobe)
  Nat Geog 125: 2 (col) Jan
    '64
CAPITOL--WASHINGTON, D. C.,
  1800
  Nat Geog 125: 2 (col) Jan
    '64

CAPITOL--WASHINGTON, D.C.,
1852
  Am Heritage 20: 48-49 (col)
  Feb '69
CAPITOL--WASHINGTON, D.C.,
1877
  Ebony 22: 114 Jan '67
CAPITOL--WASHINGTON, D.C.
(aerial view, 1930)
  Nat Geog 124: 565 (col) Oct
  '63
CAPITOL--WASHINGTON, D.C.,
1837--DOME BY CHARLES
BULFINCH
  Nat Geog 125: 3 (col) Jan '64
CAPITOL--WASHINGTON, D.C.
--FRESCOES OF CONSTAN-
TINO BRUMIDI
  Nat Geog 125: 8-9, 12-13
  (col) Jan '64
CAPITOL--WASHINGTON, D.C.
--HOUSE OF REPRESENTA-
TIVES--SPEAKER'S LOBBY
  Nat Geog 125: 32-3 (col) Jan
  '64
CAPITOL--WASHINGTON, D.C.
--PRAYER ROOM
  Nat Geog 125: 50 (col) Jan
  '64
CAPITOL--WASHINGTON, D.C.
--PRESIDENT'S ROOM
  Nat Geog 125: 52-3 (col)
  Jan '64
CAPITOL--WASHINGTON, D.C.
--ROTUNDA
  Nat Geog 125: 6-7 (col) Jan
  '64
CAPITOL--WASHINGTON, D.C.
--SENATE CHAMBER (used
1810-1859)
  Nat Geog 125: 56-7 (col) Jan
  '64
CAPITOL--WASHINGTON, D.C.
--SENATE MARBLE ROOM
  Nat Geog 125: 54 (col) Jan
  '64
CAPITOL--WASHINGTON, D.C.
--SENATE RECEPTION ROOM
  Nat Geog 125: 38-9 (col) Jan
  '64
CAPITOL--WASHINGTON, D.C.
--SENATE WING
  Nat Geog 125: 19 (col) Jan
  '64

CAPITOL--WASHINGTON, D.C.
--STATUARY HALL
  Nat Geog 125: 14-17 (col)
  Jan '64
CAPITOL--WASHINGTON, D.C.
VICE PRESIDENT'S OFFICE
  Nat Geog 125: 55 (col) Jan
  '64
CAPITOLS--CALIFORNIA
  Nat Geog 129: 660 (col) May
  '66
CAPITOLS--FLORIDA
  Nat Geog 124: 874 (col) Dec
  '63
CAPITOLS--MARYLAND (State
House)
  Nat Geog 126: 407 (col) Sept
  '64
CAPRI, ISLE OF
  Holiday 45: 64-65 (col) Jan
  '69
  Nat Geog 137: 794-809 (col)
  June '70
CARAVANS, CAMEL--SAHARA
DESERT
  Nat Geog 128: 695-9, 702-5
  (col) Nov '65
CARAVANS, CAMEL--SYRIA
  Nat Geog 124: 824-5 (col)
  Dec '63
CARAVANS, CAMEL--YEMEN
  Nat Geog 125: 430-1 (col)
  Mar '64
CARAVANS, SALT. See SALT
CARAVANS
CARAVANS, YAK--NEPAL
  Nat Geog 128: 581 (col) Oct
  '65
CARBINES. See RIFLES--
CARBINES
CARDIFF, WALES
  Nat Geog 127: 768-9 (col)
  June '65
CARDS, PLAYING--ANTIQUE
  Hobbies 72: 123 Apr '67
CARDS, PLAYING--ENGLISH
  Hobbies 68: 119 July '63
  Hobbies 69: 118 June '64
CARDS, PLAYING--FRENCH
  Hobbies 68: 119 July '63
  Hobbies 68: 119 Aug '63
CARDS, PLAYING--FRENCH
SUIT CARDS

Hobbies 68: 115 Dec '63
CARDS, PLAYING--FRENCH,
20TH CENT.
Hobbies 74: 153 Sept '69
CARDS, PLAYING--GERMAN,
18TH CENT.
Hobbies 73: 117 Jan '69
CARDS, PLAYING--GERMAN
SUIT CARDS
Hobbies 68: 115 Dec '63
CARDS, PLAYING--GERMAN,
20TH CENT.
Hobbies 73: 115 Feb '69
CARDS, PLAYING--ITALIAN
Hobbies 68: 119 Oct '63
CARDS, PLAYING--ITALIAN
SUIT CARDS
Hobbies 68: 115 Dec '63
CARDS, PLAYING--SPANISH
SUIT CARDS
Hobbies 68: 115 Dec '63
CARDS, PLAYING--TAROTS
Hobbies 73: 118-119 July '68
CARICATURES
Life 66: 40-41 (col), 44
Apr 4 '69
CARLSBAD CAVERNS--NEW
MEXICO
Nat Geog 125: 816-17 (col)
June '64
America's Wonderlands, p.
40-1 (col)
America's Wonderlands, p.
244-59 (col)
CARLSBAD CAVERNS--NEW
MEXICO (depth map)
America's Wonderlands, p.
252-3 (col)
CARMEL, CALIF.--BEACH
Nat Geog 129: 654-5 (col)
May '66
CARNIVAL--MARDI GRAS--
MAMOU, LA
Nat Geog 129: 380-1 (col)
May '66
CARNIVAL--RIO DE JANEIRO
Holiday 39: 40-51 (col) Feb
'66
Holiday 45: 88-89 (col) Feb
'69
CARPENTER SHOPS--NAZA-
RETH, ISRAEL
Nat Geog 128: 834 (col) Dec
'65

CARRIAGES. See also BUG-
GIES; CARTS; COACHES
CARRIAGES--LANDAUS
Life 55: 38-9 Nov 1 '63
CARRIAGES--PHAETONS--
ENGLAND, CIRCA 1785
(painting)
Life 55: 50 (col) Aug 9 '63
CARRIAGES--ST. AUGUSTINE,
FLA.
Nat Geog 129: 210 (col) Feb
'66
CARROUSELS. See MERRY-
GO-ROUNDS
CARTOONS (by Disney). See
MOVING PICTURES--ANI-
MATED CARTOONS--"SNOW
WHITE AND THE SEVEN
SWARFS" (by Disney)
CARTOONS--"ON STAGE"
(Leonard Starr)
Ebony 22: 49 (col) Nov '66
CARTOONS, POLITICAL--
CLEVELAND ADMINISTRA-
TION, 1885
Nat Geog 127: 702 (col) May
'65
CARTOONS, POLITICAL--MC-
KINLEY ADMINISTRATION
Nat Geog 127: 710-11 (col)
May '65
CARTOONS, POLITICAL--
FRANKLIN D. ROOSEVELT
ADMINISTRATION
Nat Geog 129: 75 Jan '66
CARTOONS, POLITICAL--
THEODORE ROOSEVELT AD-
MINISTRATION
Nat Geog 128: 541 Oct '65
CARTOONS, POLITICAL--
TRUMAN ADMINISTRATION
Nat Geog 129: 81 Jan '66
CARTOONS, POLITICAL--
WINSTON CHURCHILL, 1900
Nat Geog 128: 169 (col) Aug
'65
CARTOONS--"STEVE CANYON"
(Milton Caniff)
Ebony 22: 48 (col) Nov '66
CARTOONS--"WEE PALS"
(Morrie Turner)
Ebony 22: 52 Nov '66
CARTRIDGES--MINIE BALLS

(used in U.S. Civil War)
Nat Geog 127: 450 (col) Apr
'65
CARTS, BULLOCK--CEYLON
Nat Geog 129: 457 (col) Apr
'66
CARTS, DECORATED--SPAIN
Nat Geog 127: 314-15 (col)
Mar '65
CARTS, OCEAN-GOING--BRIT-
TANY
Nat Geog 127: 488 (col)
Apr '65
CARTS, VIKING
Nat Geog 126: 715 (col) Nov
'64
CARVINGS, WOOD
Am Heritage 20: 18, 20-22
(col), 23 Dec '68
CASS CAVE--WEST VIRGINIA
Nat Geog 125: 824-5 (col)
June '64
CASSETTE TELEVISION
Life 69: 46 (col), 47-48, 49-
50, 52-53 (col) Oct 16 '70
CASTILLO DE SAN MARCOS
NATIONAL MONUMENT--
ST. AUGUSTINE, FLA.
Nat Geog 129: 196-7, 204,
220-7 (col) Feb '66
CASTLE OF ST. PETER--
TURKEY (built by Crusaders)
Nat Geog 124: 148-9 (col)
July '63
CASTLE, GUTENBERG--GER-
MANY
Nat Geog 131: 480-481, 494-
498 (col) Apr '67
CASTLES--AMBOISE--FRANCE
Nat Geog 129: 850-1 (col)
June '66
CASTLES--ANGERS--FRANCE
Nat Geog 129: 864 (col)
June '66
CASTLES--AZAY-LE-RIDEAU--
FRANCE
Nat Geog 129: 860 (col)
June '66
CASTLES--BALMORAL--SCOT-
LAND
Life 56: 79 (col) Mar 6 '64
CASTLES--BERKELEY--ENG-
LAND

Nat Geog 125: 632 (col) May
'64
CASTLES--BLOIS--FRANCE
Nat Geog 129: 842-3 (col)
June '66
CASTLES--BRODICK--SCOT-
LAND
Nat Geog 128: 84-5 (col)
July '65
CASTLES--CAERNARVON--
WALES
Nat Geog 127: 742-3 (col)
June '65
CASTLES--CARDIFF--WALES
Nat Geog 127: 758-9 (col)
June '65
CASTLES--CARRICKFERGUS--
NORTHERN IRELAND
Nat Geog 126: 248-9 (col)
Aug '64
CASTLES--CASTELO DA PENA
--PORTUGAL
Nat Geog 128: 471 (col) Oct
'65
CASTLES--CHAMBORD--
FRANCE
Nat Geog 129: 846-7 (col)
June '66
CASTLES--CHAUMONT--
FRANCE
Nat Geog 129: 854 (col)
June '66
CASTLES--CHENONCEAUX--
FRANCE
Nat Geog 129: 825, 854-5
(col) June '66
CASTLES--CHEVERNY--
FRANCE
Nat Geog 129: 848-9 (col)
June '66
CASTLES--CONWAY--WALES
Nat Geog 127: 754-5 (col)
June '65
CASTLES--FRANCE
Nat Geog 126: 192 (col) Aug
'64
CASTLES--GLAMIS--SCOTLAND
Nat Geog 125: 615 (col) May
'64
CASTLES--HARLECH--WALES
Nat Geog 127: 767 (col) June
'65
CASTLES--HASTINGS (ruins)--

ENGLAND
Nat Geog 130: 238 (col) Aug
'66
CASTLES--KENILWORTH--ENG-
LAND
Life 56: 58-9 (col) Apr 24
'64
CASTLES--KRAK DES CHEVA-
LIERS--SYRIA
Nat Geog 124: 798-9 (col)
Dec '63
CASTLES--LANGEAIS--FRANCE
Nat Geog 129: 856 (col) June
'66
CASTLES--MIDDLEHAM--ENG-
LAND
Nat Geog 125: 643 (col) May
'64
CASTLES--NEUSCHWANSTEIN--
GERMANY
Nat Geog 128: 382 (col) Sept
'65
CASTLES--ST. MICHAEL'S
MOUNT (off Cornwall Coast)
--ENGLAND
Nat Geog 125: 880-97 (col)
June '64
CASTLES--SAUMUR--FRANCE
Nat Geog 129: 861 (col)
June '66
CASTLES--SPAIN
Life 61: 34-41 (col) Sept 2
'66
CASTLES--USSE--FRANCE
Nat Geog 129: 858-9 (col)
June '66
CASTLES--WINDSOR--ENG-
LAND
Nat Geog 125: 660-1 (col)
May '64
CASTLE, YORK--TANGIER
Look 28: 51-58 (col) Jan 28
'64
CATAMARANS
Life 68: 28-31 (col) Feb 6
'70
CATHEDRAL--BARCELONA (un-
finished)
Holiday 47: 40-1 (col) June '70
CATHEDRAL, CHARTRES
Nat Geog 136: 856-881 (col)
Dec '69
CATHEDRAL--TOLEDO, SPAIN

Life 55: 64-75 (col) Dec 13
'63
CATHEDRALS--COVENTRY (old)
--COVENTRY, ENGLAND
Nat Geog 125: 634 (col) May
'64
CATHEDRALS--EXETER--
EXETER, ENGLAND
Nat Geog 124: 235 (col) Aug
'63
CATHEDRALS--NOTRE DAME--
PARIS
Life 55: 34-36 (col) Aug 9
'63
CATHEDRALS--ST. BASIL'S--
MOSCOW
Nat Geog 124: 534-5 (col)
Oct '63
Nat Geog 129: front cover,
298, 315 (col) Mar '66
CATHEDRALS--ST. LOUIS--
ST. LOUIS (interior)
Nat Geog 128: 635 (col) Nov
'65
CATHEDRALS--ST. MARK'S--
VENICE
Life 56: 58-9 (col) Feb 21
'64
CATHEDRALS--ST. PATRICK'S
--NEW YORK
Nat Geog 126: 103 (col) July
'64
CATHEDRALS--ST. PAUL'S--
LONDON
Nat Geog 128: 212-15, 225
(col) Aug '65
CATHEDRALS--ST. PETER'S--
ROME
Life 55: 22-3, 26 (col) July
5 '63; 56-7 (col) July 12
'63; 34-34A Oct 11 '63
CATHEDRALS--SANTIAGO DE
COMPOSTELA--SANTIAGO,
SPAIN
Nat Geog 127: 319 (col) Mar
'65
CATHEDRALS--TOLEDO--
TOLEDO, SPAIN
Life 55: 64-75 (col) Dec 13
'63
CATHEDRALS--WASHINGTON--
WASHINGTON, D. C.
Nat Geog 126: 758 (col) Dec
'64

CATHOLIC CHURCH. See COL-
LEGE OF CARDINALS--
CATHOLIC CHURCH
CAVE DWELLERS--ANATOLIAN
FARMERS
Nat Geog 138: 126-146 (col)
July '70
CAVES. See also CARLSBAD
CAVERNS; CASS CAVE;
CUMBERLAND CAVERNS;
MAMMOTH CAVE
CAVES AND CAVERNS--WIND
CAVE--BLACK HILLS, S.D.
America's Wonderlands, p.
154 (col)
CAVES OF ALTAMIRA (near
Santander)--SPAIN
Nat Geog 127: 318 (col) Mar
'65
CAVES--UNITED STATES
Nat Geog 125: 802-37 (col)
June '64
CAYMEN ISLANDS--CARIB-
BEAN
Travel 134: 44, 46, 48 (col)
July '70
CENTRAL PARK, 18TH CEN-
TURY--NEW YORK CITY
Life 59: 56 Dec 24 '65
CEVENNES--FRANCE
Holiday 36: 88-93 (col) Nov
'64
CEYLON
Nat Geog 129: 447-97 (col)
Apr '66
CHACO NATIONAL MONUMENT
--N. MEXICO
America's Wonderlands, p.
288-90 (col)
CHAD LAKE
Nat Geog 130: 166-7 (col)
Aug '66
CHAIR--"JEWISH SEAT" OF
THE SUPREME COURT
Life 68: 70 Mar 27 '70
CHAIR LIFTS. See CABLE-
WAYS
CHALETS. See HOUSES--
CHALETS
CHALICES
Life 59: 60-61 (col) Nov 5
'65
CHAMPLAIN (Lake) VALLEY

COUNTRY
Nat Geog 132: 154-201 (col)
Aug '67
CHAPEL OF THE TRANSFIG-
URATION--WYOMING
Nat Geog 128: 891 (col) Dec
'65
CHAPELS--U.S. AIR FORCE
ACADEMY--COLORADO
SPRINGS, COLO.
Nat Geog 128: 346-7 (col)
Sept '65
CHAPELS--URGUP, TURKEY
(built by early Christians)
Nat Geog 124: 810 (col) Dec
'63
CHARTWELL (home of Winston
Churchill)--ESSEX, ENGLAND
Nat Geog 128: 178-9 (col)
Aug '65
CHATEAUX. See CASTLES
CHEER LEADERS
Life 55: 68 (col) Sept 27 '63
CHESAPEAKE BAY BRIDGE-
TUNNEL
Nat Geog 125: 592-611 (col)
Apr '64
CHESAPEAKE BAY COUNTRY
Nat Geog 126: 370-411 (col)
Sept '64
CHESLER PARK--UTAH
America's Wonderlands, p.
225 (col)
CHICAGO
Holiday 41: 68-69 (col) Mar
'67
Life 67: 51 Dec 12 '69
CHICAGO--AERIAL VIEW
Life 59: 71 (col) Dec 24 '65
CHICAGO AT NIGHT
Holiday 41: 70-73 (col) Mar
'67
CHICAGO--HISTORY (founding
in 1779)
Ebony 19: 170-2, 174 Dec
'63
CHICAGO MONUMENT (dedi-
cated to Negro soldiers who
fought in World War I)
Ebony 18: 110 Sept '63
CHICAGO--PARKS--GRANT
PARK
Nat Geog 124: 694-5 (col)
Nov '63

CIVIL WAR (U. S.)--SURVIVORS
  Life 65: 62-71 Nov 29 '68
CIVILIAN CONSERVATION CORPS.
  See UNITED STATES--CIVIL-
  IAN CONSERVATION CORPS
CLASSROOMS--CHINA (People's
  Republic)
  Nat Geog 126: 612 (col) Nov
  '64
CLASSROOMS--ESKIMO CHIL-
  DREN
  Nat Geog 125: 723 (col) May
  '64
CLASSROOMS--MALAYSIA
  Nat Geog 124: 780 (col) Nov
  '63
CLASSROOMS--NEPAL (Sherpa
  children)
  Nat Geog 130: 572 (col) Oct
  '66
CLASSROOMS--SAUDI ARABIA
  Nat Geog 129: 14 (col) Jan
  '66
CLASSROOMS, STREET--
  MAURITANIA
  Nat Geog 130: 190-1 (col)
  Aug '66
CLIFF DIVING
  Life 55: 43-6 Sept 6 '63
CLIFF DWELLINGS, INDIAN
  (N. American)--MESA
  VERDE NATIONAL PARK
  Nat Geog 125: 156-9, 163,
  165-70, 172, 182-9, 192-
  3 (col) Feb '64
CLIFF DWELLINGS--MESA
  VERDE, COLORADO
  America's Wonderlands, p.
  302-3 (col)
CLIFF DWELLINGS--MONTE-
  ZUMA CASTLE--ARIZONA
  America's Wonderlands, p.
  332 (col)
CLIFF DWELLINGS--NAVAJO
  NATIONAL MONUMENT--
  ARIZONA
  America's Wonderlands, p.
  316-19 (col)
CLIFF DWELLINGS--WETHER-
  ILL MESA PROJECT (Mesa
  Verde National Park)
  America's Wonderlands, p.
  6-7 (col)

America's Wonderlands, p.
  304-7, 310-11 (col)
CLIFF PALACE--MESA VERDE
  NATIONAL PARK
  America's Wonderlands, p.
  300-1 (col)
CLIFF PALACE--MESA VERDE
  NATIONAL PARK (painting)
  America's Wonderlands, p.
  298-9 (col)
CLIFFS--AUSTRALIA
  Life 67: 46-47 Nov 14 '69
CLOCKS--BIG BEN--LONDON
  Nat Geog 125: 649 (col) May
  '64
  Nat Geog 129: 771 (col) June
  '66
CLOCKS, GRANDFATHER
  Hobbies 68: 24-25 Jan '64
CLOCKS, JAPANESE LANTERN
  Hobbies 76: 126-127 Apr '71
CLOWNS
  Ebony 25: 155-6 (col), 157-9,
  160, 162 Nov '69
CLUBS--OXFORD AND CAM-
  BRIDGE UNIVERSITY CLUB
  --LONDON (interior)
  Nat Geog 129: 756-7 (col)
  June '66
COACHES. See also CARRI-
  AGES
COACHES, ENGLISH--GLASS
  COACH (used for royal
  weddings since 1910)
  Life 56: 78 (col) Mar 6 '64
COACHES, ENGLISH--STATE
  COACH OF LORD MAYOR
  OF LONDON
  Nat Geog 129: 746-7 (col)
  June '66
COACHES, SIGHTSEEING, 1904
  Nat Geog 130: 460-1 Oct '66
COAL MINERS--WALES
  Nat Geog 127: 738, 763 (col)
  June '65
COAL MINERS' LAMPS. See
  LAMPS, COAL MINERS'
COAT OF ARMS--ARMSTRONG
  Nat Geog 130: 539 (col) Oct
  '66
COAT OF ARMS--ELLIS
  Nat Geog 130: 539 (col) Oct
  '66

COAT OF ARMS--GROSVENOR
Nat Geog 130: 539 (col) Oct
'66
COAT OF ARMS--MOORE
Nat Geog 130: 539 (col) Oct
'66
COAT OF ARMS--ROOSEVELT
Nat Geog 129: 77 (col) Jan
'66
COAT OF ARMS--WOOD
Nat Geog 130: 539 (col)
Oct '66
COCK FIGHTING--PHILIPPINES
Nat Geog 130: 328 (col)
Sept '66
COCOPAH INDIANS. See IN-
DIANS OF NORTH AMERICA
--COCOPAH
COIN COLLECTION, LOUIS E.
ELIASBERG
Look 28: 54-55 (col) Dec 29
'64
COINS--SPAIN--DOUBLOONS
(era of Philip V)
Nat Geog 127: 1-3, 26-9,
37 (col) Jan '65
COINS--SPAIN--PIECES OF
EIGHT (era of Philip V)
Nat Geog 127: 5, 26-7 (col)
Jan '65
COINS--TONGA--KOULA
PIECES
Life 55: 44 (col) Oct 11 '63
COLISEUMS. See STADIUMS
COLLAGES
Sch Arts 63: 16-17 Dec '63
Sch Arts 68: 10-11 Mar '69
Sch Arts 69: 6-10 Jan '70
COLLECTIVE SETTLEMENTS--
ISRAEL
Nat Geog 138: 364-91 (col)
Sept '70
Nat Geog 127: 396-7, 404-5
(col) Mar '65
Nat Geog 128: 862-5 (col)
Dec '65
COLLEGE OF CARDINALS--
CATHOLIC CHURCH
Look 29: 24, 25-8 (col), 32
Aug 24 '65
COLLEGES AND UNIVERSITIES.
See Names of Colleges and
Universities, e.g. VIRGINIA.

UNIVERSITY; etc.
COLOMBIA
Travel 126: 51-54 (col) Aug
'66
Life 62: 62-63 (col) Apr 14
'67
Nat Geog 128: 234-273 (col)
Aug '70
COLOMBO, CEYLON
Nat Geog 129: 452-3 (col)
Apr '66
COLORADO
Nat Geog 136: 158-179, 182-
201 (col) Aug '69
COLORADO RIVER
America's Wonderlands, p.
140, 162-3 (col)
Holiday 41: 50-55 (col) June
'67
Am Heritage 20: 52, 55 (col)
Oct '69
Holiday 49: 50-53 (col) May/
June '71
COLOSSEUM--ROME
Nat Geog 137: 742-743 (col)
June '70
COLOSSUS. See Names of De-
ceased with Subdivision
Colossus, e.g. RAMESES II--
COLOSSUS
COLUMBUS, OHIO--AERIAL
VIEW
Ebony 20: 120 Mar '65
COMBINE MACHINES
Nat Geog 125: 626-7 (col)
May '64
Nat Geog 129: 370 (col) Mar
'66
COMBS
Hobbies 69: 28-29 Apr '64
COMMAND AND SERVICE
MODULES--PROJECT APOL-
LO. See SPACE VEHICLES
--U. S.--PROJECT APOLLO
COMMUNAL LIVING
Life 67: cover (col), 16B,
16C-23 (col) July 18 '69
COMMUNES--CHINA (People's
Republic)
Nat Geog 126: 636-7 (col)
Nov '64
COMMUNICATIONS SATELLITES
Life 58: 63-64 May 7 '65

COMMUNICATIONS SATELLITES
--U. S.--SYNCOM II
Life 55: 47-8 Sept 20 '63
COMPUTING MACHINES. See
CALCULATING MACHINES
--COMPUTERS
CONESTOGA WAGONS. See
COVERED WAGONS
CONGRESS--UNITED STATES.
See UNITED STATES--
CONGRESS
CONTROL ROOMS--SPACE
FLIGHT. See SPACE
FLIGHT--CONTROL ROOMS
CONVENTIONS, POLITICAL.
See POLITICAL CONVEN-
TIONS
COPPER MINES--ALASKA--
1939
Life 70: 40 (col) Jan 8 '71
COPPER MINES--PHILIPPINES
Nat Geog 130: 341 (col)
Sept '66
COPPER MINES, OPEN-CUT--
UTAH
Nat Geog 125: 570 (col) Apr
'64
COPPERSMITHS--IRAQ
Nat Geog 130: 748 (col)
Dec '66
CORAL REEFS
Life 69: 50-57 (col) Oct 23
'70
CORDILLERA VILLCABAMBA.
See VILCABAMBA, CORDIL-
LERA
CORFU ISLAND
Holiday 40: 58-65 (col) Oct
'66
CORNWALL, ENGLAND
Holiday 36: 34-39 (col) Aug
'64
CORONATION CEREMONIES
(22 Uganda martyrs)
Ebony 20: front cover, 23-
26 (col), 28-30 Jan '65
CORONATION CEREMONIES--
IRAN
Life 63: 28-34 (col) Nov 10
'67
Nat Geog 133: 300-321 (col)
Mar '68
CORREGIDOR (ruins)--PHILIP-

PINES
Nat Geog 130: 350 (col) Sept
'66
COSMONAUTS. See ASTRO-
NAUTS
COSTA RICA--ANTIQUITIES
Nat Geog 128: 144-5 (col)
July '65
COSTUME, ACADEMIC
Life 55: 78-9 (col) Sept 27
'63
Life 56: 45 Mar 6 '64
Nat Geog 128: 116 July '65;
556 Oct '65; 628 (col)
Nov '65
COSTUME, AFGHANISTAN
Look 32: 45-55 (col) Sept
17 '68
COSTUME, AFRICAN
Ebony 22: 151-2, 154-5 (col)
May '67
Look 31: 36-40 (col) July 25
'67
Ebony 23: 167-8 (col), 170
Nov '67
Life 66: 88-89 (col) Jan 10
'69
COSTUME, AMERICAN. See
also COSTUME--U. S.
COSTUME, AMERICAN MOD-
ERN. See also COSTUME--
U. S.
COSTUME, AMERICAN MOD-
ERN
Holiday 34: 56-67 July '63
Ebony 18: 81-2, 84 Aug '63
Life 55: 46-51 (col) Aug 16
'63
Look 27: 68 (col), 69, 71
Sept 24 '63
Ebony 18: 140 (col), 141,
144-6, 148, 150 Oct '63
Ebony 19: 173-4, 176, 178
Apr '64
Look 28: 82-83 (col), 85-86
June 16 '64
Sports Illus 21: 37-43 (col)
Sept 14 '64
Ebony 19: 126-7 (col) Sept
'64
Ebony 20: 162-4 (col), 166,
168 Dec '64
Look 29: 48-53 (col) Jan 26
'65

COSTUME, AMERICAN MOD-
ERN--BLAZERS (jackets for
all occasions)
Look 28: 46, 48, 50, 52
Mar 24 '64
Sports Illus 35: 42 (col), 43
Aug 23 '71
COSTUME, AMERICAN MOD-
ERN--COATS
Look 29: 82, 84-85 Nov 2
'65
COSTUME, AMERICAN MOD-
ERN--EVENING DRESSES
Ebony 18: 128-30 July '63
Look 27: 210, 212, 214
Oct 22 '63
Life 55: 133-136 (col), 137-
138 Nov 15 '63
Ebony 19: 176-7 (col), 178-
80, 182 May '64
Ebony 19: front cover (col)
Oct '64
Ebony 20: 95 (col), 96 Jan
'65
Ebony 21: 202 (col), 203
Nov '65
Holiday 38: 78-83 (col) Nov
'65
Ebony 22: 179-80 (col) Dec
'66
Ebony 23: 194 (col), 195
Oct '68
Ebony 25: 151-3 (col) Dec
'69
Holiday 49: 80-83 (col) Dec/
Jan '71
COSTUME, AMERICAN MOD-
ERN--FALL AND WINTER
FASHIONS 1963
Ebony 19: 155-6, 158, 160-
1 Nov '63
COSTUME, AMERICAN MOD-
ERN--FALL FASHIONS 1965
Life 59: 45-46 Aug 20 '65
COSTUME, AMERICAN MOD-
ERN--FALL FASHIONS 1967
Ebony 22: 120 (col), 121
Sept '67
COSTUME, AMERICAN MOD-
ERN--FALL FASHIONS 1971
Ebony 26: 150 (col), 152, 154,
156, 158 (col) Sept '71
COSTUME, AMERICAN MOD-

ERN--HOT PANTS
Life 70: 36-39 (col) Jan 29
'71
COSTUME, AMERICAN MOD-
ERN--LEATHER
Look 29: 96-98 (col) Sept 7
'65
COSTUME, AMERICAN MOD-
ERN (patchwork)
Look 34: 42-46 (col) Aug 25
'70
COSTUME, AMERICAN MOD-
ERN--SLEEPWEAR
Look 28: 42-44, 46 (col) Aug
11 '64
COSTUME, AMERICAN MOD-
ERN--SPORTING LOOK, 1964
Holiday 35: 78-81 (col) June
'64
COSTUME, AMERICAN MOD-
ERN--SPORTING LOOK, 1965
Holiday 37: 54-59 (col) June
'65
COSTUME, AMERICAN MOD-
ERN--SPORTING LOOK, 1967
Holiday 41: 80-85 (col) Feb
'67
Holiday 41: 64-69 (col) Apr
'67
COSTUME, AMERICAN MOD-
ERN--SPRING AND SUMMER
FASHIONS 1967
Ebony 22: 116-8, 120-1 (col)
Apr '67
COSTUME, AMERICAN MOD-
ERN--SPRING AND SUMMER
FASHIONS 1970
Ebony 25: 142-4, 146-7, 149-
52 (col) Apr '70
COSTUME, AMERICAN MOD-
ERN--SPRING FASHIONS
1964
Ebony 19: 124 (col), 125
Feb '64
Ebony 19: 130-2, 134 Mar
'64
COSTUME, AMERICAN MOD-
ERN--SPRING FASHIONS
1965
Ebony 20: 116 (col), 117
Feb '65
Ebony 20: 133-4, 136, 154
(col) Mar '65

COSTUME, AMERICAN MOD-
ERN--SPRING FASHIONS
1967
Ebony 22: 102-3 (col), 104,
106, 108 Feb '67
Ebony 22: 122-3 (col) Mar
'67
COSTUME, AMERICAN MOD-
ERN--SPRING FASHIONS
1968
Ebony 23: 116 (col), 117
Jan '68
COSTUME, AMERICAN MOD-
ERN--SUMMER FASHIONS
1964
Look 28: 73 (col), 74 June
30 '64
COSTUME, AMERICAN MOD-
ERN--SUMMER FASHIONS
1965
Life 58: 99-100 May 28 '65
Ebony 20: 140-2 (col), 144,
146 June '65
COSTUME, AMERICAN MOD-
ERN--SUMMER FASHIONS
1966
Ebony 21: 132-3 (col), 135-
6, 138-40 Apr '66
COSTUME, AMERICAN MOD-
ERN--SUMMER FASHIONS
1970
Ebony 25: 156 (col), 157, 164
Apr '70
Ebony 25: 137-9 (col), 140, 142,
144 (col), 145 May '70
COSTUME, AMERICAN MOD-
ERN--VINYL
Look 29: 69-70 (col) Oct 19
'65
COSTUME--AMISH MENNON-
ITES. See MENNONITES
COSTUME, ARABS
Holiday 34: 98 (col) Nov '63
Nat Geog 126: 835, 839, 846-
7 (col) Dec '64
Life 61: 80-82 (col) Aug 19
'66
COSTUME--ARABS. See also
COSTUME--EGYPT; COSTUME
--JORDAN; COSTUME--
SAUDI ARABIA; COSTUME--
SYRIA; COSTUME--YEMEN

COSTUME--AUSTRIA
Nat Geog 128: 44, 48 (col)
July '65
COSTUME--BALI
Nat Geog 124: 436, 439-46,
448-51, 454-8 (col) Sept
'63
COSTUME--BARDS--WALES
Nat Geog 127: 730-3 (col)
June '65
COSTUME, BASEBALL. See
BASEBALL CLUBS
COSTUME--BASQUES IN THE
UNITED STATES
Nat Geog 129: 884-5 (col)
June '66
COSTUME--BATHING SUITS
(modern)
Ebony 19: 107 (col), 108,
110, 112 Feb '64
Look 28: 59-60, 62-63 (col)
June 2 '64
Look 28: M8-M11 Dec 15
'64
Ebony 21: 116-17 Feb '66
Life 60: 118-120 (col) June
10 '66
Look 30: 52-53 (col) Aug 23
'66
Ebony 22: 112, 113 (col)
Jan '67
Ebony 25: 116-18, 120, 122
(col) Jan '70
Holiday 41: 68-73 (col) June
'67
Life 64: 66-67 (col) May 3
'68
Look 33: 44-49 (col) Feb 4
'69
Holiday 45: 50-53 (col) Feb
'69
Life 66: 64-66 (col) May 16
'69
Ebony 24: 134-6, 138 July
'69
Look 34: 30-35 (col) Feb 10
'70
Life 69: cover, 46-53 (col)
July 10 '70
Look 35: cover, 40-47 (col)
Feb 9 '71
Look 35: 54-60, 62 (col) May
18 '71

Ebony 26: front cover (col)
July '71
COSTUME--BATHING SUITS--
(1960's)
Nat Geog 124: 356-7 (col)
Sept '63
Nat Geog 128: 257 (col) Aug
'65
Life 58: 46-55 (col), 57,
Jan 8 '65
Life 106 (col) Dec 26 '69
COSTUME--BATHING SUITS
(in the Philippine Islands)
Holiday 48: 58-61 (col) Sept-
Oct '70
COSTUME, BATHING SUITS--
SWEDISH
Life 65: cover (col) Sept
27 '68
COSTUME--BATHING SUITS,
TOPLESS, 1964
Life 57: 54B-55, 57 July 10
'64
COSTUME--BEDOUINS. See
BEDOUINS
COSTUME--BEST DRESSED
NEGRO WOMEN, 1964
Ebony 19: 184-6, 188 (col),
189, 192-4 May '64
COSTUME--BEST DRESSED
NEGRO WOMEN, 1965
Ebony 20: 161-4, 166, 168
(col) May '65
COSTUME--BEST DRESSED
NEGRO WOMEN, 1966
Ebony 21: 48-50 (col), 52-4,
56, 58 (col) May '66
COSTUME--BEST DRESSED
NEGRO WOMEN, 1967
Ebony 22: 162-4, 166, 168-
70 (col) May '67
COSTUME--BEST DRESSED
NEGRO WOMEN, 1968
Ebony 23: 172-4, 176, 178-
9 (col) June '68
COSTUME--BEST DRESSED
NEGRO WOMEN, 1971
Ebony 26: 162-4, 166, 168-
70 (col) May '71
COSTUME, BIBLICAL, CIRCA
1800 B.C. (paintings)
Nat Geog 130: 742-3, 746-7,
754-5, 778, 782, 784, 788-

9 (col) Dec '66
COSTUME, BIBLICAL--DURING
THE LIFE OF JESUS CHRIST
Life 56: 56-66 (col) Mar 27
'64
COSTUME--BOLIVIA
Nat Geog 126: 298, 316-18
(col) Sept '64
Nat Geog 129: 153, 156-9,
163-4, 166, 170-1, 174-9,
185, 187, 189-95 (col) Feb
'66
COSTUME, BOWLING--AUS-
TRALIAN WOMEN
Nat Geog 124: 366-7 (col)
Sept '63
COSTUME, BOWLING--WOMEN
Life 55: 61, 64 Nov 8 '63
COSTUME--BRAZIL (Queen
Isabel Valenca)
Ebony 20: 33 (col) Sept '65
COSTUME--BRIDES. See also
WEDDINGS
COSTUME--BRIDES--RUSSIA
Nat Geog 129: 341 (col) Mar
'66
COSTUME--BRITTANY
Nat Geog 126: 189 (col) Aug
'64
Nat Geog 127: 471-3, 475,
478, 480, 482-3, 485, 487-
8, 491-3, 498-500, 503
(col) Apr '65
COSTUME--BUDDHIST PRIESTS
(students)--CEYLON
Nat Geog 129: 486 (col) Apr
'66
COSTUME--BUDDHIST PRIESTS
--VIETNAM (Republic)
Nat Geog 127: 865 (col) June
'65
COSTUME--BURMA
Nat Geog 124: 928-9 (col)
Dec '63
COSTUME--BURNOOSES
Nat Geog 125: 372-3 (col)
Mar '64
COSTUME--CAMBODIA
Nat Geog 126: 515-17, 526-7,
538-45, 548-51 (col) Oct
'64
COSTUME--CANADA--MAYOR
OF OTTAWA

Nat Geog 124: 96 (col) July
'63
COSTUME--CEYLON
Nat Geog 129: 447-9, 455-9,
461-8, 472-4, 477-85,
494-7 (col) Apr '66
COSTUME, CHILDREN'S (American)
Look 27: 58-60 (col), 61 Dec
31 '63
COSTUME--CHILDREN'S--PLAY
SUITS OF HEROES
Look 29: 64-67 (col) Aug 24
'65
COSTUME--CHILDREN'S--
RUSSIA
Look 31: 66-67 (col) Dec 26
'67
COSTUME, CHILDREN--20TH
CENTURY
Look 28: 38-40 (col) Sept 8
'64
Look 31: M6-M8 Sept 5 '67
Life 63: 63-66 Sept 22 '67
Look 32: 54-57 (col) Mar 19
'68
COSTUME--CHINA (People's Republic)
Life 55: 28-9 July 19 '63;
34 Aug 16 '63
Life 57: 97-102 (col) July
17 '64
COSTUME--CHINA--MANCHU
WOMAN, CIRCA 1910
Nat Geog 124: 538 (col) Oct '63
COSTUME, CHINESE
Holiday 34: 94 (col) Nov '63
Life 71: 59-65 (col) Dec 10 '71
COSTUME, COATS
Ebony 21: 104-6, 108 Jan '66
Ebony 22: 145 (col), 146, 148
Apr '67
COSTUME--COSTA RICA
Nat Geog 128: 124, 127-9,
131-3, 139, 141-3, 145,
147, 150 (col) July '65
COSTUME--COWBOYS. See
COWBOYS
COSTUME--CRICKET. See
CRICKETERS
COSTUME--CRUSADERS, 11TH
CENT. (paintings)
Nat Geog 124: 803, 808-9,

816-17, 820, 822-3, 844-5,
849-51, 853 (col) Dec '63
COSTUME--DIVERS (1960's)
Nat Geog 124: 138, 141, 144-
5, 150-1 (col) July '63
COSTUME--DRESSES--PICTURE-
BOOK
Life 69: 38-39 (col) July 17
'70
COSTUME, ECCLESIASTICAL.
See also COSTUME--BUD-
DHIST PRIESTS; COSTUME--
LAMAS
COSTUME, ECCLESIASTICAL--
CATHOLIC CHURCH--CARDI-
NALS
Life 55: front cover, 24-8
(col) July 5 '63
Nat Geog 128: 634 (col) Nov
'65
COSTUME, ECCLESIASTICAL--
CATHOLIC CHURCH--POPES
Life 55: 22, 26-8 (col) July
5 '63
Nat Geog 126: 823, 825 (col)
Dec '64
Nat Geog 129: 105 (col) Jan
'66
COSTUME, ECCLESIASTICAL--
GREEK ORTHODOX CHURCH
Life 56: 26, 28 (col) Mar 27
'64
Nat Geog 124: 132 (col) July
'63
Nat Geog 125: 86-8, 90-4, 96,
102, 104, 111-12, 127 (col)
Jan '64
Nat Geog 126: 818, 823 (col)
Dec '64
Nat Geog 128: 840 (col) Dec
'65
COSTUME--ECUADOR
Nat Geog 126: 338-45 (col)
Sept '64
COSTUME--EGYPT
Nat Geog 127: 586-7, 591-2,
594-6, 604-5, 610-13, 620-
1, 624-7, 631 (col) May
'65
COSTUME--ENGLAND. See also
COSTUME--WALES
COSTUME--ENGLAND, 11TH
CENT. (Bayeux Tapestry)

Nat Geog 130: 206-51 (col)
Aug '66
COSTUME--ENGLAND, 16TH
CENT. (1558-1603)--ELIZA-
BETHAN PERIOD (paintings)
Life 56: 60-76 (col) Apr 24
'64
COSTUME--ENGLAND, 17TH
CENT. (painting)
Nat Geog 125: 654-6 (col)
May '64
COSTUME--ENGLAND, 18TH
CENT. (paintings)
Life 55: 49-50, 54-5 (col)
Aug 9 '63
COSTUME--ENGLAND, 19TH
CENT. (painting)
Life 55: 51 (col) Aug 9 '63
COSTUME--ENGLAND, 20TH
CENT. (1950-59)--EVENING
DRESS
Nat Geog 128: 196 Aug '65
COSTUME--ENGLAND, 20TH
CENT. (1960-65)
Life 59: 65-6 Sept 17 '65
COSTUME--ENGLAND, 20TH
CENT. (1960-66)
Nat Geog 129: 746, 748-9,
756-7, 759-60, 766-7,
776-82, 784-5, 787-91
(col) June '66
COSTUME--ENGLAND, 20TH
CENT. (1960-66)--MORNING
DRESS
Nat Geog 129: 767 (col) June
'66
COSTUME--ENGLAND, 20TH
CENT. (1960-66)--ROCKERS
Nat Geog 129: 780-1 (col)
June '66
COSTUME--ENGLAND--HORSE
SHOW RING GUARD (pink
coat; gray topper)
Nat Geog 124: 243 (col) Aug
'63
COSTUME--ENGLAND--LORD
MAYOR OF LONDON
Nat Geog 128: 219 (col)
Aug '65
COSTUME--ENGLAND--LORD
MAYOR OF PLYMOUTH
Nat Geog 124: 217 (col) Aug
'63

COSTUME--ENGLAND--PEERS
Life 57: 48 Nov 20 '64
Nat Geog 129: 754-5 (col)
June '66
COSTUME--ENGLAND--POR-
TREEVE
Nat Geog 124: 240 (col) Aug
'63
COSTUME--ENGLAND--SPORT
STYLES (1960-66)
Holiday 40: 66-71 (col) Sept
'66
COSTUME--ESKIMOS. See
ESKIMOS
COSTUME--ETHIOPIA
Nat Geog 127: front cover,
548-552, 557-61, 563-5,
568-9, 571-2, 574-82 (col)
Apr '65
Nat Geog 128: 290 (col) Aug
'65
COSTUME--ETHIOPIA (painting)
Ebony 20: 90 (col) June '65
COSTUME--EUROPE, 20TH
CENT. (1910-19)
Life 55: 71-88 (col) Nov 22
'63
COSTUME--EVENING DRESSES
(by noted courturiers)
Look 29: 80-84 (col) Sept
21 '65
Life 59: 67 (col), 68, 71
Nov 12 '65
Life 59: 146-147 (col), 150
Nov 19 '65
COSTUME, FEATHERS
Life 61: 57-58 Oct 28 '66
Life 62: 87-90 (col), 92 June
2 '67
COSTUME--FINLAND
Life 60: 60-9 (col) June 24
'66
COSTUME--FRANCE, 20TH
CENT. (1910-19)
Life 55: 71 (col) Nov 22 '63
COSTUME--FRANCE, 20TH
CENT. (1960-66)
Nat Geog 129: 829-30, 834-5,
840-2, 844-5, 852-3, 856-
7, 859, 865-8 (col) June
'66
COSTUME, FRENCH MODERN
Ebony 20: 164-6, 168-70, 172

sented at President Kennedy's funeral, Nov. 1963)
Nat Geog 125: 310-11, 314-16, 318-20, 322-5, 335-7, 340-1, 344-5, 351 (col) Mar '64

COSTUME, MILITARY--U. S., 20TH CENT. (1917-18)--WORLD WAR I--ARMY
Nat Geog 128: 559 Oct '65
Nat Geog 129: 82 Jan '66

COSTUME, MILITARY--U. S., 20TH CENT. (1917-18)--WORLD WAR I--ARMY--GENERALS
Nat Geog 128: 174 Aug '65

COSTUME, MILITARY--U. S., 20TH CENT. (1930-39)--AIR FORCE--LIEUTENANTS (pilots)
Nat Geog 128: 294 Sept '65

COSTUME, MILITARY--U. S., 20TH CENT. (1941-45) WORLD WAR II--ARMY
Nat Geog 129: 91 Jan '66

COSTUME, MILITARY--U. S., 20TH CENT. (1941-45)--WORLD WAR II--ARMY--GENERALS
Life 56: 32-3 (col) Apr 17 '64
Life 57: 83, 85, 88 July 17 '64
Nat Geog 128: 156-7 Aug '65
Nat Geog 129: 91 Jan '66

COSTUME, MILITARY--U. S., 20TH CENT. (1960-66)--AIR FORCE--BLACK KNIGHTS (pilots)
Nat Geog 128: 336 (col) Sept '65

COSTUME, MILITARY--U. S., 20TH CENT. (1960-66)--AIR FORCE--GENERALS
Nat Geog 128: 291, 295-6, 308 (col) Sept '65

COSTUME, MILITARY--U. S., 20TH CENT. (1960-66)--ARMY
Life 55: 36-36A Nov 1 '63

COSTUME, MILITARY--U. S., 20TH CENT. (1960-66)--ARMY--GENERALS

Nat Geog 127: 837, 855 (col) June '65

COSTUME, MILITARY--U. S., 20TH CENT. (1960-66)--NAVAL AVIATION CADETS
Nat Geog 124: 894 (col) Dec '63

COSTUME, MILITARY--U. S., 20TH CENT. (1960-66)--NAVY--ADMIRALS
Nat Geog 127: 148-9, 181 (col) Feb '65

COSTUME, MILITARY--U. S., 20TH CENT. (1960-66)--NAVY--VICE ADMIRALS
Nat Geog 127: 148 (col) Feb '65

COSTUME, MILITARY--U. S., 20TH CENT. (1960-66)--U. S. MILITARY ACADEMY CADETS
Life 56: 34-5 (col) Apr 17 '64

COSTUME, MILITARY--U. S., 20TH CENT. (1960-66)--U. S. NAVAL ACADEMY MIDSHIPMEN
Nat Geog 126: 408-9 (col) Sept '64

COSTUME, MILITARY--U. S., 20TH CENT. (1960-66)--VIETNAMESE WAR
Life 56: front cover (col) Mar 20 '64; front cover, 42-3 (col) June 12 '64
Life 61: 60, 68-9 July 8 '66
Nat Geog 127: front cover, 39, 43, 49-50, 55, 57, 62, 64 (col) Jan '65; 855, 857 (col) June '65
Nat Geog 129: 274, 293, 295 (col) Feb '66

COSTUME, MILITARY--VIETNAM (Republic)
Life 56: 35, 38-40 (col) June 12 '64
Nat Geog 127: 834-5, 861, (col) June '65
Nat Geog 129: 274-7, 288, 294 (col) Feb '66

COSTUME, MILITARY--VIETNAM (Republic)--GENERALS IN VARIOUS BRANCHES OF

SERVICE
Life 56: 22-3 Feb 14 '64
Nat Geog 127: 836-7, 846-7
(col) June '65
COSTUME, MILITARY--YEMEN
Nat Geog 125: 416-17 (col)
Mar '64
COSTUME--MODERN (by noted
couturiers)
Life 68: 38-44 (col) Mar 13
'70
COSTUME--MOUNTAIN CLIMB-
ERS. See MOUNTAIN
CLIMBERS
COSTUME--MOZAMBIQUE
Nat Geog 126: 196-7, 201,
206-8, 210-13, 220-1,
224-7 (col) Aug '64
COSTUME--NAUTICAL STYLES
Am Heritage 15: 36-37 Feb
'64
COSTUME--NEPAL--MUSTANG
KINGDOM
Nat Geog 128: front cover,
578, 580, 582-3, 586-90,
592, 595, 598-601, 604 (col)
Oct '65
COSTUME--NEW BRITAIN (is-
land)
Nat Geog 129: 792-8, 800-17
(col) June '66
COSTUME--NIGERIA
Nat Geog 124: 578-9 (col)
Oct '63
COSTUME--NUBIA
Nat Geog 124: 589, 596-601,
603, 606-12, 614, 616-21
(col) Oct '63
Nat Geog 127: 620-1, 626-7
(col) May '65
COSTUME--OVERALLS
Life 55: 21 (col) Sept 6 '63
COSTUME, PALESTINIAN
WOMEN
Life 68: 28 (col) June 12 '70
COSTUME--PANTS SUITS
Ebony 24: 162 (col) Mar '69
Ebony 24: 168 (col), 169
Aug '69
COSTUME--PARKAS
Nat Geog 125: 456, 464 (col)
Mar '64; 702, 711, 714-17,
719-22, 732, 735 (col) May
'64

COSTUME--PARKAS--MOUNTAIN
CLIMBERS--MOUNT EVEREST
Nat Geog 124: 473, 488-9, 500-
2 (col) Oct '63
COSTUME--PERU
Nat Geog 125: 217, 221-2,
224-5, 228-30, 232-3, 239-
40, 251 (col) Feb '64
COSTUME--PHILIPPINES
Nat Geog 130: 301, 303-5,
308, 314, 316-18, 322-5,
328-31, 334-6, 338-41,
345, 347-9, 351 (col) Sept
'66
Holiday 38: 30 Aug '65
COSTUME--PLASTICS
Life 58: 91-92 Apr 9 '65
COSTUME--POLICE. See
POLICE; POLICEWOMEN
COSTUME--PORTUGAL
Nat Geog 128: 453-5, 461,
466-70, 473-83, 485-7,
490-2, 494, 496, 499
(col) Oct '65
Life 66: 64-8 (col) Jan 24
'69
COSTUME--RENAISSANCE
Life 65: 128-132 (col) Dec
6 '68
COSTUME--ROMAN CENTURION
Life 56: 65 (col) Mar 27 '64
COSTUME--ROMAN GOVERNOR
Life 56: 64 (col) Mar 27 '64
COSTUME--RUMANIA
Nat Geog 128: 70, 72-3 (col)
July '65
COSTUME--RUSSIA
Look 31: 40-45 (col) June
27 '67
COSTUME--RUSSIA, 20TH
CENT. (1910-19)
Life 55: front cover, 104A,
105-7 Oct 18 '63
COSTUME--RUSSIA, 20TH
CENT. (1910-19)--SCHOOL-
BOYS
Nat Geog 124: 536-7 (col)
Oct '63
COSTUME--RUSSIA, 20TH
CENT. (1960-66)
Life 55: entire issue (col)
Sept 13 '63
Nat Geog 129: 300-3, 306-7

311-13, 316-21, 324-9,
333, 335-6, 340-1, 344-
5, 350-1 (col) Mar '66
COSTUME--SALVATION ARMY
WOMEN
Nat Geog 124: 227 (col) Aug
'63
COSTUME, SAMOA
Holiday 34: 97 (col) Nov '63
COSTUME--SARAWAK
Nat Geog 126: 335 (col)
Sept '64
COSTUME--SAUDI ARABIA
Nat Geog 129: front cover,
11, 13-21, 30-3, 35, 38-
40, 43-50, 52-3 (col) Jan
'66
COSTUME--SCOTLAND. See
also TARTANS
COSTUME--SCOTLAND
Nat Geog 128: 82-3, 88-95
(col) July '65
Sports Illus 26: 63-5 (col)
Oct 14 '68
COSTUME--SENEGAL
Nat Geog 130: 196-7, 202-3
(col) Aug '66
COSTUME, SHAKESPEAREAN--
"THE COMEDY OF ERRORS"
(painting)
Nat Geog 125: 662 (col) May
'64
COSTUME, SHAKESPEAREAN--
"HAMLET"
Life 56: front cover, 83-7,
91-2, 95-6, 98 Apr 24 '64
COSTUME, SHAKESPEAREAN--
"HAMLET" (movie)
Life 56: 78B-81, 95, 99 Apr
24 '64
COSTUME, SHAKESPEAREAN--
"HENRY V"
Life 56: 102 May 1 '64
COSTUME, SHAKESPEAREAN--
"MIDSUMMER NIGHT'S
DREAM"
Life 70: 64-67 (col), 69 Apr
9 '71
COSTUME, SHAKESPEAREAN--
"OTHELLO"
Life 56: 80B-85 May 1 '64
COSTUME, SHAKESPEAREAN--
"OTHELLO" (painting)

Nat Geog 125: 655 (col) May
'64
COSTUME, SHAKESPEAREAN--
"RICHARD III" (painting)
Nat Geog 125: 635, 659 (col)
May '64
COSTUME, SHAKESPEAREAN--
"TAMING OF THE SHREW"
Life 55: 120, 123 Sept 20 '63
Look 30: 58-63 (col) Oct 4
'66
COSTUME, SHAKESPEAREAN--
"THE TEMPEST"
Life 61: 42-3 (col) July 8
'66
COSTUME--SHEIKS. See
SHEIKS
COSTUME--SHERPAS. See
SHERPAS--NEPAL
COSTUME--SIKKIM
Nat Geog 124: 708-27 (col)
Nov '63
COSTUME--SINGAPORE
Nat Geog 130: 268, 270-5,
282-95, 297 (col) Aug '66
COSTUME--SKI STYLES
Look 28: 52 Feb 25 '64
Life 60: 97 (col), 98, 103-
104 Feb 18 '66
Look 30: 64-65 (col), 66,
68 Nov 29 '66
Sports Illus 27: 47-54, 57
(col) Nov 13 '67
Look 32: 52-55 (col) Feb 6
'68
Sports Illus 31: 61-71 (col)
Nov 17 '69
COSTUME--SLEEPWEAR
Look 29: 60, 61 (col), 64
Dec 28 '65
Ebony 23: 158, 160 June '68
Ebony 26: 161-2, 164-5 Apr
'71
COSTUME--SOUTHEAST ASIA
Holiday 43: 80-85 (col) Feb
'68
COSTUME--SPAIN
Ebony 19: 135-8 Sept '64
Nat Geog 127: 293, 300-1,
303-5, 312-21, 324-5,
330, 335-9 (col) Mar '65
Look 30: 68-70, 73 Nov 1 '66
COSTUME, SPORTS

Look 27: 49-52 (col) July
   16 '63
Look 27: 70-75 (col) Nov
   19 '63
Ebony 19: 98-100, 102 Jan
   '64
Look 28: M9-M10, M12
   Mar 10 '64
Look 28: 60-64 (col) Nov 3
   '64
Life 58: 49-50 Jan 29 '65
Ebony 20: 94 (col) Jan '65
Ebony 20: 104-5 (col), 106,
   108 Feb '65
Sports Illus 22: 53-57 (col)
   Feb 15 '65
Sports Illus 22: 53-57 (col)
   Mar 15 '65
Ebony 20: 175-6, 178, 180,
   188 (col), 189 Apr '65
Look 29: 54-58 (col) July 27
   '65
Sports Illus 23: 35-38 (col)
   Sept 6 '65
Sports Illus 23: 64-65 Oct 25
   '65
Life 59: 144-145 (col), 149
   Nov 19 '65
Sports Illus 24: 91-94 (col)
   Apr 4 '66
Holiday 39: 78-81 (col) Apr
   '66
Ebony 21: 181-2 (col), 184,
   186 June '66
Sports Illus 25: 51-55 (col)
   Dec 12 '66
Life 62: 48-59 (col) Jan 27
   '67
Ebony 22: 156, 159-160, 162
   (col) June '67
Life 63: 44-49 (col) July 21
   '67
Holiday 42: 98-103 (col) Sept
   '67
Look 31: 44-45 (col) Nov 14
   '67
Ebony 23: 153-4, 156 (col)
   July '68
Look 32: 45 (col) July 23 '68
Sports Illus 29: 34-36 (col),
   37 Aug 12 '68
Holiday 44: 84-89 (col) Sept
   '68

Holiday 44: 96-101 (col) Nov
   '68
Sports Illus 30: 27-34 (col)
   Jan 13 '69
Ebony 24: 166, 167 (col)
   Apr '69
Look 33: 34-37 (col) Apr 1
   '69
Life 66: 74-78 (col) Apr 18
   '69
Ebony 24: 166-8, 170 June
   '69
Sports Illus 30: 23-26 (col)
   June 30 '69
Holiday 46: 56-59 (col) Nov
   '69
Sports Illus 32: 35-42 (col)
   Jan 12 '70
Look 34: 36-39 (col), 40
   Mar 24 '70
Sports Illus 32: 41-43 (col)
   Apr 20 '70
Look 34: 67-68 (col), 69
   June 2 '70
Ebony 25: 116 (col), 167
   Oct '70
Sports Illus 33: 52-54 (col)
   Oct 5 '70
Holiday 48: 36-43 (col) Nov
   '70
Ebony 26: 106-9 (col) Jan '71
Ebony 26: 154-5 May '71
Ebony 26: 156-8, 160 (col)
   June '71
COSTUME--SUEDE
   Ebony 18: 172 (col), 173
      Sept '63
COSTUME--SWEATERS
   Look 28: 52-53 (col), 54-55
      Aug 25 '64
COSTUME--SWEATERS, BULKY
   Life 55: 115 (col) Oct 25 '63
COSTUME--SWEATSHIRTS
   Life 69: 40-41 (col) July 17
      '70
COSTUME, SWEDEN
   Life 65: 88-98 (col) Sept 27
      '68
COSTUME--SYRIA
   Nat Geog 124: 826 (col) Dec
      '63
   Nat Geog 128: 266-7, 269-71
      (col) Aug '65

Nat Geog 130: 759-65 (col)
Dec '66
COSTUME--TENNIS, 1960's
Life 59: 48-50, 52 Aug 13 '65
COSTUME--"THE WET LOOK"
Life 66: 61-62 (col) Apr 11
'69
COSTUME, THEATRICAL--
"ADRIADNE AND NAXOS"
Ebony 20: 86 Mar '65
COSTUME, THEATRICAL--
"AFTER THE FALL"
Life 56: 64A-65 Feb 7 '64
COSTUME, THEATRICAL--
"AIDA"
Nat Geog 126: 88-9 (col)
July '64
Ebony 21: 94 Aug '66
COSTUME, THEATRICAL--
"ANTONY AND CLEOPATRA"
Ebony 22: 184-5 (col), 186
Dec '66
COSTUME, THEATRICAL--
"APPLAUSE"
Life 68: 54A-54C (col) Apr
3 '70
COSTUME, THEATRICAL--
"THE BALLAD OF THE SAD
CAFE"
Life 55: 33 Nov 22 '63
COSTUME, THEATRICAL--
"BARBER OF SEVILLE"
Ebony 20: 84 (col) Mar '65
COSTUME, THEATRICAL--
"BECKET" (movie)
Life 56: 81-2 (col) Mar 13
'64
COSTUME, THEATRICAL--
"CAMELOT"
Nat Geog 130: 834 (col) Dec
'66
COSTUME, THEATRICAL--
"CELEBRATION"
Life 66: 82-83 (col) Mar 14
'69
COSTUME, THEATRICAL--
"THE DEPUTY"
Life 56: 28D Mar 13 '64
COSTUME, THEATRICAL--
"DYLAN"
Life 56: 62 June 5 '64
COSTUME, THEATRICAL--
"FALSTAFF"

Ebony 21: 85-6 Jan '66
COSTUME, THEATRICAL--
"THE FANTASTICKS"
Life 57: 75-6, 78, Oct 16
'64
COSTUME, THEATRICAL--
"THE GOLDEN COCKEREL"
Ebony 20: 86 Mar '65
COSTUME, THEATRICAL--
"GOOD MORNING, MISS
DOVE"
Life 56: 37 Feb 21 '64
COSTUME, THEATRICAL--
"THE GREATEST STORY
EVER TOLD" (movie)
Life 56: 54-67 (col) Mar 27
'64
COSTUME, THEATRICAL--
"HAIR"
Ebony 25: 120-1 (col), 122,
126 May '70
COSTUME, THEATRICAL--
"HELLO, DOLLY"
Life 56: front cover, 107-11
(col) Apr 3 '64
Ebony 23: 83-7 (col) Jan '68
COSTUME, THEATRICAL--
"HERE'S LOVE"
Life 55: 34-5 Nov 22 '63
COSTUME, THEATRICAL--
"LA TRAVIATA"
Life 56: 37, 40-1 Mar 13
'64
COSTUME, THEATRICAL--
"LORD OF THE FLIES"
(movie)
Life 55: 96-100 Oct 25 '63
COSTUME, THEATRICAL--
"LUTHER"
Life 55: 125-6 Oct 11 '63
COSTUME, THEATRICAL--
"MAME"
Life 60: 88, 89-92 (col)
June 17 '66
COSTUME, THEATRICAL--
"MOTHER COURAGE"
Life 57: 112B-114 Sept 18 '64
COSTUME, THEATRICAL--
"MY FAIR LADY"
Look 28: 60-61 (col), 62, 64
Feb 25 '64
COSTUME, THEATRICAL--
"OH, WHAT A LOVELY WAR"

COSTUME--U.S., 20TH CENT.
(1900-09)
Nat Geog 124: 518, 520, 523,
529-33, 566 Oct '63
Nat Geog 130: 456-61 Oct '66
COSTUME--U.S., 20TH CENT.
(1900-09)--RIDING COSTUME
Nat Geog 130: 469 Oct '66
COSTUME--U.S., 20TH CENT.
(1901-33)--PRESIDENTS OF
U.S.
Nat Geog 128: 540, 546-8,
552, 555, 558-62, 564-6,
568, 571-2 (col) Oct '65
COSTUME--U.S., 20TH CENT.
(1910-19)
Nat Geog 124: 554-5, 582,
Oct '63
Nat Geog 128: 108-9, 112-13
July '65
COSTUME--U.S., 20TH CENT.
(1910-19)--RIDING COSTUME
Nat Geog 124: 546 Oct '63
COSTUME--U.S., 20TH CENT.
(1920-29)
Life 55: 58 July 26 '63
Nat Geog 124: 543 Oct '63
COSTUME--U.S., 20TH CENT.
(1920-29)--EVENING DRESS
Nat Geog 124: 556, 563 Oct
'63
COSTUME--U.S., 20TH CENT.
(1930-39)
Nat Geog 124: 570-1, 582-3
Oct '63
Nat Geog 128: 114-5 July '65
COSTUME--U.S., 20TH CENT.
(1930-39)--EVENING DRESS
Life 55: 133 Dec 6 '63
COSTUME--U.S., 20TH CENT.
(1933-63)--PRESIDENTS OF
U.S.
Nat Geog 129: 70, 72, 75, 79-
80, 83, 87-90, 94, 97-100,
104-5, 107-12, 114-15 (col)
Jan '66
COSTUME--U.S., 20TH CENT.
(1950-59)--EVENING DRESS
Nat Geog 128: 117 July '65
COSTUME--U.S., 20TH CENT.
(1960-66)
Life 55: 32-32A July 12 '63
Nat Geog 126: 58, 68-9, 79,

86-7, 94, 101 (col) July
'64
COSTUME--U.S., 20TH CENT.
(1960-66)--CHILDREN
Life 56: 98, 101 June 12 '64
COSTUME--U.S., 20TH CENT.
(1960-66)--COLLEGE GIRLS
Life 55: 46-51 (col) Aug 16
'63
COSTUME--U.S., 20TH CENT.
(1960-66)--EVENING DRESS
Life 57: 48-55 (col) Aug 28
'64
Nat Geog 129: 108 Jan '66
Nat Geog 130: 595, 610, 624-
7 (col) Nov '66
COSTUME--U.S., 20TH CENT.
(1960-66)--HIGH SCHOOL
STUDENTS
Life 55: 66-79 (col) Sept 27
'63; 68-79 (col) Oct 11 '63
COSTUME--U.S., 20TH CENT.
(1960-66)--MORNING DRESS
Nat Geog 130: 598-9, 636 Nov
'66
COSTUME, VELVET SUITS
Look 27: 110-111 (col) Nov
5 '63
COSTUME--VIETNAM (Republic)
Nat Geog 126: 414-15, 418,
421, 426-8, 430, 432-3
(col) Sept '64
Nat Geog 127: 43, 46-7, 52-3,
59-60, 65 (col) Jan '65;
834-5, 842, 844-5, 849-54,
865-6, 868-71 (col) June
'65
COSTUME--WALES
Nat Geog 127: 734, 742, 748,
750, 769 (col) June '65
COSTUME, WEDDING
Ebony 19: 200-2, 204, 206
June '64
Ebony 20: 185-6, 188, 190
May '65
COSTUME, WESTERN U.S.
Look 32: 54-57 (col) Aug 6
'68
COSTUME--WINDWARD ISLANDS
Nat Geog 128: 762-6, 772-5,
780-2, 786-7, 790-3, 797,
799-801 (col) Dec '65
COSTUME--YEMEN

Nat Geog 125: 402-5, 407,
410, 415-17, 422-3, 426-
33, 435-9, 441-4 (col)
Mar '64
COSTUME--YUGOSLAVIA
Nat Geog 128: 59-61 (col)
July '65
COSTUME DESIGN BY BAL-
MAIN, 1963
Life 55: 80 (col) Aug 30 '63
COSTUME DESIGN BY BLACK
DESIGNERS
Look 35: 50-54 (col) Apr 20
'71
COSTUME DESIGN BY BROOKS,
1968
Ebony 23: 179-80, 184 (col)
Aug '68
Life 65: 71-72 Nov 22 '68
COSTUME DESIGN BY CAPUC-
CI, 1964
Look 28: 122 May 19 '64
COSTUME DESIGN BY CAPUC-
CI, 1966
Ebony 22: 170 (col) Nov '66
COSTUME DESIGN BY CAPUC-
CI, 1967
Ebony 23: 154-5 (col) Nov '67
COSTUME DESIGN BY CARDIN,
1963
Life 55: 79 (col) Aug 30 '63
COSTUME DESIGN BY CARDIN,
1964
Look 28: 126 May 19 '64
COSTUME DESIGN BY CARDIN,
1965
Life 59: 46-47 (col) Sept 3
'65
COSTUME DESIGN BY CARDIN,
1966
Ebony 22: 172 (col) Nov '66
COSTUME DESIGN BY CARDIN,
1967
Ebony 23: 152 (col) Nov '67
COSTUME DESIGN BY CARDIN,
1968
Life 64: 33 Mar 1 '68
Life 65: 62 (col) Aug 30 '68
Ebony 202 (col) Oct '68
COSTUME DESIGN BY CARDIN,
1969
Life 66: 47 (col) Feb 28 '69
Ebony 25: 140-2, 144A, 146A

(col) Nov '69
COSTUME DESIGN BY CARDIN,
1971
Ebony 27: 196, 200 (col) Nov
'71
COSTUME DESIGN BY CHALLIS,
1968
Life 65: 74-75, 78 (col), 80
Nov 15 '68
COSTUME DESIGN BY CHANEL,
1964
Life 56: 123 Mar 6 '64
COSTUME DESIGN BY CHANEL,
1965
Life 59: 50 Sept 3 '65
COSTUME DESIGN BY COUR-
REGES, 1964
Look 28: 126 May 19 '64
Look 28: M11 Oct 6 '64
COSTUME DESIGN BY COUR-
REGES, 1965
Life 58: 47, 48-49 (col), 52-
54 May 21 '65
Look 29: 98-100 July 13 '65
Life 59: 52A Sept 3 '65
COSTUME DESIGN BY COUR-
REGES, 1968
Life 65: 60 (col) Aug 30 '68
Ebony 23: 208 (col) Oct '68
COSTUME DESIGN BY COUR-
REGES, 1969
Life 66: 47 (col) Feb 28 '69
Ebony 25: 142 (col) Nov '69
COSTUME DESIGN BY DIOR,
1963
Life 55: 78-9 (col) Aug 30
'63
COSTUME DESIGN BY DIOR,
1964
Look 28: 123 May 19 '64
COSTUME DESIGN BY DIOR,
1967
Ebony 23: 152 (col) Nov '67
COSTUME DESIGN BY DIOR,
1968
Life 64: 33 Mar 1 '68
Ebony 23: 179 (col) Aug '68
Life 65: 58-59 (col) Aug 30
'68
Ebony 23: 203 (col) Oct '68
COSTUME DESIGN BY DIOR,
1969
Life 66: 46 (col) Feb 28 '69

Life 55: 81 Aug 30 '63
COSTUME DESIGN BY ST.
LAURENT, 1964
Life 56: 119-21 (col) Mar 6
'64
Look 28: 122 May 19 '64
Look 28: 84-87 July 14 '64
COSTUME DESIGN BY ST.
LAURENT, 1965
Life 59: 48 (col), 50 Sept 3
'65
COSTUME DESIGN BY ST.
LAURENT, 1966
Life 60: 28 Mar 4 '66
Ebony 22: 169 (col) Nov '66
COSTUME DESIGN BY ST.
LAURENT, 1967
Ebony 23: 154 (col) Nov '67
COSTUME DESIGN BY ST.
LAURENT, 1968
Life 64: 32, 36 Mar 1 '68
Life 65: 60 (col) Aug 30 '68
Life 65: 53 (col) Sept 6 '68
Ebony 23: 208 (col) Oct '68
COSTUME DESIGN BY ST.
LAURENT, 1969
Life 66: 46 (col) Feb 28 '69
Ebony 25: 140-1 (col) Nov '69
COSTUME DESIGN BY SARMI,
1964
Life 57: 54 (col) Aug 28 '64
COSTUME DESIGN BY "SLAVA."
See COSTUME DESIGN BY
ZAITSEV
COSTUME DESIGN BY TIFFEAU,
1964
Life 57: 69-70 (col) Oct 2 '64
COSTUME DESIGN BY UNGARO,
1967
Ebony 23: 153 (col) Nov '67
COSTUME DESIGN BY UNGARO,
1968
Life 65: 61 (col) Aug 30 '68
COSTUME DESIGN BY UNGARO,
1969
Ebony 25: 142 (col) Nov '69
COSTUME DESIGN BY UNGARO,
1971
Ebony 27: 196, 198 (col) Nov
'71
COSTUME DESIGN BY VALEN-
TINO, 1968
Life 65: 107-108 (col) Oct 11
'68

COSTUME DESIGN BY VANDER-
BILT (Gloria)
Life 65: 86-88 (col) Oct 4
'68
COSTUME DESIGN BY ZAITSEV
("Slava"), 1963
Life 55: 113-14 Sept 13 '63
COTTAGES--COLONIAL PERI-
OD--PLYMOUTH, MASS.
(replicas)
Nat Geog 130: 824-5 (col)
Dec '66
COTTON PICKERS--BOLIVIA
Nat Geog 129: 191 (col) Feb
'66
COUNTRY STORE. See STORE,
COUNTRY
COUPS D'ETAT. See REVOLU-
TIONS
COURCHEVEL--FRENCH ALPS
Holiday 34: 98-99, 102-103
(col) Dec '63
COURTHOUSES--APPOMATTOX,
VA. (place of surrender by
General Lee to General Grant
ending U.S. Civil War, April
1865)
Nat Geog 127: 458-9, 461 (col)
Apr '65
COURTHOUSES--HUDSON
COUNTY--NEW YORK STATE
Am Heritage 17: 26, 27-29
(col) Oct '66
COURTHOUSES--MANCHESTER,
VT.
Life 55: 118 Oct 11 '63
COURTHOUSES--ST. LOUIS (Old
Courthouse where Dred Scott's
trial held, 1847)
Nat Geog 128: 619 (col) Nov
'65
COVERED WAGONS
Nat Geog 128: 642, 652-3, 655
(col) Nov '65
COVERED WAGONS--OREGON
TRAIL (painting)
Nat Geog 127: 100-1 (col)
Jan '65
COWBOYS
Life 68: 39-47 Apr 3 '70
COWBOYS--BOLIVIA
Nat Geog 129: 190 (col)
Feb '66

COWBOYS--COSTA RICA
Nat Geog 128: 150 (col) July
'65
COWBOYS--LOUISIANA (Acadians)
Nat Geog 129: 366-7 (col)
Mar '66
COWBOYS--PORTUGAL
Nat Geog 128: 496 (col) Oct
'65
COWBOYS--SPAIN
Nat Geog 127: 315 (col) Mar
'65
COWBOYS--U. S. --EARLY 19TH
CENT.
Am Heritage 14: 16-31 Oct
'63
COWBOYS--WYOMING
Nat Geog 129: 558 (col) Apr
'66
COZUMEL ISLAND--CARIBBEAN
Life 58: 120-123 (col), 125
Mar 5 '65
CRAB RACING--HARD CRAB
DERBY--CRISFIELD, MD.
Nat Geog 126: 390-1 (col)
Sept '64
CRADLEBOARDS. See PA-
POOSE BOARDS
CRATER, HALEAKALA--HAWAII
America's Wonderlands, p.
540-1 (col)
CRATER, SUNSET--ARIZONA
America's Wonderlands, p.
326-9 (col)
CRATER LAKE--OREGON
America's Wonderlands, p.
42 (col)
America's Wonderlands, p.
408-11 (col)
CRATERS OF THE MOON NA-
TIONAL MONUMENT--IDAHO
America's Wonderlands, p.
240 (col)
CREE INDIANS. See INDIANS
OF NORTH AMERICA--CREE
CREMATION--INDIA
Life 56: front cover, 37-40
(col) June 5 '64
CRETE
Life 62: 62-71 (col) Feb 17
'67
Life 65: 20-23 (col) July 19
'68

CRICKETERS--ENGLAND
Nat Geog 129: 767 (col) June
'66
CRISPUS ATTUCKS MONUMENT
--BOSTON
Ebony 18: 108 Sept '63
CROAGH PATRICK--IRELAND'S
HOLY MOUNTAIN
Look 29: 78-79 (col), 81-82
Mar 23 '65
CROQUET
Holiday 42: 50-53 (col) Oct
'67
CROSS OF SCRIPTURES--
CLONMACNOISE ABBEY--
IRELAND
Look 35: 46 (col) Mar 23 '71
CROSSES, COPTIC
Nat Geog 127: front cover,
550 (col) Apr '65
CROSSES, IVORY, 12TH CENT.
Life 56: 119-20 (col) June
12 '64
CROW INDIANS. See INDIANS
OF NORTH AMERICA--CROW
CROWNS, ENGLISH--IMPERIAL
STATE CROWN
Life 56: 75 (col) Mar 6 '64
CROWNS--ETHIOPIAN
Ebony 19: 30 (col) Oct '64
CRUISERS. See WARSHIPS
CRUSADES (route of First Cru-
sade retraced)
Nat Geog 124: 797-855 (col)
Dec '63
CRYPT LAKE
America's Wonderlands, p.
134-5 (col)
CRYSTALS
Nat Geog 134: 278-295 (col)
Aug '68
CUBA--HISTORY--BLOCKADE,
1962
Nat Geog 129: 106-7 Jan '66
CUBAN BLOCKADE. See CUBA
--HISTORY--BLOCKADE
CUMBERLAND CAVERNS--TEN-
NESSEE
Nat Geog 125: 806-7 (col)
June '64
CUMBERLAND GAP--TENNES-
SEE
Nat Geog 140: 592-621 (col)
Nov '71

CURRENT RIVER--MISSOURI
America's Wonderlands, p.
60 (col)
CUSTER MASSACRE, 1876. See
BATTLES--LITTLE BIG HORN
CYCLORAMA--PICKETT'S
CHARGE (visitors' center at
Gettysburg)
Nat Geog 124: 22-3 (col)
July '63
CYCLOS. See PEDICABS
CYPRUS
Look 28: 30-37 June 2 '64
CYPRUS--CYPRIOT-TURKISH
WAR, 1964
Life 57: 20-5 (col) Aug 21
'64
CZECHOSLOVAKIA
Nat Geog 133: 152-193 (col)
Feb '68

D

D-1 (artificial satellite). See
ARTIFICIAL SATELLITES--
FRANCE--D-1
DACHAS. See HOUSES--
DACHAS
DAKAR, SENEGAL
Nat Geog 130: 200-1 (col) Aug
'66
DAMASCUS
Nat Geog 130: 767 (col) Dec
'66
DAMS. See Names of Dams,
e. g. GLEN CANYON DAM;
etc.
DANCE--FLAMENCO--SPAIN
Nat Geog 127: 332-3 (col)
Mar '65
DANCE--FRUG
Life 57: 57 Aug 7 '64
DANCE--HIGHLAND FLING--
NOVA SCOTIA
Nat Geog 125: 874 (col) June
'64
DANCE--LIMBO--ANTIGUA
(island)
Nat Geog 130: 503 (col) Oct
'66
DANCE, MODERN. See MOD-
ERN DANCE

DANCERS--AUSTRIA
Nat Geog 124: 568-9 (col)
Oct '63
DANCERS--BALI
Nat Geog 124: 442-3 (col)
Sept '63
DANCERS--BOLIVIA
Nat Geog 129: 163 (col) Feb
'66
DANCERS--CAMBODIA
Nat Geog 126: 520, 531 (col)
Oct '64
DANCERS--CEYLON
Nat Geog 129: 479 (col) Apr
'66
DANCERS--CHINA (People's
Republic)
Nat Geog 126: 626-7 (col)
Nov '64
DANCERS--DEVIL DANCERS--
BOLIVIA
Nat Geog 129: 193 (col) Feb
'66
DANCERS, INDIAN (N. Ameri-
can)--HOPIS
Nat Geog 125: 552-3 (col)
Apr '64
DANCERS--MALAYSIA
Nat Geog 124: 746-7 (col)
Nov '63
DANCERS--POLAND
Nat Geog 127: 733 (col) June
'65
DANCERS--RUSSIA
Life 55: 125-6 Sept 13 '63
DANCERS--SPAIN
Nat Geog 127: 330-1 (col)
Mar '65
DANUBE RIVER
Nat Geog 128: 34-79 (col)
July '65
Holiday 40: 28-33, 35-37 (col),
86-87 Aug '66
DEAD SEA
Nat Geog 130: 774-5 (col)
Dec '66
DEATH VALLEY--CALIFORNIA
Holiday 38: 69, 72-73 (col)
Oct '65
America's Wonderlands, p.
370-2, 373-4 (col)
Nat Geog 137: 68-103 (col)
Jan '70

DIAMANT (rocket) See ROCK-
  ETS--CARRIERS--FRANCE
  --DIAMANT
DIAMOND, CARTIER
  Life 67: 65-66A Nov 14 '69
DIAMOND, HOPE (Winston's
  gift to the Smithsonian Insti-
  tute)
  Life 59: 96 (col) Nov 19 '65
  Life 67: 66B Nov 14 '69
DIAMOND--IDOL'S EYE
  Life 67: 66B Nov 14 '69
DIAMOND, KRUPP
  Life 67: 66B Nov 14 '69
DIAMONDS, UNCUT
  Nat Geog 130: 171 (col) Aug
    '66
  Life 67: 93 Dec 12 '69
DINOSAUR NATIONAL MONU-
  MENT--UTAH--COLO.
  America's Wonderlands, p.
    232, 234-7 (col)
DINOSAUR QUARRY CENTER--
  UTAH--COLO.
  America's Wonderlands, p.
    239 (col)
DINOSAURS--DIPLODOCUS
  America's Wonderlands, p.
    238
DIRIGIBLES. See AIRSHIPS
DISASTERS. See EXPLOSIONS;
  FLOODS; HURRICANES; SUB-
  MARINE DISASTERS
DISNEYLAND
  Nat Geog 124: 158-60, 183-
    207 (col) Aug '63
  Nat Geog 129: 610-11 (col)
    May '66
  Look 35: 18-25 (col) Apr 6
    '71
DIVERS
  Life 59: 41 (col) Sept 3 '65
  Ebony 21: 71-2, 74, 76-8
    May '66
  Ebony 23: 40-1 Apr '68
  Sports Illus 35: 27-30 (col)
    Aug 16 '71
DIVERS, JAPANESE (Ama)
  (block prints)
  Nat Geog 140: 124-134 (col)
    July '71
DIVING
  Nat Geog 124: 413-14 (col)

  Sept '63
  Nat Geog 125: 469, 475, 483,
    487-9, 493, 500 (col) Apr
    '64
  Nat Geog 126: 809 (col) Dec
    '64
DIVING APPARATUS
  Life 59: 42 Sept 3 '65
  Life 65: 64-68, 70-71, 74-75
    (col) Oct 4 '68
DIVING APPARATUS--SCUBA
  DIVERS
  Nat Geog 125: 837 (col) June
    '64
DIVING APPARATUS--STEINKE
  HOOD (aid to breathing)
  Nat Geog 125: 780 (col) June
    '64
DIVING, CLIFF. See CLIFF
  DIVING
DIVING--GREAT BAHAMA BANK
  Nat Geog 138: 346-363 (col)
    Sept '70
DIVING EXPLORATIONS--
  FLORIDA
  Ebony 22: 99-101 (col), 102,
    104-5 Mar '67
DIVING EXPLORATIONS--PRO-
  JECT TEKTITE--GREAT
  LAMESHUR BAY, VIRGIN
  ISLANDS
  Life 66: 30-35 (col) Mar 7
    '69
DIVING SAUCERS (models)
  Nat Geog 125: 479, 502, 505,
    507 (col) Apr '64
DIVING SAUCERS--CAPTAIN
  JACQUES YVES COUSTEAU'S
  DIVING SAUCER
  Nat Geog 125: 795 (col) June
    '64
DIVINING ROD
  Life 55: 143-4 Oct 18 '63
DOG SHOW--WESTMINSTER
  KENNEL CLUB
  Life 70: 38-45 (col) Feb 12
    '71
DOG SLEDS, ESKIMO
  Nat Geog 125: 715 (col)
    May '64
DOG SLEDS--ONTARIO (province)
  CANADA
  Nat Geog 124: 433-4 (col)
    Sept '63

DOG TEAMS, ESKIMO
Nat Geog 125: 714, 718 (col)
May '64
DOG TEAMS--GREENLAND
HUSKIES
Nat Geog 127: 254-5, 266-7,
272-3, 275-9 (col) Feb
'65
DOG TEAMS--ONTARIO (prov-
ince) CANADA
Nat Geog 124: 433-4 (col)
Sept '63
DOGS, SENTRY--POLICE
Life 58: 107-108 Apr 23 '65
DOLL CLOTHES, 1830-1880
Hobbies 70: 40-41 Feb '66
DOLL HOUSES
Hobbies 69: 116 Mar '64
DOLLS, BABY
Hobbies 69: 36-37 Sept '64
DOLLS, BARBIE
Life 55: 73-5 (col) Aug 23
'63
DOLLS, BISQUE-HEADED
Hobbies 72: 40-41 May '67
Hobbies 74: 42-43 Aug '69
DOLLS, BRU
Hobbies 69: 37-38, 40 Aug
'64
Hobbies 70: 36, 38 Feb '65
DOLLS, BUTTON
Hobbies 73: 50-51 Jan '69
DOLLS, CHINA-HEADED
Hobbies 71: 40-41, 44 Feb
'67
DOLLS, CHINESE
Hobbies 70: 38-39 Apr '65
DOLLS, CHRISTMAS CRIB
FIGURINES
Hobbies 69: 36, 38 Dec '64
DOLLS--DUMP BABIES
Hobbies 74: 46-7 Nov '69
DOLLS--"FIRST LADY" DOLLS
OF EVYAN COLLECTION
Ebony 22: 138 Dec '66
DOLLS, FRENCH
Hobbies 68: 39 Dec '63
Hobbies 69: 36-37, 40 July
'64
DOLLS, JAPANESE
Hobbies 70: 38-40 Apr '65
Hobbies 75: 48-49 May '70
DOLLS, LOOFA

Hobbies 70: 36-37 June '65
DOLLS, MECHANICAL
Hobbies 72: 38-39 Aug '67
DOLLS, PAPIER-MACHE
Hobbies 69: 36-37, 40 June
'64
Instr 75: 63 Feb '66
DOLLS, PARIAN
Hobbies 76: 41 Dec '71
DOLLS, PEDDLER
Hobbies 68: 37 Dec '63
DOLLS, PINCUSHION
Hobbies 73: 41 June '68
DOLLS--SAMUEL F. PRYOR
CHRISTMAS EXHIBIT--
NATIONAL GEOGRAPHIC
SOCIETY 1965
Hobbies 71: 40 Jan '67
DOLLS--SASCHA MORGEN-
THALER'S
Look 28: 71-73 Dec 29 '64
DOLLS, WAX
Hobbies 70: 38-39 Aug '65
DOLLS, WOOD--SCHOENHUT
Hobbies 76: 40 June '71
DOLLS, WOODEN
Hobbies 71: 39-40 Aug '66
Hobbies 76: 44 Apr '71
Hobbies 76: 42 May '71
DOLOMITES
Nat Geog 128: 394-5 (col)
Sept '65
DOME OF THE ROCK--JERU-
SALEM. See MOSQUES--
DOME OF THE ROCK--
JERUSALEM
DOMINICA (island). See WIND-
WARD ISLANDS
DOMINICAN REPUBLIC--
REVOLUTION
Life 58: 30-38B (col), 38C
May 14 '65
Look 29: 38-43 June 15 '65
DOOR PENINSULA--WISCONSIN
Nat Geog 135: 346-371 (col)
Mar '69
DOUBLOONS. See COINS--
SPAIN--DOUBLOONS
DOUGLASS, FREDERICK--
MEMORIAL--STATEN ISLAND,
N. Y.
Ebony 18: 109 Sept '63
DOVE-COTES, 16TH CENT.

EDWARD VII, KING OF GREAT
BRITAIN--FUNERAL RITES,
MAY 20, 1910
Life 55: 72-5 (col) Nov 22 '63
EGYPT
Holiday 35: 68-73, 75 (col)
June '64
EGYPT, ANCIENT
Life 64: 42-59 (col) Apr 5
'68
Life 64: 58-77 (col) Apr 12
'68
Life 64: 62-75 (col) Apr 19
'68
EGYPT--ANTIQUITIES
Travel 123: 30-35 Jan '65
Nat Geog 127: 583-633 (col)
May '65
EIFFEL TOWER--PARIS
Life 56: 54 (col) May 1 '64
Nat Geog 126: 187 (col) Aug
'64
Life 69: 74-75 Dec 4 '70
Life 71: 59 (col) Aug 21 '71
EINSTEIN AND CHARLES PRO-
TEUS STEINMETZ (photo-
graph)
Life 53 Apr 23 '65
EISENHOWER, DWIGHT D. --
FUNERAL RITES
Life 66: front cover, 24-31
(col), 32-34 Apr 11 '69
EL MORRO NATIONAL MONU-
MENT--NEW MEXICO
America's Wonderlands, p.
283-5 (col)
ELBA ISLAND
Travel 136: 31, 33, 35 (col)
Nov '71
ELIZABETH II, QUEEN OF
GREAT BRITAIN--BIRTHDAY
PARADE ("trooping the col-
our")
Nat Geog 129: 790-1 (col)
June '66
ELIZABETH II, QUEEN OF
GREAT BRITAIN--OPENING
PARLIAMENT
Nat Geog 129: 753-5 (col)
June '66
ELLESMERE ISLAND
Nat Geog 128: 692-3 (col)
Nov '65

EMBLEMS--UNITED STATES
Am Heritage 18: 49-63 (col)
Feb '67
ERIE CANAL
Life 59: 52 Dec 24 '65
Am Heritage 19: 22-31 (col)
Oct '68
ERIE, LAKE
Am Heritage 22: 14-15 (col),
17, 18-23 (col), (18th
Cent. paintings) Apr '71
ERIGBAAGTSA INDIANS. See
INDIANS OF SOUTH AMERI-
CA--BRAZIL--ERIGBAAGTSA
ESCAPE CAPSULES, AIRPLANE.
See PILOT EJECTION SEATS,
CAPSULES; etc.
ESKIMOS--ALASKA
Holiday 35: 88-93 (col) Apr
'64
Nat Geog 128: 684-5 (col)
Nov '65
Nat Geog 139: 188-217 (col)
Feb '71
ESKIMOS--BANKS ISLAND
Nat Geog 125: 702-35 (col)
May '64
ESKIMOS--GREENLAND
Nat Geog 127: 262 (col) Feb
'65
ETCHING--SCHOOL PROJECTS
Instr 73: 29 Jan '64
ETHIOPIA
Nat Geog 127: 548-82 (col)
Apr '65
Holiday 41: 58-67 (col) June
'67
Nat Geog 137: 186-211 (col)
Feb '70
Life 69: 46-55 (col) Nov 27
'70
ETNA, MOUNT
Life 70: 28-29 (col) May 28
'71
ETRUSCAN TOMBS
Holiday 34: 47-49, 51 (col)
Sept '63
EUCHARIST CONGRESS--
BOGOTA, COLOMBIA
Life 65: 64-67 (col) Sept 6
'68
EUPHRATES RIVER
Nat Geog 130: 750-1 (col)

Dec '66

EUROPA (rocket). See ROCK-
ETS--CARRIERS--EUROPE--
EUROPA I

EUROPE--GALLERIES AND
MUSEUMS
Holiday 39: 105-10 (col)
June '66

EUROPEAN WAR, 1914-1918.
See WORLD WAR I

EVEREST, MOUNT
Life 55: 68-9, 71 (col) Sept
20 '63
Nat Geog 130: 560, 565 (col)
Oct '66
Life 71: 22-7 (col), 28-9
July 2 '71

EVEREST, MOUNT--CONQUEST
BY AMERICANS, 1963
Life 55: front cover, 68-92
(col) Sept 20 '63
Nat Geog 124: 460-73 (col)
Oct '63

EVERGLADES--FLORIDA
Life 69: 30-31 (col) July 4
'70

EVERGLADES NATIONAL PARK
--FLORIDA
America's Wonderlands, p.
420-7, 430-1 (col)
Nat Geog 132: 508-553 (col)
Oct '67

EVERS, MEDGAR--FUNERAL
RITES
Ebony 18: 142 Sept '63

EXCAVATIONS (archeology).
See also FOSSILS; MAN,
PREHISTORIC

EXCAVATIONS (archeology)--
MEXICO
America's Wonderlands, p.
294-5

EXERCISES, PHYSICAL
Look 29: 88-90, 92 Aug 24
'65
Look 32: 87-93 May 14 '68

EXHIBITIONS. See Names of
Cities with Subdivision Exhi-
bitions, e.g. MOSCOW--
EXHIBITIONS; etc.

EXPLORER (artificial satellite).
See ARTIFICIAL SATELLITES
--U. S. --EXPLORER

EXPLORERS, CAVE
Ebony 23: 144-7 Apr '68

EXPLOSIONS--FAIRGROUNDS
COLISEUM--INDIANAPOLIS,
IND. , 1963
Life 55: 44-44A Nov 15 '63

EXPO '67--MONTREAL
Instr 76: 172-175 Feb '67
Look 31: 48-53 (col) Apr 4
'67
Life 62: 32-41 (col) Apr 28
'67
Nat Geog 131: 604-607, 610-
617 (col) May '67
Ebony 22: 140-1, 144, 146,
148, 150, 152 (col) June
'67

EXPO '70--JAPAN
Look 33: 61-65 (col), 66
Oct 21 '69
Life 67: 60D-60F Nov 28 '69
Travel 133: 66-68 Feb '70
Life 68: 37-43, 45 (col) Mar
27 '70

EXPRESS HIGHWAYS
Nat Geog 133: 194-221 (col)
Feb '68
Life 66: 24D-35 (col) May
30 '69

EXPRESS HIGHWAYS--INTER-
STATE HIGHWAY SYSTEM
Nat Geog 129: 96 (col) Jan
'66

EXPRESS HIGHWAYS--TOKYO
Nat Geog 126: 454-5 (col)
Oct '64

EYE MAKEUP
Life 59: 98-101 (col), 103
Oct 29 '65

EYEGLASSES. See SUN
GLASSES

F

FACTORIES, CIGAR--PHILIP-
PINES
Nat Geog 130: 325 (col) Sept
'66

FACTORIES, TRUCK--CHINA
(People's Republic)
Nat Geog 126: 622-3 (col)
Nov '64

FAEROES ISLANDS
  Nat Geog 138: 410-441 (col)
    Sept '70
FANEUIL HALL--BOSTON (interior)
  Nat Geog 130: 796-7 (col)
    Dec '66
FANS, MOURNING
  Hobbies 68: 26-28 July '63
FANS, SPANISH
  Nat Geog 129: 203 (col) Feb
    '66
FARMERS--EGYPT
  Nat Geog 127: 596 (col) May
    '65
FARMS--ISRAEL
  Nat Geog 128: 850-1 (col)
    Dec '65
FASHION. See COSTUME
FASHION SHOWS--SPRING COL-
  LECTION--LA COUPOLE,
  PARIS
  Life 68: 48-50 (col) Feb 27
    '70
FASTS AND FEASTS--HINDU
  SACRIFICIAL FEAST--BALI
  Nat Geog 124: 446-7 (col)
    Sept '63
FATIMA (Pope Paul's Visit)
  Life 62: 32-35 (col) May 26
    '67
FELLAHIN. See FARMERS--
  EGYPT
FENCING
  Ebony 20: 125-8 Mar '65
  Ebony 25: 52-5 Jan '70
FERRIES
  Nat Geog 128: 91 (col) July
    '65; 618-19, 641 (col)
    Nov '65
FERRIES, SAIL-DRIVEN
  Nat Geog 129: 156 (col) Feb
    '66
FERRYBOATS
  Am Heritage 15: 38-49 Apr
    '64
FESTIVAL OF THE ARTS TO-
  DAY--BUFFALO, N. Y.
  Life 58: 63 (col), 64, 66,
    68 Apr 23 '65
FESTIVAL OF NEGRO ARTS
  Life 60: 83-8 (col) Apr 22
    '66

Ebony 21: 97-9 (col), 100-2,
    104, 106 July '66
FESTIVALS. See also MUSIC
  FESTIVALS
FESTIVALS, BEER--OKTOBER-
  FEST--MUNICH, GERMANY
  Holiday 38: 70-75 (col) Nov
    '65
FESTIVALS--BOLEY ROUND-
  UP--OKLAHOMA
  Ebony 20: 100, 102, 104-5
    Nov '64
FESTIVALS--IRAN--2500TH
  ANNIVERSARY OF FOUNDING
  OF PERSIAN EMPIRE
  Life 71: 22, 23-29 (col) Oct
    29 '71
FESTIVALS--NEW GUINEA
  Nat Geog 136: 148-156 (col)
    July '69
FESTIVALS, SNOW--JAPAN
  Nat Geog 134: 824-833 (col)
    Dec '68
FETAL SURGERY (monkey)
  Life 59: 62-63 (col) Sept 10
    '65
FETUS
  Life 59: 60-9 (col) Sept 10
    '65
FIDDLERS--OLDTIME FID-
  DLERS' CONTEST--WEISER,
  IDA.
  Life 55: 89-90 July 12 '63
FIGUREHEADS OF SHIPS
  Life 57: 58-9 (col) July 24
    '64
  Nat Geog 126: 381 (col)
    Sept '64
FIJI ISLANDS
  Travel 125: 51-54 (col) Apr
    '66
  Ebony 26: 84-8 (col) Feb '71
FINGER LAKES REGION--NEW
  YORK
  Holiday 41: 62-67 (col) May
    '67   •
FINLAND
  Holiday 40: 64-67 (col) Nov
    '66
  Nat Geog 133: 588-629 (col)
    May '68
  Holiday 46: 70-73 (col) Oct
    '69

FIORDS--NORWAY
  Nat Geog 125: 284-5 (col)
    Feb '64
FIRE APPARATUS. MOTOR
  (paintings of proposed new
  pumpers and tenders for
  New York)
  Life 56: 24 Mar 20 '64
FIRE APPARATUS--STEAM
  (early 18" high model)
  Life 61: 69 (col) Dec 9 '66
FIRE ENGINES. See FIRE
  APPARATUS. MOTOR
FIRE ISLAND RESORT (near
  New York City)
  America's Wonderlands, p.
    477 (col)
FIRE-WALKERS--CEYLON
  Nat Geog 129: 482-3 (col)
    Apr '66
FIREARMS. See ARQUE-
  BUSES; MUSKETS; RIFLES
FIRES--SAINT LAURENT--
  DU-PONTE, FRANCE, 1970
  Life 69: 40-42 Nov 13 '70
FISH NETS. See FISHING
  NETS
FISHERMEN--PHILIPPINES
  Nat Geog 130: 320-1, 339
    (col) Sept '66
FISHERMEN--PORTUGAL
  Nat Geog 128: 453, 474-9
    (col) Oct '65
  Nat Geog 133: 572-83 (col)
    Apr '68
FISHING BOATS--BOLIVIA
  Nat Geog 129: 168-9 (col)
    Feb '66
FISHING BOATS--SALMON
  SEINERS--ALASKA
  Nat Geog 127: 788 (col)
    June '65
FISHING BOATS, SHRIMP
  Nat Geog 127: 644-5, 648-9
    (col) May '65
  Nat Geog 129: 354-5 (col)
    Mar '66
FISHING, EEL--NORTHERN
  IRELAND
  Nat Geog 126: 256 (col) Aug
    '64
FISHING NETS--MARSEILLES,
  FRANCE

Nat Geog 126: 160 (col) Aug
    '64
FISHING, OYSTER--CHESA-
  PEAKE BAY
  Nat Geog 126: 372 (col) Sept
    '64
FISHING, SHRIMP
  Nat Geog 127: 651 (col) May
    '65
  Ebony 21: 131-4, 136 Nov '65
FISHING, TUNA
  Life 71: 60-67 (col), 68 Dec
    3 '71
FLAGS--ST. LOUIS
  Nat Geog 128: 605 (col) Nov
    '65
FLAGS--UNITED STATES--15-
  STAR DESIGN, 1803
  Nat Geog 126: 667 (col) Nov
    '64
FLAGS--UNITED STATES--
  PLACED ATOP MOUNT
  EVEREST BY AMERICAN
  EXPEDITION, 1963
  Nat Geog 124: 475 (col)
    Oct '63
FLATBOATS
  Nat Geog 127: 667 (col) May
    '65
FLESH-PIERCING CEREMONY--
  CEYLON
  Nat Geog 129: 480 (col) Apr
    '66
FLIGHT SIMULATORS
  Life 66: 26 (col) Feb 28 '69
FLOODS--ALASKA
  Life 63: 24-25 (col) Sept 1
    '67
FLOODS--ITALY
  Life 61: 28, 29-31 (col), 32-
    9 Dec 16 '66
  Nat Geog 132: 1-43 (col) July
    '67
  Life 69: 44-45 Oct 30 '70
FLOODS--ITALY--VAIONT
  DAM, 1963
  Life 55: 30-41 Oct 25 '63
FLOODS--U. S.
  Life 58: 20-27, cover (col)
    Jan 8 '65
  Life 58: 34-35 (col) Apr 30
    '65
  Life 66: 53-56 (col), 57-58,

59 (col) Apr 25 '69
Nat Geog 136: 574-591 (col)
    Oct '69
FLORENCE, ITALY
    Holiday 46: 28-34 (col), 36-
    37, 42-43 (col) Sept '69
FLORIDA
    Nat Geog 124: 858-903 (col)
    Dec '63
FLORIDA--GULF COAST
    Holiday 41: 70-77 (col) May
    '67
FLORIDA KEYS
    Nat Geog 139: 72-93 (col)
    Jan '71
FOLIES BERGERE--PARIS
    Holiday 45: 92-93 (col) Apr
    '69
FOOD--HYPER-GROWING
    Life 66: 38-51 (col) Jan 24
    '69
FOOD STORES. See also
    MARKETS; SUPERMARKETS
FOOD STORES--LENINGRAD
    Life 55: 28-9 Sept 13 '63
FOOD VENDORS. See VEND-
    ING MACHINES, FOOD
FOODS--CANDY
    Ebony 22: 172 (col), 174,
    176 Dec '66
FOODS, FRENCH
    Life 58: 106-107 (col) Apr
    30 '65
FOODS, ITALIAN
    Look 29: 68 (col) Aug 24 '65
FOODS, MEXICAN
    Look 31: 31-33 (col) Mar 21
    '67
    Life 66: 84-85 (col) June 6
    '69
FOODS, SPANISH
    Look 28: 66-68 (col) Mar
    10 '64
FOODS, TURKISH
    Life 65: 114-115 (col) Sept
    27 '68
FOODS--YUGOSLAVIA
    Look 29: 88-91, 93 (col)
    June 15 '65
FOOTBALL--BOWLS
    Look 29: 85-87 Dec 28 '65
    Sports Illus 24: 26-30 Jan 3

    '66
    Sports Illus 24: 33-37 Jan
    10 '66
    Sports Illus 26: 28-35 (col)
    Jan 2 '67
    Sports Illus 32: 13-16 (col)
    Jan 12 '70
    Sports Illus 32: 11-14 (col)
    Jan 19 '70
FOOTBALL HELMETS
    Life 55: 69, 76 (col) Sept
    27 '63
FOOTBALL PROS
    Ebony 19: 70-2, 74, 76, 78,
    80 Nov '63
    Ebony 19: 32 (col), 33-4,
    36-7 Jan '64
    Ebony 20: 65-6, 129-30, 132,
    134 Dec '64
    Ebony 20: 56-8, 60-2, 64
    Jan '65
    Sports Illus 23: 23-26 (col)
    Aug 16 '65
    Ebony 20: 57-8, 60-2, 64
    Oct '65
    Look 29: 87-90 Oct 5 '65
    Life 59: 72-75 Nov 5 '65
    Ebony 21: 86, 90, 92, 144
    Dec '65
    Life 59: cover (col), 36-46
    Dec 10 '65
    Ebony 21: 70-1, 74-6 Jan '66
    Look 30: 142-143, 145-147
    Oct 18 '66
    Ebony 22: 120-2, 124, 126-8,
    130 Nov '66
    Look 30: 115-118 Nov 29 '66
    Ebony 22: 39-40, 42, 44-6,
    119-20, 122, 124, 126
    Dec '66
    Look 30: 92-97 (col) Dec
    13 '66
    Ebony 22: 77-8, 80, 82 Jan
    '67
    Ebony 23: 99-102, 104, 106-
    10 Nov '67
    Ebony 23: 25-7, 30, 32 Dec
    '67
    Sports Illus 29: 53-55, 58,
    60-61, 64-65, 67, 70-73,
    76, 79, 82, 84 (col) Sept
    16 '68

Sports Illus 29: 21-24 (col)
Sept 30 '68
Ebony 23: 159-62 Oct '68
Life 65: 105-107 Oct 18 '68
Ebony 24: 170-2 Dec '68
Ebony 24: 64-6, 68-70 Jan
'69
Ebony 25: 164-5, 168-74 Nov
'69
Ebony 25: 44-6, 48 Dec '69
Sports Illus 32: 10-12, 15-16
(col) Jan 5 '70
Ebony 26: 143-7, 150, 152,
154-5 Nov '70
Ebony 26: 131-2, 134, 136,
138-9 Dec '70
Ebony 27: 170-2, 174, 176,
178, 182, 184, 186 Nov
'71
FOOTBALL PROS--COLTS
Look 29: 90, 92-96 Sept 21
'65
Life 65: front cover, 76-81
(col) Dec 13 '68
FOOTBALL PROS--49ERS
Sports Illus 35: front cover,
55-62 (col) Sept 20 '71
FOOTBALL PROS--JETS
Life 65: 53 (col), 54 Dec
20 '68
FOOTBALL PROS--LIONS
Life 59: 85, 90A-90B Oct
22 '65
Life 69: 34-37 Nov 6 '70
FOOTBALL PROS--NAVY
Look 28: 68-72 Sept 22 '64
FOOTBALL PROS--"SUICIDE
SQUADS"
Life 71: 32-39 (col) Dec 3
'71
FOOTBALL STARS
Life 59: 57-58, 60-62 Nov
19 '65
Sports Illus 25: 21-24 (col)
Oct 10 '66
Sports Illus 33: 28-34 (col)
Aug 17 '70
Sports Illus 33: 49-52 (col)
Sept 14 '70
Life 69: 44-47 (col) Dec 4
'70
FOOTBALL STARS--ALL
AMERICA 1964

Look 28: 116 (col), 118-119,
124 Dec 15 '64
FOOTBALL STARS--ALL
AMERICA--1965
Look 29: 146 (col), 148, 150-
152, 154 Dec 14 '65
FOOTBALL STARS--ALL
AMERICA--1966
Look 30: 90 Dec 13 '66
FOOTBALL STARS--ALL
AMERICA--1967
Look 31: 117-120 Dec 12 '67
FOOTBALL STARS--ALL
AMERICA--1968
Look 32: 88-9 (col), 90-1,
93, 95, 97, 99, 100 Dec
10 '68
FOOTBALL STARS--ALL
AMERICA--1969
Look 33: 76, 78, 80 Dec 16
'69
FOOTBALL TEAMS--VIKINGS
Ebony 25: 83-6 Jan '70
FOOTBALL TEAMS--WASH-
INGTON REDSKINS
Life 71: 40-41 (col) Oct 15
'71
FOOTBALL TECHNIQUE (illus-
trating control of players)
Life 61: 76-91 (col) Oct 14
'66
FOOTBALL TRAINING
Look 28: 28-32 Oct 6 '64
FOREST FIRES
Life 71: 28-33 (col) July 23
'71
FORTS--BELOGRADCHIK--
BULGARIA (built by Ottoman
Turks)
Nat Geog 128: 67 (col) July
'65
FORTS--CAROLINE (near Jack-
sonville)--FLA.
Nat Geog 129: 214-15 (col)
Feb '66
FORTS--FORT OF GRAND
PORTAGE OF FUR TRADERS
--LAKE SUPERIOR SHORE
Nat Geog 124: 420 (col) Sept
'63
FORTS--LARAMIE--WYOMING
(on the Oregon Trail)
Nat Geog 128: 652 (col) Nov

'65

FORTS--McHENRY--BALTI-
MORE, MD.
Nat Geog 126: 400-1 (col)
Sept '64

FORTS--ROMAN--QASR IBRIM,
EGYPT
Nat Geog 127: 629 (col) May
'65

FORTS--SACSAHUAMAN--
PERU (built by Incas)
Nat Geog 125: 252-3 (col)
Feb '64

FORTS--ST. SEBASTIAN--
MOZAMBIQUE
Nat Geog 126: 208 (col)
Aug '64

"FORTY-NINERS. " See
MINERS, GOLD--"FORTY-
NINERS"

FOSSILS--AFRICA (discovered
by Louis S. B. Leakey)
Nat Geog 127: 195, 197, 203,
208-15 (col) Feb '65

FOUNDRIES--19TH CENT. --
COLD SPRING, N. Y. (paint-
ing)
Nat Geog 127: 660-1 (col)
May '65

FOUNTAINS--"MEETING OF
THE WATERS"--UNION
STATION--ST. LOUIS
Nat Geog 128: 611 (col) Nov
'65

FRANKFURT, GERMANY
Holiday 41: 74-76, 78-79
(col) Jan '67

FREEZERS. See REFRIGERA-
TION AND REFRIGERATING
MACHINERY (used for ca-
daver preservation)

FREMONT, JOHN C. --PLANT-
ING U. S. FLAG IN ROCKY
MOUNTAINS, 1842
Nat Geog 128: 657 (col) Nov
'65

FRENCH RIVIERA
Nat Geog 131: 799-835 (col)
June '67

FRIGATES. See WARSHIPS--
U. S. --FRIGATES

FROG 1 (guided missile). See
GUIDED MISSILES--RUSSIA--

FROG 1

FUJIYAMA, MOUNT
Nat Geog 124: 573 (col) Oct
'63

FUNERAL RITES AND CERE-
MONIES. See name of per-
son, e. g., KENNEDY, JOHN
F. --FUNERAL RITES

FUNRYU 2 (guided missile).
See GUIDED MISSILES--
JAPAN--FUNRYU 2

FUR COATS, WRAPS, etc.
Ebony 21: 173 (col), 174,
176, 178 Dec '65
Life 59: 95-96 Dec 10 '65
Ebony 21: 103 Jan '66
Ebony 21: 67-8 Aug '66
Life 61: 85-86 Nov 4 '66
Look 31: 94-99 (col) Oct 3
'67
Ebony 23: 204 (col) Oct '68
Sports Illus 29: 60-61 Dec 9
'68
Ebony 24: 178-80, 182, 184
(col) Dec '68
Life 65: 100-104 (col) Dec
13 '68
Life 67: 76-79 (col) Oct 31
'69
Ebony 25: 154, 156 Dec '69
Life 68: 68-70 Feb 27 '70
Sports Illus 33: 51-53 (col)
Nov 16 '70

FUR TRADERS (mountain men
of the West)
Nat Geog 128: 651 (col) Nov
'65

FUR TRADERS--HUDSON'S BAY
CO. , 1828
Nat Geog 124: 413 (col)
Sept '63

FUR TRADERS' CARAVAN
(leaving St. Louis, 1830)
Nat Geog 128: 652-3 (col)
Nov '65

FURNITURE, CHILDREN'S
Life 70: 64-66 (col) Apr 30
'71

FURNITURE--MILANESE
Life 66: 48-54 (col) Mar 14
'69

FURNITURE, PLASTIC
Look 35: 50-51 (col) Mar 9
'71

G

GALAPAGOS ISLANDS
  Nat Geog 131: 540-585 (col)
    Apr '67
  Sports Illus 32: 36-42 (col)
    June 8 '70
  Holiday 48: 52-55 (col) Sept-
    Oct '70
GALILEE
  Nat Geog 128: 832-65 (col)
    Dec '65
GALILEE, SEA OF
  Nat Geog 128: 832-3, 842-3,
    849, 860 (col) Dec '65
GALLEONS. See SHIPS--
  GALLEONS
GALLERY OF MODERN ART--
  NEW YORK
  Life 56: 52 Feb 7 '64; 65
    (col) Apr 3 '64
GAMES, CHILDREN'S
  Grade Teach 85: 124-125 (col)
    Nov '67
  Life 68: 67-68 Mar 6 '70
GANGES RIVER
  Nat Geog 140: 445-483 (col)
    Oct '71
GARDENS, PUBLIC
  Holiday 38: 91-96 (col) July
    '65
GATES--MICKLEGATE BAR--
  YORK, ENGLAND
  Nat Geog 125: 636-7 (col)
    May '64
GEBEL ADDA, EGYPT
  Nat Geog 127: 624-5 (col)
    May '65
GEMINI PROJECT. See AS-
  TRONAUTS; GLIDERS; SPACE
  FLIGHT--MANNED FLIGHTS;
  SPACE FLIGHT SIMULATORS;
  SPACE VEHICLES--U.S.,
  etc. with subdivision PRO-
  JECT GEMINI
GEMS
  Nat Geog 140: 838-863 (col)
    Dec '71
  Holiday 50: 38-40 (col) Sept/
    Oct '71
GEMS--STAR RUBY
  Nat Geog 140: 834 (col) Dec
    '71

GENOA
  Holiday 39: 36-37 (col) Jan
    '66
GEOMETRIC FIGURES
  Grade Teach 84: 61-63 Dec
    '66
GEORGETOWN--WASHINGTON,
  D.C.
  Nat Geog 126: 757 (col) Dec
    '64
GERMANY. See also EAST
  GERMANY
GERMANY
  Travel 122: 54-58 Sept '64
  Holiday 36: 57-63 (col) Oct
    '64
  Travel 127: 55-58 (col) Apr
    '67
GERMANY (after World War II)
  Look 29: 29-33 (col) May 4
    '65
GETTYSBURG FARM (home of
  Dwight D. Eisenhower)--
  NEAR GETTYSBURG, PA.
  Nat Geog 124: 26-7 (col)
    July '63
GETTYSBURG, PA.
  Nat Geog 124: 6-9 (col) July
    '63
GETTYSBURG, PA.--SHRINES
  OF THE CIVIL WAR
  Nat Geog 124: 4-13, 24-5,
    30 (col) July '63
GEYSERS--"OLD FAITHFUL"--
  YELLOWSTONE NATIONAL
  PARK
  Nat Geog 128: 892-3 (col)
    Dec '65
  Nat Geog 129: 563-4 (col)
    Apr '66
  America's Wonderlands, p.
    66, 71 (col)
GEYSERS--"OLD FAITHFUL"--
  YELLOWSTONE NATIONAL
  PARK (winter scene)
  Nat Geog 129: 555 (col) Apr
    '66
GHOST TOWNS
  Travel 134: 34-39 (col) Oct
    '70
GIANT FOREST
  America's Wonderlands, p.
    30-1, 32-3 (col)

GIANT'S CAUSEWAY--NORTH-
ERN IRELAND
Nat Geog 126: 255 (col) Aug
'64
GIBRALTAR
Holiday 41: 70-71 (painting,
col) Feb '67
Travel 133: 30-31 (col), 32,
33 (col) June '70
GLACIER BAY
America's Wonderlands, p.
534-5 (col)
GLACIER, GRINNELL--MON-
TANA
America's Wonderlands, p.
124-5 (col)
GLACIER, TAZLINA
Life 70: 34 (col) Jan 8 '71
GLACIER NATIONAL PARK
Holiday 34: 32-33 (col) Aug
'63
Nat Geog 125: 580-3 (col)
Apr '64
America's Wonderlands, p.
110, 114-5 (col)
GLACIERS
Nat Geog 125: 456-7 (col)
Mar '64; 588-9 (col) Apr
'64
Nat Geog 128: 380-1 (col)
Sept '65
GLACIERS--ALASKA
Nat Geog 131: 195-217 (col)
Feb '67
GLACIERS--BERG--BRITISH
COLUMBIA
Nat Geog 125: 588 (col) Apr
'64
GLACIERS--COLUMBIA ICE
FIELD--ALBERTA
Nat Geog 130: 384-5 (col)
Sept '66
GLACIERS--MENDENHALL--
ALASKA
Nat Geog 127: 794-5 (col)
June '65
GLACIERS--RHONE--SWITZER-
LAND
Nat Geog 128: 381 (col) Sept
'65
GLASS BLOWING
Sch Arts 64: 29-33 Jan '65
GLASS, MEDICINE

Hobbies 68: 84-85 Jan '64
GLASSWARE (from Toledo
Museum of Art)
Look 34: 22-25 (col) Sept
8 '70
GLASSWARE, ANCIENT
Nat Geog 126: 346-68 (col)
Sept '64
GLASSWARE, ANCIENT--
CORNING GLASS CENTER--
CORNING, N. Y.
Nat Geog 126: 348, 352, 354-
5, 362, 366, 368 (col)
Sept '64
GLASSWARE, ENGLISH
Hobbies 68: 84-85 July '63
GLEN CANYON DAM
Nat Geog 125: 558 (col) Apr
'64
GLIDERS
Sports Illus 25: 28-34 (col)
Aug 1 '66
Nat Geog 131: 48-73 (col)
Jan '67
Sports Illus 33: 18-21 July
13 '70
GLIDERS (aeronautics)--PARA-
GLIDERS--PROJECT GEMINI
(models)
Nat Geog 125: 370 (col) Mar
'64
GLIDERS (aeronautics)--SAIL-
PLANES
Nat Geog 128: 387 (col) Sept
'65
GLIDERS (aeronautics)--SAIL-
PLANES--GERMANY, 1928
(rocket powered)
Hist of Rocketry and Space
Travel, p. 66
GLOUCESTER, MASS.
Nat Geog 130: 836-7 (col) Dec
'66
GOLD MINES--CARLIN MINE--
NEVADA
Nat Geog 133: 668-679 (col)
May '68
GOLDEN GATE BRIDGE--SAN
FRANCISCO
Life 55: 34A Oct 11 '63
Nat Geog 129: 646-7 (col)
May '66
Holiday 38: 85 (col) Oct '65

GOLF COURSES--FLORIDA
Sports Illus 24: 30-38 (col)
Jan 24 '66
GOLF COURSES--HARBOUR
TOWN, S. CAROLINA
Sports Illus 33: 30-34 (col)
Nov 9 '70
GOLF COURSES--HAZELTINE,
MINN.
Sports Illus 32: 37-39, 42-43
(col) June 15 '70
GOLF COURSES--PALM SPRINGS,
CAL.
Sports Illus 20: 27-34 (col)
Jan 13 '64
GOLF COURSES, WORLD'S
Travel 132: 29, 31 (col) Nov
'69
GOLF TECHNIQUE
Sports Illus 23: 32-38 (col)
Aug 9 '65
GOLF TECHNIQUE BY GAY
BREWER (drawings)
Sports Illus 27: 31-37 Aug
7 '67
GOLF TECHNIQUE BY CLAUDE
HARMON (sketches)
Sports Illus 20: 39-47 (col)
Apr 27 '64
Sports Illus 20: 70-76 (col)
May 4 '64
GOLF TECHNIQUE BY TONY
LEMA
Sports Illus 22: 40-47 (col),
49-50 Feb 15 '65
Sports Illus 22: 40-47 (col), 49-
50 Mar 15 '65
Sports Illus 22: 51-55 Mar
22 '65
GOLF TECHNIQUE BY JACK
NICKLAUS (drawings)
Sports Illus 26: 47 (col) Jan
2 '67
GOLF TECHNIQUE BY ARNOLD
PALMER
Sports Illus 23: 37-43 (draw-
ings) July 5 '65
Sports Illus 23: 37-43 (draw-
ings) Aug 2 '65
Look 30: 64-66, 68 Aug 9 '66
GOLF--TOURNAMENTS--
MASTERS, 1964
Life 56: 42-42A Apr 24 '64

GOLF--TOURNAMENTS--U.S.
OPEN, 1963
Life 55: 34B-34C July 5 '63
GOLFERS--AMATEUR TITLE
WINNERS
Sports Illus 32: 47-49 (col)
Apr 6 '70
GOLFERS--PROS
Life 56: 42-42A Apr 24 '64
Sports Illus 22: 35-40 (col)
Apr 5 '65
Sports Illus 24: 58, 59-66
(col), 67 Apr 4 '66
Sports Illus 24: 36 (col), 39-
41, 43 Apr 18 '66
Sports Illus 24: 86 (col) Apr
25 '66
Sports Illus 32: 15-16 (col)
Apr 20 '70
Sports Illus 32: 19-20 (col)
May 18 '70
Sports Illus 32: 24-25 June
1 '70
Sports Illus 32: 15-16 (col)
June 29 '70
Sports Illus 33: 13-14 (col)
July 20 '70
Sports Illus 31: 29-34 (col)
Sept 1 '69
Sports Illus 34: 23-24 (col)
Mar 8 '71
GONDOLAS--VENICE
Life 56: 56-7 (col) Feb 21
'64
GONDOLAS, FERRY--VENICE
Life 56: 60-1 (col) Feb 21
'64
GONDOLAS, OVERHEAD--
DISNEYLAND
Nat Geog 124: 189 (col)
Aug '63
GRAND CANYON
Nat Geog 125: 554-5 (col)
Apr '64
America's Wonderlands, p.
160-7 (col)
America's Wonderlands, p.
20-21 (col)
Life 71: 40-41, 43 (col) July
2 '71
GRAND CANYON--GEOLOGIC
CROSS SECTION
America's Wonderlands,

p. 169 (col)

GRAND CAYMEN
Holiday 43: 94-95 (col) Jan '68

GRAND TETON NATIONAL PARK--WYOMING
America's Wonderlands, p. 92-5 (col)
America's Wonderlands, p. 4-5 (col)

GRAPES--HARVESTING--FRANCE
Nat Geog 129: 844-5 (col) June '66

GRAPES--VINEYARDS--PORTUGAL
Nat Geog 128: 490-1 (col) Oct '65

GRAPES--VINEYARDS--SWITZERLAND
Nat Geog 128: 362-3 (col) Sept '65

GRAVE RUBBINGS
Look 27: M6-M7 Aug 27 '63
Sch Arts 65: 21-23 June '66

GREAT BRITAIN--NORMAN CONQUEST (Bayeux Tapestry)
Nat Geog 130: 206-51 (col) Aug '66

GREAT LAKES
Life 65: 36-47 (col) Aug 23 '68

GREAT RIFT VALLEY
Nat Geog 128: 254-90 (col) Aug '65

GREAT SALT DESERT--UTAH
Nat Geog 125: 564-5 (col) Apr '64
Nat Geog 132: 252-263 (col) Aug '67

GREAT SMOKEY MOUNTAINS NATIONAL PARK
America's Wonderlands, p. 450-1, 453-61 (col)
America's Wonderlands, p. 62-3 (col)
Nat Geog 134: 522-549 (col) Oct '68

GREAT WALL OF CHINA
Life 57: 102 (col) July 17 '64
Nat Geog 124: 577 Oct '63
Life 70: 22-23 (col) Apr 30 '71

"GREAT WHITE FLEET"--WORLD CRUISE MISSION, 1907 (sent by T. Roosevelt)
Am Heritage 15: 30 (painting, col), 42-43 Feb '64

GREAT WHITE THRONE--ZION NATIONAL PARK--UTAH
America's Wonderlands, p. 192-3 (col)

GREECE
Travel 123: 51-54 (col) May '65

GREEK ISLANDS
Holiday 39: 62-71 (col) Jan '66

GREENLAND
Nat Geog 132: 264-279 (col) Aug '67
Travel 129: 51-53 (col) June '68

GREENWICH VILLAGE--NEW YORK
Nat Geog 126: 94 (col) July '64

GRENADA (island). See WINDWARD ISLANDS

GRINDING BINS, INDIAN (N. American)--MESA VERDE NATIONAL PARK
Nat Geog 125: 198-9 (col) Feb '64

GRINDING BINS, INDIAN (N. American)--PUEBLOS, 20TH CENT.
Nat Geog 125: 198 (col) Feb '64

GRIST MILLS--WALES
Nat Geog 127: 753 (col) June '65

GROTTO OF THE ANNUNCIATION--NAZARETH, ISRAEL
Nat Geog 127: 422-3 (col) Mar '65

GUADALAJARA
Nat Geog 131: 412-441 (col) Mar '67

GUADELOUPE ISLAND
Holiday 42: 54-55, 57-59 (col) Aug '67

GUAM
Holiday 42: 56-57, 59-61 (col) July '67

GUATEMALA

Holiday 50: 46-50 (col) Sept/
Oct '71
GUIDED MISSILES.   See also
ROCKETS
GUIDED MISSILES
Ebony 20: 106 Mar '65
GUIDED MISSILES--ENGLAND--
LARNYX, 1927 (radio con-
trolled)
Hist of Rocketry and Space
Travel, p. 38
GUIDED MISSILES--ENGLAND--
RED TOP
Hist of Rocketry and Space
Travel, p. 144
GUIDED MISSILES--ENGLAND--
STOOGE--ANTIAIRCRAFT
MISSILE (used in World War
II)
Hist of Rocketry and Space
Travel, p. 90
GUIDED MISSILES--ENGLAND--
THUNDERBIRD 2
Hist of Rocketry and Space
Travel, p. 147
GUIDED MISSILES--FRANCE--
TOPAZE
Hist of Rocketry and Space
Travel, p. 142
GUIDED MISSILES--GERMANY--
GROUND-TO-GROUND MIS-
SILES (developed during
World War II)
Hist of Rocketry and Space
Travel, p. 115
GUIDED MISSILES--GERMANY--
SURFACE-TO-AIR MISSILES
(developed during World War
II)
Hist of Rocketry and Space
Travel, p. 110
GUIDED MISSILES--JAPAN--
FUNRYU 2 (developed during
World War II)
Hist of Rocketry and Space
Travel, p. 89
GUIDED MISSILES--"POLARIS"
Ebony 19: 46-7, 50 May '64
GUIDED MISSILES--"POLARIS"--
LAUNCHING FROM SUBMA-
RINE
Life 68: 66-69 (col) Apr 3
'70

GUIDED MISSILES--RUSSIA,
1964
Life 57: 42-3 (col) Nov 20
'64
GUIDED MISSILES--RUSSIA--
ANTI-MISSILE MISSILES,
1965
Hist of Rocketry and Space
Travel, p. 147
GUIDED MISSILES--RUSSIA--
FROG 1
Hist of Rocketry and Space
Travel, p. 140
GUIDED MISSILES--RUSSIA--
SHYSTER
Hist of Rocketry and Space
Travel, p. 140
GUIDED MISSILES--RUSSIA--
SKEAN
Hist of Rocketry and Space
Travel, p. 140
GUIDED MISSILES--SWEDEN--
SAAB 305A
Hist of Rocketry and Space
Travel, p. 142
GUIDED MISSILES--U. S. --
ATLAS (U. S.'s first inter-
continental ballistic missile)
Hist of Rocketry and Space
Travel, p. 134
GUIDED MISSILES--U. S. --BAT
(used in World War II)
Hist of Rocketry and Space
Travel, p. 102
GUIDED MISSILES--U. S. --
HONEST JOHN
Life 61: 24 (col) July 8 '66
GUIDED MISSILES--U. S. --
HOUND DOG, 1966 (jet pro-
pelled)
Hist of Rocketry and Space
Travel, p. 143
GUIDED MISSILES--U. S. --
JUPITER, 1958 (U. S.'s first
successful intermediate range
ballistic missile)
Hist of Rocketry and Space
Travel, p. 128
GUIDED MISSILES--U. S. --
JUPITER C
Hist of Rocketry and Space
Travel, bet. p. 100-1 (col)

GUIDED MISSILES--U. S. --
LITTLE LARK (developed
during World War II)
Hist of Rocketry and Space
Travel, p. 98

GUIDED MISSILES--U. S. --
MINUTEMAN--IN SILO
Life 57: 35 Nov 6 '64
Nat Geog 129: 575 (col) Apr
'66

GUIDED MISSILES--U. S. --
NAVAHO (1950's)
Hist of Rocketry and Space
Travel, p. 123

GUIDED MISSILES--U. S. --
NIKE-ZEUS, 1959
Hist of Rocketry and Space
Travel, p. 146

GUIDED MISSILES--U. S. --
SPRING NIKE-X, 1965
Hist of Rocketry and Space
Travel, p. 146

GUIDED MISSILES--U. S. --
TITAN 2
Hist of Rocketry and Space
Travel, p. 136
Nat Geog 125: 362, 365
(col) Mar '64
Nat Geog 127: 142 (col) Jan
'65
Nat Geog 128: 319 (col) Sept
'65

GUIDED MISSILES--U. S. --
TITAN 2--IN SILO
Hist of Rocketry and Space
Travel, p. 136

GUIDED MISSILES--U. S. --
LAUNCHING FROM SHIPS--
TALOS (antiaircraft)
Nat Geog 127: 182 (col) Feb
'65

GUIDED MISSILES--U. S. --
LAUNCHING FROM SUB-
MARINE BOATS--CONTROL
PANELS
Nat Geog 127: 152 (col) Feb
'65

GUIDED MISSILES--U. S. --
LAUNCHING FROM SUBMA-
RINE BOATS--POLARIS
Hist of Rocketry and Space
Travel, p. 132
Nat Geog 127: 150 (col)

Feb '65

GUIDED MISSILES--U. S. --
LAUNCHING FROM SUBMA-
RINE BOATS--SUBROC
Life 55: 49-54 Dec 13 '63

GUIDED MISSILES--U. S. --
LAUNCHING FROM SUBMA-
RINE BOATS--SUBROC (dia-
gram)
Nat Geog 127: 172-3 (col)
Feb '65

GUIDED MISSILES--U. S. --
LAUNCHING FROM UNDER-
GROUND SILOS--MINUTE-
MAN (intercontinental bal-
listic missile)
Hist of Rocketry and Space
Travel, p. 137
Nat Geog 128: 312-13 (col)
Sept '65

GUNBOATS. See WARSHIPS--
U. S. --GUNBOATS

GUNS. See ARQUEBUSES;
BAZOOKAS; BLOWGUNS;
CANNON; MUSKETS; RIFLES

GYPSIES, PORTUGUESE--
CALDAS DA RAINHA, PORTU-
GAL
Look 31: 58-63 (col) Aug 8
'67

H

HAIR BRUSHES, STRAW--
INDIAN (N. American)--
PUEBLOS, 20TH CENT.
Nat Geog 125: 208 (col)
Feb '64

HAIR DRYERS--RUSSIA
Life 55: 98-9 Sept 13 '63

HAIR STYLES
Ebony 18: 128-30, 132 Oct
'63
Ebony 19: 149-50, 152 Nov
'63
Ebony 19: 151-2, 154 Dec
'63
Ebony 19: 93-6 Jan '64
Ebony 19: 114-16 Feb '64
Ebony 19: 143-5 Mar '64
Ebony 19: 180-2, 184 Apr
'64

Ebony 19: 172-4 May '64
Ebony 19: 208-9 June '64
Ebony 19: 119-20, 122 Aug
  '64
Ebony 19: 112, 114 Sept '64
Ebony 19: 152-3 Oct '64
Ebony 20: 158, 160, 162 Nov
  '64
Ebony 20: 158, 160 Dec '64
Ebony 20: 83-4 Jan '65
Ebony 20: 130-1 Mar '65
Ebony 20: 171-2 Apr '65
Ebony 20: 181-2 May '65
Ebony 20: 149-50 June '65
Ebony 20: 120-2 July '65
Ebony 20: 126, 128 Sept '65
Ebony 20: 114-6 Oct '65
Ebony 21: 205-6, 208 Nov '65
Ebony 26: 121-2 (col), 124
  June '71
HAIR STYLES--WASHERWO-
  MAN LOOK
Life 67: 57-58 Dec 12 '69
HAIRDRESSING--ETHIOPIA
Nat Geog 127: 551-2, 563-
  4, 571 (col) Apr '65
HAIRDRESSING, INDIAN (N.
  American)--PUEBLOS, 20TH
  CENT.
Nat Geog 125: 208 (col) Feb
  '64
HAITI
Holiday 46: 30-31 (col) Nov
  '69
HALIFAX, NOVA SCOTIA
Nat Geog 125: 862-3 (col)
  June '64
HALLOWE'EN--FOLK ART
Life 69: 68-71 (col) Oct 30
  '70
HALL'S CROFT (home of John
  Hall, William Shakespeare's
  son-in-law)--STRATFORD-
  ON-AVON
Nat Geog 125: 617, 623 (col)
  May '64
HANDBALL
Life 71: 45-46, 50 (col) Oct
  8 '71
HARBORS. See Names of Cities
  with Subdivision Harbor, e.g.
  NEW YORK (city)--HARBOR;
  SAN DIEGO, CALIF. --

HARBOR; etc.
HAREM HOUSES. See HOUSES,
  HAREM
HARLEM, NEW YORK CITY'S
Look 28: 22-6, 29 July 28
  '64
Ebony 19: 168-9, 172, 174,
  176, 178 Oct '64
HARPERS FERRY, W. VA. --
  JOHN BROWN RAID, 1859
Nat Geog 127: 120 Jan '65
HARQUEBUSES. See ARQUE-
  BUSES
HARRISON, WILLIAM HENRY--
  MOURNING RIBBON
Nat Geog 127: 95 Jan '65
HARTFORD, CONN. --AERIAL
  VIEW
Ebony 20: 118 Mar '65
Life 59: 85 (col) Dec 24 '65
HARTFORD, CONN. --CONSTI-
  TUTION PLAZA
Look 29: cover, 44-46 (col)
  Sept 21 '65
HARTFORD, HUNTINGTON--
  GALLERY OF MODERN ART
  --NEW YORK. See GAL-
  LERY OF MODERN ART--
  NEW YORK
HARVESTING. See GRAPES--
  HARVESTING; RICE, WILD--
  HARVESTING; WHEAT--
  HARVESTING; etc.
HARVESTING MACHINERY.
  See also COMBINE MACHINES;
  THRESHING MACHINES
HARVESTING MACHINERY,
  WHEAT--CHINA (People's
  Republic)
Nat Geog 126: 614-15 (col)
  Nov '64
HATS. See HEADDRESS
HAVASUPAI INDIANS. See
  INDIANS OF NORTH AMER-
  ICA--HAVASUPAI
HAWAII
Life 59: 84-99 (col) Oct 8
  '65
Holiday 42: 62-65, 67-69
  (col) July '67
Look 33: 23-28, 30 (col)
  Apr 29 '69
Holiday 46: 56-61 (col)

Oct '69
Sports Illus 32: 31-32 (col)
    Jan 12 '70
Travel 134: 62-67 Oct '70
HAYES, RUTHERFORD B. --
    CABINET
    Ebony 22: 118 Jan '67
HEAD START, PROJECT.
    See PROJECT HEAD START
HEADDRESS, ACADEMIC--
    MORTARBOARDS
    Nat Geog 128: 628 (col) Nov
    '65
HEADDRESS--ARABS. See
    HEADDRESS--EGYPT; HEAD-
    DRESS--JORDAN; HEADDRESS
    --SAUDI ARABIA; HEADDRESS
    --SYRIA; HEADDRESS--YE-
    MEN
HEADDRESS--BEDOUINS
    Nat Geog 128: 276-7, 282
    (col) Aug '65
    Nat Geog 129: front cover,
    30-3, 35 (col) Jan '66
HEADDRESS, BIBLICAL--
    DURING THE LIFE OF
    JESUS CHRIST
    Life 56: 56-66 (col) Mar 27
    '64
HEADDRESS--BOLIVIA
    Nat Geog 129: 153, 157-9,
    163, 166, 170-1, 174-7,
    179, 185, 187, 189-91,
    194-5 (col) Feb '66
HEADDRESS--COIFS, LACE--
    BRITTANY
    Nat Geog 127: 472, 498-9
    (col) Apr '65
HEADDRESS--DUTCH GUIANA
    (Surinam)
    Ebony 22: 36-7 (col), 38
    May '67
HEADDRESS--EGYPT
    Nat Geog 127: 586-7, 591-2,
    594-5, 604-5, 612-13,
    620-1, 624-7, 631 (col)
    May '65
HEADDRESS--ENGLAND, 16TH
    CENT. (1558-1603)--ELIZA-
    BETHAN PERIOD (paintings)
    Life 56: 60-4, 67, 70, 72A-
    72B, 78A Apr 24 '64

HEADDRESS--ENGLAND, 17TH
    CENT. (painting)
    Nat Geog 125: 654-6 (col)
    May '64
HEADDRESS--ENGLAND--
    YEOMEN WARDERS--TOWER
    OF LONDON
    Nat Geog 129: 782 (col) June
    '66
HEADDRESS--ETHIOPIA
    Nat Geog 127: front cover,
    550, 572, 577-80 (col)
    Apr '65
HEADDRESS--HATS, BRETON
    --BRITTANY
    Nat Geog 127: 491 (col) Apr
    '65
HEADDRESS--HATS--GRAY
    TOPPERS
    Nat Geog 124: 371 (col) Sept
    '63
    Nat Geog 129: 767, 776-7
    (col) June '66
HEADDRESS--HATS, LAMP-
    SHADE--BOLIVIA
    Nat Geog 129: 163 (col)
    Feb '66
HEADDRESS--HATS, PLUMED
    (worn by Governor General
    of Australia)
    Nat Geog 124: 313 (col) Sept
    '63
HEADDRESS--HATS, STOVE-
    PIPE--WALES
    Nat Geog 127: 737, 730 (col)
    June '65
HEADDRESS--HATS, STRAW--
    VIETNAM (Republic)
    Nat Geog 126: 539 (col) Oct
    '64
HEADDRESS--HATS, WITCHES'
    Nat Geog 127: 755 (col) June
    '65
HEADDRESS--INDIA
    Life 56: front cover, 32-42A
    (col) June 5 '64
HEADDRESS, INDIAN (N. Ameri-
    can)--CHIPPEWA
    Nat Geog 124: 429 (col) Sept
    '63
HEADDRESS--JORDAN
    Nat Geog 126: 785, 792, 798-

HELICOPTERS, MILITARY--
U. S. --TWIN-ENGINE (lifting
damaged small helicopter--
Vietnamese War)
Nat Geog 129: 285 (col) Feb
'66
HELLS CANYON
Holiday 47: 52-53 (col) May
'70
HEMISFAIR, 1968--SAN AN-
TONIO, TEXAS
Look 32: 67-70 (col) May
28 '68
HEMP FLAILING, HAND--
YUGOSLAVIA
Nat Geog 128: 60 (col) July
'65
HERALDRY. See COAT OF
ARMS
HERMES (rocket). See ROCK-
ETS--U. S. --HERMES
(The) HERMITAGE (home of
Andrew Jackson)--NASH-
VILLE, TENN.
Nat Geog 127: 89 (col) Jan
'65
HIGH SIERRAS
Holiday 47: 62-65 (col) May
'70
HIGH WIRE ACT--KARL WAL-
LENDA
Life 69: 39-40 July 31 '70
HIJACKERS--PALESTINIAN
GUERRILLAS
Life 69: 30-37 Sept 18 '70
HILLWOOD--GEORGIAN MAN-
SION BELONGING TO MAR-
JORIE MERRIWEATHER
POST
Life 59: 54-59 (col) Nov 5
'65
HIMALAYAS
Life 58: 56-67 (col) May 28
'65
Nat Geog 130: 548, 559-61,
565 (col) Oct '66
HINDU KUSH
Life 55: 18-27 Aug 9 '63
HISTORIC HOUSES, ANTE-BEL-
LUM--CHATILLON-DEMENIL
HOUSE--ST. LOUIS
Nat Geog 128: 630 (col) Nov
'65

HOCKEY (game in action)
Look 29: 88-89 Jan 26 '65
Life 60: 34 Mar 4 '66
Sports Illus 24: 31-34 (col)
Apr 25 '66
Life 64: 42-55 (col) Feb 2
'68
Sports Illus 28: 31-33 (col)
Mar 18 '68
Sports Illus 29: 29-30 (col)
Dec 2 '68
Sports Illus 32: cover (col),
22-23 Mar 2 '70
Sports Illus 32: 18-21 Apr 6
'70
Sports Illus 34: 15-18 (col)
Apr 26 '71
HOCKEY--BRUINS--BOSTON
Life 68: 30-33 (col) Feb 27
'70
Sports Illus 32: 19-20 (col)
May 4 '70
Life 70: 46-48 (col) Apr 9
'71
HOCKEY--MAPLE LEAFS--
TORONTO
Nat Geog 124: 66-7 (col)
July '63
Holiday 45: 70-71 (col) Feb
'69
HOHOKAM INDIANS. See INDI-
ANS OF NORTH AMERICA--
HOHOKAM
HOLOGRAMS (three dimensional
pictures with use of lasers)
Nat Geog 129: 669 (col) May
'66
Nat Geog 130: 875 (col) Dec
'66
HOME OF ADAMS FAMILY.
See ADAMS HOUSE
HOME OF WINSTON CHURCHILL.
See CHARTWELL
HOME OF DWIGHT D. EISEN-
HOWER. See GETTYSBURG
FARM
HOME OF ULYSSES S. GRANT
--GALENA, ILL. (interior)
Nat Geog 127: 684 (col) May
'65
HOME OF JOHN HALL (William
Shakespeare's son-in-law).

See HALL'S CROFT
HOME OF HELEN HAYES--
NYACK, N.Y.
Life 55: 99-101 (col) Nov 1
'63
HOME OF WILLIAM RANDOLPH
HEARST. See SAN SIMEON,
CALIF.
HOME OF HERBERT HOOVER--
WEST BRANCH, IA.
Nat Geog 128: 576 (col) Oct
'65
HOME OF ANDREW JACKSON.
See (The) HERMITAGE
HOME OF THOMAS JEFFER-
SON. See MONTICELLO
HOME OF LYNDON B. JOHN-
SON. See LBJ RANCH
HOME OF ABRAHAM LINCOLN
--SPRINGFIELD, ILL.
Nat Geog 127: 670-1 (col)
May '65
HOME OF ALFRED LUNTS'--
GENESEE DEPOT, WIS.
Life 55: 76-8 July 26 '63
HOME OF JAMES MADISON.
See MONTPELIER
HOME OF JAMES MONROE.
See OAK HILL
HOME OF FRANKLIN D. ROOSE-
VELT--HYDE PARK, N.Y.
Nat Geog 129: 76 (col) Jan
'66
HOME OF THEODORE ROOSE-
VELT. See SAGAMORE HILL
HOME OF WILLIAM SHAKE-
SPEARE (birthplace)--STRAT-
FORD-ON-AVON
Nat Geog 125: 624-5 (col)
May '64
HOME OF MARTIN VAN BUREN
--KINDERHOOK, N.Y.
Nat Geog 127: 93 (col) Jan
'65
HOME OF CORNELIUS VANDER-
BILT. See THE BREAKERS
HOME OF GEORGE W. VANDER-
BILT. See BILTMORE
HOME OF GEORGE WASHING-
TON. See MOUNT VERNON
HOME OF JAMES WILSON (pa-
ternal grandfather of Woodrow
Wilson)--COUNTY TYRONE,

NORTHERN IRELAND
Nat Geog 126: 257 (col) Aug
'64
HOME OF WOODROW WILSON
--STAUNTON, VA.
Nat Geog 128: 557 (col) Oct
'65
HONEST JOHN (guided missile).
See GUIDED MISSILES--U.S.
--HONEST JOHN
HONG KONG
Nat Geog 127: 186-7 (col) Feb
'65
Travel 132: 30, 31 (col), 32,
33 (col), 34 Aug '69
Nat Geog 140: 540-573 (col)
Oct '71
HONOLULU
Nat Geog 136: 500-531 (col)
Oct '69
Holiday 46: 62-63 (col) Oct
'69
HOOVER DAM--LAKE MEAD
America's Wonderlands, p.
183 (col)
HORNS, HUNTING. See
HUNTING HORNS
HORSE RACING--EPSOM
DERBY
Sports Illus 32: 15-18 (col)
June 15 '70
HORSE RACING--KENTUCKY
DERBY
Sports Illus 32: 24-25 Apr
27 '70
Sports Illus 32: 22-24, 26
(col) May 11 '70
HORSE RACING--LONGCHAMP
--PARIS
Sports Illus 24: 47-50 (col)
June 6 '66
HORSE RACING--FROM HARRY
T. PETER'S AMERICA ON
STONE LITHOGRAPHY COL-
LECTION IN THE SMITH-
SONIAN INSTITUTION
Am Heritage 18: 33-48 (col)
Dec '66
HORSE RACING--SANTA ANITA
DERBY
Sports Illus 26: 19-20 (col)
Mar 13 '67
HORSE RACING--SARATOGA

Sports Illus 33: 28-34 (col)
Aug 3 '70
HORSE RACING--STEEPLE-
CHASE
Life 58: 60-61 Apr 9 '65
Sports Illus 34: 23-28 (col)
Feb 8 '71
Holiday 50: 28-31 (col) Sept/
Oct '71
HORSE SHOW--KANSAS CITY
AMERICAN ROYAL
Sports Illus 25: 47-50 (col)
Oct 10 '66
HORSE SHOW--ROYAL EASTER
--SYDNEY, AUSTRALIA
Nat Geog 124: 350 (col)
Sept '63
HORSE SHOW--SCOTTSDALE,
ARIZ.
Look 27: 46-49 (col) Oct 8
'63
Sports Illus 24: 29-32 (col)
Feb 21 '66
HORSES, HUNTING
Nat Geog 128: 636-7 (col)
Nov '65
HORSES, JUMPING
Life 56: 100 Feb 7 '64
Nat Geog 124: 242 (col) Aug
'63
HORSES, RACE--KELSO
Life 55: 126-9 (col) Nov 22
'63
HORSES, RACE--MAN O'WAR,
1919
Life 55: 58 July 26 '63
HORSES, RACE--NATIVE
DANCER
Life 57: 53 (col) Aug 14 '64
HORSES, WILD
Nat Geog 139: 94-109 (col)
Jan '71
HOTEL, REGENCY--HYATT
HOUSE, ATLANTA, GA.
Life 63: 79-80 (col) July 21
'67
HOTEL, RITZ-CARLTON--
BOSTON
Holiday 45: 84-87 (col) Apr
'69
HOTELS--BANFF SPRINGS--
ALBERTA

Nat Geog 130: 369 (col) Sept
'66
HOTELS--JACKSON LAKE LODGE
--WYOMING
Nat Geog 129: 560-2 (col)
Apr '66
HOTELS--PRINCE OF WALES
--WATERTON-GLACIER
INTERNATIONAL PEACE
PARK--CANADA--U. S.
Nat Geog 130: 356-7, 361
(col) Sept '66
HOTELS--SARATOGA SPRINGS,
N. Y. (razed in 1945)
Life 55: 57 July 5 '63; 54-5
July 26 '63
HOTELS--WALDORF-ASTORIA--
GRAND BALLROOM--NEW
YORK
Nat Geog 126: 79 (col) July
'64
HOT ROD CAR
Sports Illus 33: 23-26 (col)
July 27 '70
HOUND DOG (guided missile).
See GUIDED MISSILES--U. S.
--HOUND DOG
HOUSE BOATS
Holiday 35: 88-9 (col) Feb
'64
Life 57: 93 (col) Aug 14 '64
HOUSE BOATS, MODERN
Life 69: 30-3 (col) Aug 14
'70
HOUSE OF LORDS. See
PARLIAMENT BUILDINGS--
HOUSE OF LORDS--LONDON
HOUSEBOATS. See HOUSE
BOATS
HOUSES. See also APART-
MENT HOUSES; COTTAGES;
HUTS; PENTHOUSES
HOUSES, ADOBE--NUBIA
Nat Geog 124: 616-17 (col)
Oct '63
HOUSES, AMERICAN. See
ARCHITECTURE, DOMESTIC;
COTTAGES--COLONIAL
PERIOD
HOUSES, BAMBOO--PHILIP-
PINES
Nat Geog 130: 304 (col) Sept
'66

HOUSES, MODERN--THREE
LEVEL
Life 59: 142-146 (col) Oct
15 '65
HOUSES, MODERN--TOWER-
LIKE
Life 59: 82-85 (col), 87 Aug
13 '65
HOUSES, MODERN--VACATION-
HOUSE DESIGNS
Life 58: 90-93 (col), 97 Apr
16 '65
Life 58: 124-127 (col), 129
May 7 '65
Life 60: 84-87 (col), 89
Feb 11 '66
Sports Illus 25: 56-59 Oct
17 '66
Sports Illus 26: 42 (col), 44-
46 Feb 27 '67
Life 62: 80-83 (col), 85 June
30 '67
Life 63: 108-111 (col), 113
Sept 8 '67
Holiday 42: 62-65 (col) Oct
'67
Life 64: 73-75 (col), 77 Feb
2 '68
Life 65: 115-117 (col), 118
Sept 13 '68
Life 65: 126-9 (col), 131
Nov 22 '68
Holiday 45: 88-91 (col) Apr
'69
Life 69: 66-69 (col) July 10
'70
Sports Illus 33: 42-45 Sept
28 '70
HOUSES, MOORISH--PORTUGAL
Nat Geog 128: 498 (col) Oct
'65
HOUSES, MULTILEVEL--CARIB-
BEAN ISLAND OF BEQUIA
Life 66: 70-72 (col) Feb 21
'69
HOUSES, PLANTATION--
LOUISIANA (ante-bellum)
Nat Geog 129: 382 (col) Mar
'66
HOUSES, PRESIDENTS'. See
also under the name of the
House, e.g., MONTICELLO--

(home of Thomas Jefferson)
CHARLOTTESVILLE, VA.
HOUSES, PRESIDENTS' (from
George Washington to Lyndon
B. Johnson)
Life 65: 12-13 July 5 '68
HOUSES, ROCK--PORTUGAL
Nat Geog 128: 483 (col) Oct
'65
HOUSES, ROW--LONDON
Nat Geog 129: 760 (col) June
'66
HOUSES--ST. AUGUSTINE, FLA.
(city's oldest, 1720's)
Nat Geog 129: 200-1 (col)
Feb '66
HOUSES, SLANT-WALLED--
SWITZERLAND
Nat Geog 128: 365 (col) Sept
'65
HOUSES, SOD (19th cent.)
(painting)
Nat Geog 128: 668 (col) Nov
'65
HOUSES, STONE
Life 58: 88-91 (col), 93 June
4 '65
Life 66: 86-88 (col) Apr 11
'69
HOUSES, THATCHED (near
Dartmouth)--ENGLAND
Nat Geog 124: 220-1 (col)
Aug '63
HOUSES, THATCHED--TRIS-
TAN DA CUNHA (island)
Nat Geog 125: 66-8 (col) Jan
'64
HOUSES, TIN MINERS'--BOLIVIA
Nat Geog 129: 182-3 (col)
Feb '66
HOUSES, UNDERGROUND--
PLAINVIEW, TEX.
Life 56: 51, 54 Apr 24 '64
HOUSES ON STILTS--DAHOMEY
Nat Geog 130: 178-9 (col)
Aug '66
HOUSES ON STILTS--MALAY-
SIA
Nat Geog 124: 776 (col) Nov
'63
HOUSES ON STILTS--VIETNAM
(Republic)

Nat Geog 127: 59 (col) Jan
'65; 850-1 (col) June '65
HOUSEWARMINGS--RUSSIA
Life 55: 40-1 Sept 13 '63
HOUSING--HEXAHEDRON
Life 67: 102-103 (col), 104-
105 Dec 5 '69
HOUSING PROJECTS--ATHENS,
GREECE
Nat Geog 124: 129 (col) July
'63
HOUSING PROJECTS--CHURCH
SPONSORED--BOSTON,
MASSACHUSETTS
Ebony 20: 116 July '65
HOUSING PROJECTS--CHURCH
SPONSORED--CORSICANA,
TEXAS
Ebony 20: 119 July '65
HOUSING PROJECTS--CHURCH
SPONSORED--DALLAS,
TEXAS
Ebony 20: 118 July '65
HOUSING PROJECTS--CHURCH
SPONSORED--KANSAS CITY,
KANSAS
Ebony 20: 117 July '65
HOUSING PROJECTS--CHURCH
SPONSORED--LITTLE ROCK,
ARKANSAS
Ebony 20: 118 July '65
HOUSING PROJECTS--CHURCH
SPONSORED--LOS ANGELES,
CALIFORNIA
Ebony 20: 119 July '65
HOUSING PROJECTS--CHURCH
SPONSORED--ROXBURY'S
SECTION--BOSTON
Ebony 20: 118 July '65
HOUSING PROJECTS--CHURCH
SPONSORED--SAN ANTONIO,
TEXAS
Ebony 20: 116 July '65
HOUSING PROJECTS--CHURCH
SPONSORED--WASHINGTON,
D. C.
Ebony 20: 116-17 July '65
HOUSTON, TEXAS
Nat Geog 132: 338-377 (col)
Sept '67
Holiday 43: 55, 59 (col) Apr
'68

HOUSTON, TEXAS--AERIAL
VIEW
Ebony 20: 120 Mar '65
HOUSTON ASTRODOME. See
STADIUMS--ASTRODOME--
HOUSTON, TEX.
HOVENWEEP NATIONAL
MONUMENT--UTAH-COLO.
America's Wonderlands, p.
312 (col)
HOWARD UNIVERSITY COL-
LEGE OF MEDICINE
Ebony 18: 168 Sept '63
HUDSON RIVER
Life 57: 64-5 (col) July 24
'64
HUDSON RIVER COUNTRY
Holiday 40: 40-55 (col) Oct
'66
HUNGARY
Nat Geog 139: 444-483 (col)
Apr '71
HUNTING HORNS
Nat Geog 129: 839 (col) June
'66
HUNTINGTON-HARTFORD GAL-
LERY OF MODERN ART--
NEW YORK. See GALLERY
OF MODERN ART--NEW
YORK
HURDLING
Ebony 19: 63-6 Apr '64
HURLING
Sports Illus 27: 41-44 (col)
Aug 28 '67
HURRICANE DISASTER--
"CAMILLE"--MISSISSIPPI
GULF COAST
Life 69: 78-83 Sept 18 '70
HURRICANE DISASTER--
"FLORA"--HAITI
Life 55: 34-43 Oct 18 '63
HURRICANES
Am Heritage 20: 10, 12-15
Aug '69
HURRICANES--BETSY--GRAND
ISLA, LA., SEPTEMBER
1965
Life 59: 44C-44D Sept 24
'65
Nat Geog 129: 358-9 (col)
Mar '66

HURRICANES--DORA--JACK-
SONVILLE, FLA., SEP-
TEMBER 1964
Life 57: 36-41 (col) Sept
25 '64
HURRICANES--FLORA--CUBA
AND HAITI, OCTOBER 1963
Life 55: 34-43 Oct 18 '63;
36B-37 Nov 1 '63
HUTS--SAIGON
Nat Geog 127: 848 (col) June
'65
HUTS, THATCHED--YEMEN
Nat Geog 125: 442-3 (col)
Mar '64
HUTTERITE COLONIES--SOUTH
DAKOTA
Nat Geog 138: 98-125 (col)
July '70
HYDROFOILS
Nat Geog 127: 610-11 (col)
May '65
Nat Geog 128: 352 (col) Sept
'65
Nat Geog 130: 454-5 (col)
Oct '66

I

IBIZA ISLAND
Holiday 47: 33-37 (col) June
'70
ICE--POLAR REGIONS
Nat Geog 128: 670-91 (col)
Nov '65
ICE BOATS
Sports Illus 22: 31-37 (col)
Jan 4 '65
Sports Illus 22: 31-37 (col)
Jan 11 '65
ICE BREAKING VESSELS--U. S.
--ATKA
Nat Geog 127: 184 (col) Feb
'65
ICE BREAKING VESSELS,
ATOMIC POWERED--RUSSIA
--LENIN
Life 57: 30-34C (col) July 17
'64
ICE CREAM
Look 52-55 (col) July 13 '71

ICE ISLANDS. See ARCTIC
RESEARCH LABORATORY--
ICE STATION NO. 2; ICE--
POLAR REGIONS
ICEBREAKERS. See ICE
BREAKING VESSELS
ICELAND
Holiday 34: 56-61 (col) Sept
'63
Nat Geog 136: 228-265 (col)
Aug '69
Holiday 46: 54-57 (col) Dec
'69
Life 71: 42-49 (col) July 30
'71
ILE DE LA CITE--PARIS
Nat Geog 133: 680-719 (col)
May '68
ILLINOIS
Nat Geog 131: 748-797 (col)
June '67
ILLUSTRATION OF BOOKS AND
PERIODICALS. See BOOK
CHARACTERS
IMMIGRANTS--LANDING AT
NEW YORK HARBOR, 1887
Nat Geog 127: 700 (col) May
'65
INAUGURATIONS--INAUGURAL
ADDRESS--GEORGE WASH-
INGTON, 1789 (engraving)
Nat Geog 126: 642-3 (col)
Nov '64
INAUGURATIONS--INAUGURAL
PARADE--GROVER CLEVE-
LAND, 1885
Nat Geog 127: 702-3 May '65
INAUGURATIONS--LYNDON B.
JOHNSON
Life 58: 24-33 (col) Jan 29
'65
Ebony 20: 66-8 (col), 70, 72-
3 Apr '65
INAUGURATIONS--RICHARD M.
NIXON
Life 66: 18-31 (col) Jan 31
'69
INDIA
Travel 124: 51-54 (col) July
'65
Holiday 42: 38-47 (col) Oct
'67

Look 32: 31-36 (col), 37
  Mar 19 '68
Travel 136: 28-32, 34 (col)
  Sept '71
INDIAN ARTIFACTS
  Hobbies 69: 112 Nov '64
  Hobbies 69: 112-114 Dec '64
  Hobbies 70: 116-117, 124-
    125 June '65
  Hobbies 70: 114-116 July '65
  Hobbies 71: 114 Mar '66
  Hobbies 71: 114 Apr '66
  Hobbies 71: 114 Oct '66
  Hobbies 71: 112 Nov '66
  Hobbies 71: 112-113 Jan '67
  Hobbies 71: 112-113 Feb '67
  Hobbies 72: 112-113 Mar '67
  Hobbies 72: 112 Apr '67
  Hobbies 72: 112 May '67
  Hobbies 72: 112-113 June '67
  Hobbies 72: 110-112 Sept '67
  Hobbies 72: 109-110 Nov '67
  Hobbies 73: 118-120 Apr '68
  Hobbies 73: 118-121 June '68
  Hobbies 73: 120 July '68
  Hobbies 73: 112-113 Dec '68
  Hobbies 73: 110-111 Feb '69
  Hobbies 74: 111 Mar '69
  Hobbies 74: 110-112 Apr '69
  Hobbies 74: 110-112 May '69
  Hobbies 74: 110-111 June '69
  Hobbies 74: 110-111 July '69
  Hobbies 75: 142-143 Mar '70
  Hobbies 75: 154-155 Oct '70
  Hobbies 75: 154-155 Dec '70
  Hobbies 76: 150-151 Apr '71
  Life 71: 60-65 (col) July 2 '71
  Hobbies 76: 146-150 Sept '71
  Hobbies 76: 146-147 Oct '71
  America's Wonderlands, p.
    500 (col), 501-3
INDIAN ARTIFACTS--ARROW-
  HEADS
  Hobbies 75: 154-155 Feb '71
INDIAN ARTIFACTS--BASKETS
  Hobbies 71: 114 Dec '66
INDIAN ARTIFACTS--DRILLS
  Hobbies 74: 142-144 Feb '70
INDIAN ARTIFACTS--PUEBLO
  America's Wonderlands, p.
    292-3, 308-9 (col)
  America's Wonderlands, p.

308-9 (col)
INDIAN ARTIFACTS--TOOLS
  Hobbies 75: 144-145 Sept '70
INDIAN CRAFTS
  Look 27: 43 (col) Oct 8 '63
  Holiday 34: 179-181, 183-184
    (col) Dec '63
INDIAN RESERVATIONS--SUPAI
  (home of the Havasupai
  Indians)
  America's Wonderlands, p.
    176-9 (col)
INDIANS OF NORTH AMERICA.
  See also BASKETS; BURIAL
  CHAMBERS; CLIFF DWELL-
  INGS; GRINDING BINS; HAIR
  BRUSHES; JEWELRY; KIVAS;
  PAPOOSE BOARDS; POT
  RESTS; POTTERY; SAND-
  STONES; WEAVING
INDIANS OF NORTH AMERICA
  --ALASKA--TLINGIT, 20TH
  CENT.
  Nat Geog 127: 778, 789, 798-
    9 (col) June '65
INDIANS OF NORTH AMERICA
  --ANASAZI--MESA VERDE
  NATIONAL PARK (paintings)
  Nat Geog 125: 156-9, 172,
    176, 179, 186 (col) Feb '64
INDIANS OF NORTH AMERICA
  --APACHE (portrait of
  Geronimo)
  Am Heritage 17: 56 June '66
INDIANS OF NORTH AMERICA
  --ARIZ. /N. MEXICO--
  PUEBLO
  America's Wonderlands, p.
    286 (col)
INDIANS OF NORTH AMERICA
  --BLACKFOOT, 20TH CENT.
  Nat Geog 126: 573 (col) Oct
    '64
INDIANS OF NORTH AMERICA
  --CANADA--SARCEE
  Nat Geog 130: 372 (col) Sept
    '66
INDIANS OF NORTH AMERICA
  --CHIPPEWA, 20TH CENT.
  Nat Geog 124: 427-30 (col)
    Sept '63
INDIANS OF NORTH AMERICA

See EXPRESS HIGHWAYS
INVESTITURE RITES, BRITISH
--PRINCE PHILIP
Nat Geog 136: 698-715 (col)
Nov '69
IRAN
Holiday 50: 44-45 (col)
Sept/Oct '71
IRELAND
Look 30: 61-67 (col) Apr 19
'66
Travel 127: 51-54 (col) Jan
'67
Holiday 48: 48-53 (col) July
-Aug '70
ISLANDS. See Names of
Islands, e. g. ARRAN (island);
SABLE (island); etc.
ISLE ROYALE NATIONAL PARK
America's Wonderlands, p.
506-7 (col)
ISRAEL
Nat Geog 127: 394-433 (col)
Mar '65
Travel 128: 53-6 (col) Sept
'67
Holiday 42: 59, 61, 63, 65
(map) (col), 66-73, 91-
99 (col) Dec '67
ITALY
Travel 123: 53-6 (col) Apr
'65
Holiday 48: 32-8, 40-3 (col)
July-Aug '70
ITALY, SOUTHERN
Holiday 36: 38-9, 42-7 (col)
Sept '64
IWO JIMA--STATUE--MARINE
CORPS WAR MEMORIAL--
"ACROSS THE POTOMAC
FROM WASHINGTON, D. C. "
Nat Geog 126: 780 (col) Dec
'64
IZEMBECK WILDLIFE RANGE
--ALASKA
Life 70: 42-43 (col) Jan 8
'71

J

JACKSON, ANDREW--ASSAS-
SINATION ATTEMPT ON

PRESIDENT JACKSON, JAN-
UARY 30, 1835
Nat Geog 127: 86 Jan '65
JACKSON HOLE, WYOMING
America's Wonderlands, p.
94-5 (col), 98-9
JACKSON HOLE SKI AREA--
WYOMING
Nat Geog 129: 592-3 (col)
Apr '66
JACKSON LAKE--WYOMING
Nat Geog 128: 886-7 (col)
Dec '65
America's Wonderlands, p.
4-5 (col)
JACKSON, MISS. --GREENWOOD
CEMETERY (first burial
ground)
Ebony 21: 129 Feb '66
JACKSON, WYOMING
America's Wonderlands, p.
106 (col)
JACKSONVILLE, FLA.
Nat Geog 124: 889 (col) Dec
'63
JAMAICA
Nat Geog 132: 842-873 (col)
Dec '67
JAPAN
Life 57: entire issue Sept
11 '64
Look 29: 21-28 (col) Aug 10
'65
Travel 124: 53-56 (col) Oct
'65
Nat Geog 137: 296-339 (col)
Mar '70
JAPAN--HOKKAIDO
Nat Geog 131: 269-296 (col)
Feb '67
JAPANESE SURRENDER--END
OF WORLD WAR II. See
WORLD WAR II--JAPANESE
SURRENDER SIGNED
ABOARD U. S. S. MISSOURI
JARASH (ruins of Roman city)
--JORDAN
Nat Geog 126: 806-7 (col)
Dec '64
JARS, WATER (botijos)--
SPAIN
Nat Geog 127: 338 (col) Mar
'65

JAVA
Holiday 47: 32-37 (col) Feb
'70
Life 68: 46-57 (col) June 26
'70
Nat Geog 139: 2-43 (col) Jan
'71
JEFFERSON, THOMAS--STATUE
--UNIVERSITY OF VIRGINIA
CAMPUS--CHARLOTTES-
VILLE, VA.
Nat Geog 126: 670 (col) Nov
'64
JERUSALEM
Nat Geog 124: 838-55 (col)
Dec '63
Nat Geog 126: 790-1, 820-3,
827-47 (col) Dec '64
Nat Geog 127: 426-7 (col)
Mar '65
Nat Geog 134: 834-871 (col)
Dec '68
JERUSALEM--CONQUEST BY
FIRST CRUSADE, 1099
(painting)
Nat Geog 124: 849-51 (col)
Dec '63
JERUSALEM--ISRAEL MUSEUM
Look 29: 56-63 (col) Oct 6
'65
JERUSALEM--STREETS--VIA
DOLOROSA
Nat Geog 126: 820-1, 831
(col) Dec '64
JESUS CHRIST--BIRTHPLACE--
CHURCH OF THE NATIVITY
--BETHLEHEM, JORDAN
Nat Geog 126: 819 (col) Dec
'64
Nat Geog 128: 278 (col) Aug
'65
JESUS CHRIST--CRUCIFIXION
Life 56: 54-6, 66-7 (col) Mar
27 '64
JEWELRY--CAMBODIA
Nat Geog 126: 531, 542-3,
551 (col) Oct '64
JEWELRY, CLAY
Sch Arts 71: 16-17 Sept '71
JEWELRY--COLLARS
Life 69: 58-59 (col) Sept 18
'70

JEWELRY--ETHIOPIA
Nat Geog 127: 550-2, 568-
9, 571, 578 (col) Apr '65
JEWELRY, HORSESHOE NAIL
Sch Arts 70: 26-28 Feb '71
JEWELRY--INDIA--NOSE RINGS
Nat Geog 127: 78 (col) Jan
'65
JEWELRY--INDIA--NOSE
TRILLS
Nat Geog 129: 451 (col) Apr
'66
JEWELRY, INDIAN (N. Ameri-
can)
Nat Geog 125: 196-200, 202,
207-8, 210 (col) Feb '64
Nat Geog 128: 880 (col)
Dec '65
JEWELRY, INDIAN (S. Ameri-
can)--ERIGBAAGTSA--
BRAZIL
Nat Geog 125: 739-40, 742-6,
748-57 (col) May '64
JEWELRY, INDIAN SHELL
Hobbies 68: 112, 114 Aug '63
JEWELRY, MACRAME
Sch Arts 70: 12-13 Jan '71
JEWELRY, MODERN
Ebony 23: 92-3 (col) Oct '68
Life 66: 35 (col) Jan 24 '69
JEWELRY--NEPAL
Nat Geog 130: 546-7, 550-1,
555, 566 (col) Oct '66
JEWELRY--NUBIA
Nat Geog 124: 589 (col) Oct
'63
JEWELRY--RUSSIAN
Life 59: 60-61 (col) Nov 5
'65
JEWELRY, SHELL
Look 29: 77 (col) May 4 '65
Look 35: 40-43 (col) July 27
'71
JEWELRY--VIKINGS
Nat Geog 126: 715 (col) Nov
'64
JEWELRY, WAX
Sch Arts 63: 5-10 May '64
JEWELS--HOPE DIAMOND
Nat Geog 140: 836 (col) Dec
'71
JEWELS--TANZANIA

Life 66: 70, 72, 75-76 (col)
May 9 '69

JEWISH RITUAL--BAR MITZVAH
Look 27: 24-28, 30, 33 Aug
13 '63

JOAN OF ARC--STATUE--OR-
LEANS, FRANCE
Nat Geog 129: 840 (col)
June '66

JOB CORPS. See UNITED
STATES--JOB CORPS

JOCKEYS
Ebony 19: 63-4, 66, 68-9, 72
Feb '64
Sports Illus 24: 41-44 (col)
Apr 11 '66
Life 65: 32-35 (col) Dec 13
'68

JOCKEYS--SARATOGA SPRINGS,
N.Y., 1919
Life 55: 58-9 July 26 '63

JOCKEYS--WOMEN
Sports Illus 35: 25-28 (col)
July 5 '71

JOHN BROWN RAID, 1859.
See HARPERS FERRY,
W. VA. --JOHN BROWN RAID,
1859

JOHN F. KENNEDY CENTER
FOR THE PERFORMING
ARTS--WASHINGTON, D.C.
(painting of proposed struc-
ture)
Life 56: 47-8, 50 (col) Feb
7 '64
Nat Geog 126: 778-9 (col)
Dec '64

JOHN F. KENNEDY CENTER
FOR THE PERFORMING
ARTS--WASHINGTON, D.C.
Life 71: 30-32 (col) Sept
17 '71

JOHNSON, ANDREW--RECEIV-
ING IMPEACHMENT SUM-
MONS (drawing)
Nat Geog 127: 679 May '65

JOHNSON, ANDREW--TAILOR
SHOP--GREENEVILLE,
TENN. (drawing)
Nat Geog 127: 678 May '65

JOHNSON, LYNDON B. --
CABINET

Nat Geog 129: 115 (col) Jan
'66

JOHNSON, LYNDON B. --
SWEARING IN CEREMONY,
NOVEMBER 22, 1963
Life 55: 30-1 Nov 29 '63
Nat Geog 129: 112 Jan '66

JOHNSON, LYNDON B. --VISIT
TO NORTHERN EUROPE,
SEPT. 1963
Nat Geog 125: 268-93 (col)
Feb '64

JOHNSTOWN FLOOD, 1889
Am Heritage 17: 4-5 (painting),
6-11 June '66

JONES BEACH--LONG ISLAND,
N.Y.
Nat Geog 124: 676-7 (col)
Nov '63

JORDAN
Nat Geog 126: 790-825 (col)
Dec '64

JORDAN RIVER
Nat Geog 126: 794 (col) Dec
'64

JOSEPHINE LAKE
America's Wonderlands, p.
112-3 (col)

JOSHUA TREE NATIONAL
MONUMENT--CALIFORNIA
America's Wonderlands, p.
375

JUDO
Ebony 19: 83-4 Nov '63
Ebony 19: 102-4, 106, 108
June '64
Look 29: 64-65 Mar 9 '65
Nat Geog 127: 863 (col)
June '65
Ebony 22: 107-8, 110 Apr
'67

JUNEAU, ALASKA (night scene)
Nat Geog 127: 790-1 (col)
June '65

JUNKS
Nat Geog 126: 640 (col) Nov
'64
Nat Geog 129: 290 (col) Feb
'66

JUNKS--VIETNAM (Republic)
(used for sea patrol during
Vietnamese War)

Nat Geog 129: 288-9 (col)
Feb '66
JUPITER (guided missile). See
GUIDED MISSILES--U. S. --
JUPITER

K

KAHER (space vehicle). See
SPACE VEHICLES--EGYPT
--KAHER
KAMIKAZE AIRPLANES. See
ROCKET PLANES, MILITARY
--JAPAN--OHKA KAMIKAZES
KAPPA (rocket). See ROCKETS,
SOUNDING--JAPAN--KAPPA
KARATE
Nat Geog 126: 486-7 (col)
Oct '64
Life 61: 80-81 (col) Oct 21
'66
Ebony 23: 144-6, 148, 150
May '68
Ebony 25: 104-6, 108 June
'70
KASHMIR
Life 57: 91-7 (col) Aug 14
'64
KATMAI, MOUNT--ALASKA
America's Wonderlands, p.
46-7 (col)
KATMAI NATIONAL MONU-
MENT--ALASKA
America's Wonderlands, p.
524-9, 532-3 (col)
KATYUSHA (rocket). See
ROCKETS--RUSSIA--LAUNCH-
ING FROM TRUCK MOUNTED
RACKS--KATYUSHA
KAUAI ISLAND--HAWAII
Holiday 45: 64-65 (col) Apr
'69
KAYAKS--RUSSIA
Life 55: 44A Sept 13 '63
KENNEDY, JOHN F. See also
JOHN F. KENNEDY CENTER
FOR THE PERFORMING
ARTS--WASHINGTON, D. C.
KENNEDY, JOHN F. --ASSAS-
SINATION, NOVEMBER 22,
1963

Life 55: 22-32H Nov 29 '63
Life 57: 43-6 (col) Oct 2 '64
KENNEDY, JOHN F. --ASSAS-
SINATION--LEE OSWALD
WITH WEAPON USED TO
KILL PRESIDENT KENNEDY
Life 56: front cover, 80 Feb
21 '64
Life 57: 48 Oct 2 '64
KENNEDY, JOHN F. --CENTER
FOR THE PERFORMING
ARTS. See JOHN F. KEN-
NEDY CENTER FOR THE
PERFORMING ARTS
KENNEDY, JOHN F. --FUN-
ERAL RITES
Life 55: 38, 39-46 (col), 47
Dec 6 '63
Ebony 19: 25-8 Feb '64
Nat Geog 125: 310-11, 314-
51 (col) Mar '64
Nat Geog 130: 607 Nov '66
KENNEDY, JOHN F. --GRAVE--
ARLINGTON, VA. --NATION-
AL CEMETERY
Nat Geog 125: 348, 354-5
(col) Mar '64
Nat Geog 126: 769 (col) Dec
'64
KENNEDY, JOHN F. --MEMOR-
IAL PLAYGROUND--WASH-
INGTON, D. C.
Ebony 20: 190-4 Nov '64
KENNEDY, JOHN F. --ROCK-
ING CHAIR
Nat Geog 130: 617 (col) Nov
'66
KENNEDY, JOHN F. --SCRIM-
SHAW COLLECTION
Am Heritage 15: 8-13 Oct
'64
KENNEDY, JOHN F. --VISIT
TO EUROPE, 1963
Life 55: 30-1 July 5 '63
Nat Geog 129: 104-5 (col)
Jan '66
KENNEDY, MOUNT
Life 58: 47 Apr 2 '65
Life 58: front cover, 22, 24-
6 (col) Apr 9 '65
Nat Geog 128: 2-33 (col)
July '65

KENNEDY, MOUNT--FIRST
ASCENT, 1965
Nat Geog 128: 10-33 (col)
July '65
KENTUCKY (Blue Grass Country)
(painting)
Holiday 36: 80-5 (col) Nov
'64
KENYA, AFRICA
Nat Geog 135: 151-205 (col)
Feb '69
KETTLE, BRASS, CIRCA 1790
Nat Geog 124: 414 (col) Sept
'63
KETTLE, IRON (used for
making soap and rendering
lard)
Life 56: 60 (col) Feb 14 '64
KEY BISCAYNE
Life 66: 26-31 (col) Feb 21
'69
KIBBUTZIM. See COLLECTIVE
SETTLEMENTS--ISRAEL
KIKUYUS. See AFRICA--
NATIVE RACES--KIKUYUS
KILIMANJARO--CONQUEST BY
STEWART UDALL, 1963
Life 55: 55-64 Oct 11 '63
KITCHENS--CHINA (People's
Republic)
Nat Geog 126: 624-5 (col)
Nov '64
KITE, WHEEL-SHAPED (in-
vented by A. G. Bell)
Nat Geog 124: 530-1 Oct '63
KITT PEAK NATIONAL OB-
SERVATORY. See ASTRO-
NOMICAL OBSERVATORIES
--KITT PEAK NATIONAL
OBSERVATORY
KIVAS, INDIAN (N. American)
--MESA VERDE NATIONAL
PARK
Nat Geog 125: 156-7, 168-70,
188-9 (col) Feb '64
KLONDIKE GOLD RUSH, 1890's
Am Heritage 18: 34, 37-39,
41-42, 45-46, 48-49 Aug
'67
KOMODO ISLAND--INDONESIA
Nat Geog 134: 872-880 (col)
Dec '68

KORABL SPUTNIK (artificial
satellite). See SPACE VE-
HICLES--RECOVERY--
KORABL SPUTNIK 2--
RECOVERY CAPSULE
KOREA (South)
Nat Geog 135: 302-345 (col)
Mar '69
KREMLIN--INTERIOR--ST.
GEORGE'S HALL
Life 66: 34-35 (col) June
20 '69
KU KLUX KLAN
Life 56: 21 June 26 '64
Life 58: 28, 29-32 (col), 33-
34, 35 (col) Apr 23 '65
Life 59: 28 July 9 '65
Ebony 20: 38-9, 42 Aug '65
Ebony 22: 148 Dec '66
KU KLUX KLAN--(member cap-
tured in Reconstruction riot
at Huntsville, Ala.)
Ebony 22: 148 Dec '66
KUWAIT SHEIKDOM
Life 59: 96 (col), 97-8 Sept
17 '65

L

LABORATORIES, LANGUAGE.
See LANGUAGE LABORA-
TORIES
LACROSSE (Indian game)
Life 66: 49-56 (col) Apr 18
'69
LAKE OF THE WOODS--MIN-
NESOTA--CANADA
Nat Geog 124: 90-1 (col)
July '63
LAKES. See Names of Lakes,
e.g. JACKSON LAKE;
LOUISE, LAKE; LUGANO,
LAKE; POWELL, LAKE;
etc.
LAMPS (designed by Libbey)
Hobbies 74: 116-17, 124-5
Dec '69
LAMPS, ANTIQUE--1800-1900
Hobbies 68: 82-83 Aug '63
LAMPS, COAL MINERS'
Nat Geog 130: 362 (col) Sept
'66

LAMPS, INCANDESCENT
  (Edison's, 1879)
  Nat Geog 127: 689 May '65
LAMPS, KEROSENE
  Nat Geog 128: 567 (col)
    Oct '65
LAND RUSH--OKLAHOMA.
  See OKLAHOMA LAND RUSH
LANDAUS. See CARRIAGES
  --LANDAUS
LANDING CRAFT. See
  BARGES, LANDING
LANGUAGE LABORATORIES
  Nat Geog 130: 814 (col)
    Dec '66
LANTERN SLIDES. See
  SLIDES (photography)
LAOS
  Life 68: 30, 31 (col), 32,
    34-35 (col) Apr 3 '70
  Life 70: 20, cover, 21-29
    (col) Mar 12 '71
LA PAZ, BOLIVIA (aerial
  view)
  Nat Geog 129: 154-5 (col)
    Feb '66
LASERS
  Life 59: 70-71 (col) July
    9 '65
  Nat Geog 130: 858-81 (col)
    Dec '66
LASSEN VOLCANIC NATIONAL
  PARK
  America's Wonderlands, p.
    416-17 (col)
  Nat Geog 129: 666-7 (col)
    May '66
LAS VEGAS, NEVADA
  Holiday 44: 48-56 (col) Dec
    '68
LAUNCHING PADS FOR SPACE
  VEHICLES. See SPACE
  VEHICLES--LAUNCHING
  PADS
LAUNDRIES--WOMEN BEATING
  CLOTHES CLEAN--DANUBE
  DELTA
  Nat Geog 128: 75 (col) July
    '65
LAVA
  America's Wonderlands, p.
    544 (col)

L. B. J. RANCH (home of Lyn-
  don B. Johnson) NEAR
  JOHNSON CITY, TEX.
  Life 55: 29 Dec 13 '63
  Life 57: 72 Aug 21 '64
  Life 61: 38-9 (col) July 8
    '66
LEBANON
  Life 60: 46-53 (col) Jan 7
    '66
  Travel 128: 51-54 (col) Oct
    '67
  Nat Geog 137: 240-275 (col)
    Feb '70
LEEWARD ISLANDS
  Nat Geog 130: 488-537 (col)
    Oct '66
LEG IRONS (form of punish-
  ment)
  Nat Geog 125: 421 (col) Mar
    '64
LEIS, HAWAIIAN
  Nat Geog 131: 120-129 (col)
    Jan '67
LEISURE WORLD. See AGED--
  HOUSING--LEISURE WORLD
LENIN--MAUSOLEUM--MOSCOW
  Nat Geog 129: 299, 306-7
    (col) Mar '66
LENINGRAD
  Nat Geog 139: 635-673 (col)
    May '71
LEPTIS MAGNA (ruin of Medi-
  terranean Africa)
  Holiday 47: 66-67 (col) Feb
    '70
LE PUY, FRANCE
  Nat Geog 129: 836-7 (col)
    June '66
LES HALLES--FOOD MARKET
  --PARIS
  Life 66: 89-90 Mar 14 '69
LETTERING, STICK
  Sch Arts 65: 12-15 Jan '66
LEWIS AND CLARK EXPEDI-
  TION, 1804-06 (painting)
  Nat Geog 128: 646-7 (col)
    Nov '65
LEYTE GULF--PHILIPPINES
  Nat Geog 130: 350-1 (col)
    Sept '66
LIBRARY, VATICAN--ROME

Hobbies 70: 106 Apr '65
LIBRARY ARCHITECTURE
(Andrew Carnegie libraries)
Am Heritage 21: 60, 62-3,
Oct '70
LIBRARY ARCHITECTURE--
INTERIOR--17TH CENT.
Hobbies 70: 107 Apr '65
LIBRARY OF CONGRESS. See
UNITED STATES--LIBRARY
OF CONGRESS
LIFE JACKETS
Nat Geog 125: 781 (col) June
'64
LIGHTHOUSE--EDDYSTONE
LIGHT--PLYMOUTH HARBOR
--ENGLAND
Nat Geog 124: 212-3 (col)
Aug '63
LIGHTNING
Nat Geog 129: 565 (col) Apr
'66
LIMA, PERU
Nat Geog 125: 215 (col) Feb
'64
LIMA, PERU--STREETS--
PLAZA SAN MARTIN
Nat Geog 125: 218-19 (col)
Feb '64
LINCOLN, ABRAHAM--CABI-
NET (engraving)
Nat Geog 126: 645 Nov '64
LINCOLN, ABRAHAM (clothing
worn the day he was shot)
Am Heritage 16: 18-19 Apr
'65
LINCOLN, ABRAHAM--FUN-
ERAL RITES--NEW YORK,
1865 (painting)
Nat Geog 127: 674-5 (col)
May '65
LINCOLN, ABRAHAM--GETTYS-
BURG ADDRESS (copy of
address written in Lincoln's
hand)
Life 55: 116-17 Nov 15 '63
LINCOLN, ABRAHAM--MEM-
ORIAL--WASHINGTON, D. C.
Ebony 19: 32 Dec '64
Look 29: 26-7 (col) Apr 6 '65
LINCOLN, ABRAHAM--MOURN-
ING RIBBON

Nat Geog 130: 606 (col) Nov
'66
LINCOLN, ABRAHAM--MOURN-
ING RING
Nat Geog 127: 674 (col) May
'65
LINCOLN, ABRAHAM--SPLIT-
TING LOG (1860 campaign
poster)
Nat Geog 127: 669 (col) May
'65
LINCOLN, ABRAHAM--STATUE
(by Vinnie Ream)--CAPITOL--
WASHINGTON, D. C.
Nat Geog 125: 7 (col) Jan '64
LINCOLN CENTER FOR THE
PERFORMING ARTS--NEW
YORK CITY
Life 55: 42 Oct 4 '63
Nat Geog 126: 90-1 (col)
July '64
Holiday 36: 40-1 (col) July
'64
Holiday 44: 36-7, 39-41, 43-
5 (col) Sept '68
Holiday 47: 82-3 (col) Feb '70
LINCOLN-DOUGLAS DEBATES,
1858 (scene from old lantern
slide)
Nat Geog 127: 668-9 (col)
May '65
LINCOLN MEMORIAL--WASH-
INGTON, D. C.
Life 55: 20 (col) Sept 6 '63
Nat Geog 126: 738-9 (col)
Dec '64
Nat Geog 128: 552 Oct '65
LINCOLN PARK--CHICAGO
Holiday 41: 74-83 (col) Mar
'67
LINCOLN'S ASSASSINATION
(the search, trial, and
death of conspirators)
Life 58: 68-75 Apr 16 '65
LINCOLN'S FUNERAL TRAIN
Life 58: 76-77 Apr 16 '65
LINGERIE. See UNDERWEAR
LION TAMER
Ebony 19: 49-50, 52, 54-5
Oct '64
LISBON, PORTUGAL
Nat Geog 128: 458, 462-3

(col) Oct '65
LITHOGRAPHS
Life 68: 57-61 (col) Jan 23
'70
Sch Arts 70: 28-29 Dec '70
LITTLE LARK (guided missile.
See GUIDED MISSILES--U.S.
--LITTLE LARK
LOCKS AND KEYS
Hobbies 75: 84-85 July '70
LOCOMOTIVES, 19TH CENT.
Life 61: 70 (col), 72 Dec 9
'66
Am Heritage 19: 4 (litho-
graph, col) Feb '68
LOG CABIN--OLD FAITHFUL
INN (World's largest log
cabin)
America's Wonderlands, p.
74-5, 77 (col)
LOG STACKER, LE TOURNEAU
Nat Geog 126: 32-3 (col) July
'64
LOGGERS. See LUMBERJACKS
LOGGING. See LUMBERING
LOIRE RIVER
Nat Geog 129: 824-69 (col)
June '66
LONDON
Nat Geog 125: 648-9 (col)
May '64
Nat Geog 129: 743-91 (col)
June '66
LONDON, 1616 (drawing)
Nat Geog 125: 650-1 May '64
LONDON--PICCADILLY CIRCUS
Nat Geog 129: 748 (col) June
'66
LONDON--TRAFALGAR SQUARE
(night scene)
Nat Geog 129: 768-9 (col)
June '66
LONDON--WORLD'S FAIR, 1851
--CRYSTAL PALACE
Life 56: 53 May 1 '64
LONG ISLAND, NEW YORK
Look 29: 61-69 (col), 71-74
Sept 7 '65
LOOMS, 18TH CENT.
Life 57: 133 Oct 9 '64
LOS ANGELES, CALIFORNIA--
AERIAL VIEW

Ebony 20: 118 Mar '65
LOS ANGELES (night scene)
Nat Geog 129: 596-7 (col)
May '66
LOS ANGELES CENTER FOR
THE PERFORMING ARTS--
MUSIC CENTER--LOS
ANGELES
Nat Geog 129: 600 (col) May
'66
LOUISE, LAKE
Nat Geog 130: 374-7 (col)
Sept '66
LOURENÇO MARQUES, MO-
ZAMBIQUE
Nat Geog 126: 198-9 (col)
Aug '64
THE LOUVRE--PARIS
Holiday 35: 70-77 (col) Jan
'64
Nat Geog 139: 797-831 (col)
June '71
LUGANO, LAKE--ITALY-
SWITZERLAND
Nat Geog 128: 372-3 (col)
Sept '65
LUMBERING--ALASKA
Nat Geog 127: 780-1 (col)
June '65
LUMBERING--CANADA
Nat Geog 130: 382-3 (col)
Sept '66
LUMBERING--REDWOOD
GROVE--CALIFORNIA
Nat Geog 126: 30-1 (col)
July '64
Nat Geog 129: 676-7 (col)
May '66
LUMBERJACKS--ALASKA
Nat Geog 127: 780-1 (col)
June '65
LUNA (space probe). See
LUNAR PROBES--RUSSIA--
LUNA
LUNAR EXCURSION MODULE.
See SPACE VEHICLES--
LANDING SYSTEMS--LUNAR
EXCURSION MODULE FOR
LANDING ON MOON
LUNAR PROBES--RUSSIA--
LUNA 1 (first moon probe;
launched, 1959)

Hist of Rocketry and Space
Travel, p. 191
LUNAR PROBES--RUSSIA--
LUNA 9 (made first soft
landing on moon, 1966)
Hist of Rocketry and Space
Travel, p. 192
LUNAR PROBES--U.S. (by
Ranger 7, July 1964)
Nat Geog 126: 690-707 Nov
'64
LUNAR PROBES--U.S. (by Sur-
veyor 1, June 1966)
Hist of Rocketry and Space
Travel, p. 197
Nat Geog 130: 578-90 Oct
'66
LUNAR PROBES--U.S. --
RANGER 6
Life 56: 29 (col) Feb 14 '64
LUNAR PROBES--U.S. --SUR-
VEYOR 1 (model)
Nat Geog 130: 578, 580, 582-
4 (col) Oct '66
LUXEMBOURG
Holiday 35: 54-59 (col) Mar
'64
Travel 128: 51-54 (col) Aug
'67
Nat Geog 138: 68-97 (col)
July '70
LYNDHURST (home of Jay Gould
in Tarrytown, N.Y.)
Am Heritage 21: 49-53 (col)
Apr '70

M

MACAO (Portuguese Colony)--
CHINA
Nat Geog 135: 520-539 (col)
Apr '69
MACARTHUR, DOUGLAS--
FUNERAL RITES, 1964
Life 56: 28-31, 38 (col) Apr
17 '64
MACARTHUR, DOUGLAS--
MEMORIAL--NORFOLK, VA.
(interior)
Nat Geog 126: 376 (col) Sept
'64
MACARTHUR, DOUGLAS--RE-

TURN TO PHILIPPINES,
1944
Life 57: 82 July 10 '64
MCDONALD'S WILDERNESS
Life 69: 34-35 (col) July 4
'70
MACDONNELL RANGES--
AUSTRALIA
Nat Geog 129: 244-5 (col)
Feb '66
MACE (of Lord Mayor of Ply-
mouth, England)
Nat Geog 124: 216 (col) Aug
'63
MACHIGUENGA INDIANS. See
INDIANS OF SOUTH AMERI-
CA--PERU--MACHIGUENGA
MACHU PICCHU, PERU
Nat Geog 125: 248-9 (col)
Feb '64
MCKENZIE RIVER--OREGON
Travel 122: 31-33 July '64
MACKINAC ISLAND
Life 71: 42-43 (col) July 16
'71
MCKINLEY, MOUNT
America's Wonderlands, p.
44 (col)
America's Wonderlands, p.
510-12, 515
MACRAME
Sch Arts 69: 36-38 Jan '70
Ebony 25: 108-10, 112-13
July '70
Instr 80: 56 (col) May '71
MADAGASCAR
Nat Geog 132: 444-486 (col)
Oct '67
MADRID--PLAZA DE LA
CIBELES
Nat Geog 127: 332-3 (col)
Mar '65
MADRID--PRADO
Nat Geog 127: 336-7 (col)
Mar '65
MADRID UNIVERSITY--MADRID
Nat Geog 127: 334-5 (col)
Mar '65
MAIL BOX, RURAL
Nat Geog 124: 76 (col) July
'63
MAIL STRIKE
Life 68: 26, 28-29 Apr 3 '70

MAINE--COASTAL REGIONS
  Nat Geog 133: 798-843 (col)
    June '68
MAJORCA ISLAND--BALEARICS
  Holiday 37: 48-51 (col) Feb
    '65
  Holiday 47: 64-65 (col) Jan
    '70
MALAYSIA
  Nat Geog 124: 734-83 (col)
    Nov '63
MALI, WEST AFRICA
  Nat Geog 135: 430-448 (col)
    Mar '69
MALTA ISLAND
  Holiday 43: 68-71 (col) Feb
    '68
  Nat Geog 135: 852-879 (col)
    June '69
MAMMOTH CAVE--KENTUCKY
  Nat Geog 125: 814-15 (col)
    June '64
  America's Wonderlands, p.
    490-3 (col)
MAMMOTH HOT SPRINGS
  America's Wonderlands, p.
    70-1 (col)
MAN, PREHISTORIC--HOMO
  ERECTUS--OLDUVAI GORGE
  --TANZANIA
  Nat Geog 130: 707 (col) Nov
    '66
MAN, PREHISTORIC--HOMO
  HABILIS--OLDUVAI GORGE
  --TANZANIA
  Nat Geog 127: 197, 215 (col)
    Feb '65
  Nat Geog 130: 707 (col) Nov
    '66
MAN, PREHISTORIC--ZINJAN-
  THROPUS--OLDUVAI GORGE
  --TANZANIA
  Nat Geog 127: 197, 215 (col)
    Feb '65
  Nat Geog 130: 707 (col) Nov
    '66
MANHATTAN ISLAND--NIGHT
  LIFE
  Look 28: 32-37 (col) July 28
    '64
MANILA
  Nat Geog 130: 310-11 (col)

  Sept '66
MANNED ORBITAL LABORA-
  TORIES. See SPACE STA-
  TIONS--U. S. --MANNED
  ORBITAL LABORATORY
MANNED SPACE FLIGHT
  CENTER. See UNITED
  STATES--NASA--MANNED
  SPACECRAFT CENTER
MAP, BATTLE--BATTLEFIELDS
  OF THE AMERICAN REVO-
  LUTION
  Am Heritage 20: 28-33 Aug
    '69
MAP, BATTLE--CIVIL WAR
  Am Heritage 20: 62-63 (col)
    Feb '69
MAP, DECORATIVE--AFRICA
  Grade Teach 86: 57 (col),
    58 Oct '68
MAP, DECORATIVE--ALA-
  BAMA (showing Negro popu-
  lation in 1868)
  Ebony 21: 59 Dec '65
MAP, DECORATIVE--AMERICA
  (earliest existing map show-
  ing New World)
  Life 59: 61 (col) Oct 22 '65
MAP, DECORATIVE--CANYON-
  LANDS NATIONAL PARK
  America's Wonderlands, p.
    224 (col)
MAP, DECORATIVE--GERMANY
  Holiday 36: 45 (col) Oct '64
MAP, DECORATIVE--GREAT
  LAKES
  Holiday 43: 63-64 (col) May
    '68
MAP, DECORATIVE--ITALY
  Holiday 48: 30-31 (col) July-
    Aug '70
MAP, DECORATIVE--MEXICO
  Holiday 44: 34-35 (col) July
    '68
MAP, DECORATIVE--MOUNT
  MCKINLEY
  America's Wonderlands, p.
    512-13
MAP, DECORATIVE--ROCKY
  MOUNTAIN REGION
  America's Wonderlands, p.
    64-5 (col)

MAP   104

MAP, DECORATIVE--RUSSIA
Look 31: 40-41 (col) Oct 3
'67
MAP, DECORATIVE--SCANDI-
NAVIA
Holiday 40: 42 (col) Nov '66
MAP, DECORATIVE--SPAIN
Holiday 37: 50-51 (col) Apr
'65
MAP, DECORATIVE--UNITED
STATES--PACIFIC NORTH-
WEST (showing national parks
and monuments)
America's Wonderlands, p.
376-7 (col)
MAP, DECORATIVE--UNITED
STATES (showing school
desegregation)
Ebony 19: 97 May '64
MAP, DECORATIVE--UNITED
STATES--THE EAST (show-
ing national parks and monu-
ments)
America's Wonderlands, p.
418-19 (col)
MAP, DECORATIVE--UNITED
STATES--THE SOUTHWEST
(showing national parks and
monuments)
America's Wonderlands, p.
242-3 (col)
MAP, DECORATIVE--UNITED
STATES--THE WEST (show-
ing national parks and monu-
ments)
America's Wonderlands, p.
336-7 (col)
MAP, DECORATIVE--VIETNAM
Life 60: 34-37 (col) Feb 18
'66
Life 71: 34-35 (col) Nov 26
'71
MAP, DECORATIVE--WATER-
TON--GLACIER INTERNA-
TIONAL PEACE PARK
America's Wonderlands, p.
118-9 (col)
MAP, DECORATIVE--YO-
SEMITE NATIONAL PARK
America's Wonderlands, p.
29 (col)
MAP, DECORATIVE--ZION

NATIONAL PARK
America's Wonderlands, p.
188-9 (col)
MAPS, BATTLE--APPOMAT-
TOX CAMPAIGN, 1865
Nat Geog 127: 452-3 (col)
Apr '65
MAPS, BATTLE--GETTYSBURG
Nat Geog 124: 15-21 (col)
July '63
MAPS, BATTLE--VICKSBURG
Nat Geog 124: 44-5, 47 (col)
July '63
MAPS, DECORATIVE--DISNEY-
LAND
Nat Geog 124: 180-2 (col)
Aug '63
MAPS, DECORATIVE--JERU-
SALEM
Nat Geog 126: 831 (col) Dec
'64
MAPS, DECORATIVE--LOIRE
RIVER VALLEY--FRANCE
Nat Geog 129: 826-8 (col)
June '66
MAPS, DECORATIVE--LONDON
Nat Geog 129: 750-2 (col)
June '66
MAPS, DECORATIVE--MOSCOW
--KREMLIN
Nat Geog 129: 308-9 (col)
Mar '66
MAPS, STONE (allegedly in-
dicating lost gold mines
discovered by Peraltas in
Arizona circa 1846)
Life 56: 91-2, 94 June 12
'64
MAR-A-LAGO--WINTER HOME
OF MARJORIE MERRI-
WEATHER POST
Life 59: 62-65 (col) Nov 5
'65
MARDI GRAS. See CARNIVAL
--MARDI GRAS
MARIJUANA
Life 67: cover (col), 35
Oct 31 '69
MARINA CITY--CHICAGO.
See also APARTMENT
HOUSES--CHICAGO--MA-
RINA CITY

MARINA CITY--CHICAGO
Ebony 20: 106-8, 110, 112-14,
116 Nov '64
MARINER (space probe). See
SPACE PROBES--U.S.--
MARINER
MARKER, HISTORICAL--
MASON-DIXON LINE
Am Heritage 15: 22 Feb '64
MARKETS. See also FOOD
STORES; SUPERMARKETS
MARKETS--BOLIVIA
Nat Geog 126: 318 (col)
Sept '64
MARKETS--CAIRO
Nat Geog 127: 587 (col) May
'65
MARKETS--CHINA (People's
Republic)
Nat Geog 126: 602-3, 639
(col) Nov '64
MARKETS, FOOD
Life 62: 64-81 (col), 82,
84 May 12 '67
MARKETS--FRANCE
Nat Geog 129: 834-5 (col)
June '66
MARKETS--MOSCOW
Nat Geog 129: 318-19 (col)
Mar '66
MARKETS--SAIGON
Nat Geog 127: 844-5 (col)
June '65
MARRAKECH
Holiday 46: 44-47 (col) Dec
'69
MARTHA'S VINEYARD
Life 55: 42-52A (col) Aug 23
'63
MARTHA'S VINEYARD--
MENEMSHA'S HARBOR
Life 55: 45 (col) Aug 23 '63
Nat Geog 130: 832-3 (col)
Dec '66
MARYKNOLL SISTERS IN HONG
KONG
Look 28: 24-31 June 16 '64
MASAI. See AFRICA--NATIVE
RACES--MASAI
MASKS
Sch Arts 69: 18-19 Feb '70
Sch Arts 70: 21-28 June '71

MASKS (for the face), AFRICAN
CEREMONIAL
Nat Geog 130: 181 (col) Aug
'66
MASKS (for the face)--MAKE-
UP PROTECTORS
Life 55: 55-6 (col) Nov 22
'63
MASKS, OXYGEN. See OXY-
GEN MASKS
MASKS (with wax crayons)
Sch Arts 67: 38-39 Nov '67
MASSACHUSETTS
Nat Geog 130: 790-843 (col)
Dec '66
MATADORS
Sports Illus 25: 44-45, 47-48,
50-51 Aug 1 '66
Nat Geog 126: 166-7 (col)
Aug '64
Nat Geog 127: 324 (col) Mar
'65
Life 59: 62D, 63 (col), 64-
65, 66-68 (col) Aug 6 '65
Holiday 43: 68-71 (col) Jan
'68
Life 71: 74-79 (col) Nov 5
'71
MATANUSKA VALLEY--ALASKA.
See ALASKA--MATANUSKA
VALLEY
MATTERHORN--SWITZERLAND
Life 59: 26 (col) Aug 6 '65
Nat Geog 128: 376 (col) Sept
'65
MAUI ISLAND--HAWAII
Nat Geog 139: 514-543 (col)
Apr '71
MAW, CHAIN-LINK DREDGE
Nat Geog 124: 267 (col) Aug
'63
MAYFLOWER II (ship)
Nat Geog 130: 824 (col) Dec
'66
MECCA. See MOSQUES--
HARAM--MAKKAH; PIL-
GRIMAGES TO MECCA
MEDALS, DISTINGUISHED
PUBLIC SERVICE AWARD
(given by U.S. Navy)
Nat Geog 130: 481 (col) Oct
'66

MEDALS, DISTINGUISHED SER-
VICE (given by Theodore
Roosevelt Association)
Nat Geog 130: 480 (col) Oct
'66
MEDALS, EXPLORERS (given
by Explorers Club)
Nat Geog 130: 481 (col) Oct
'66
MEDALS--GIVEN TO PABLO
CASALS
Life 68: 81 (col) Apr 17 '70
MEDALS, GROSVENOR (given
by National Geographic Society)
Nat Geog 130: 481 (col) Oct
'66
MEDALS, HUBBARD (given by
National Geographic Society)
Nat Geog 124: 515 (col) Oct
'63
Nat Geog 127: 197 (col) Feb
'65
MEDALS, JEFFERSON PEACE
(given to Indian chiefs during
Lewis and Clark Expedition,
1804-06)
Nat Geog 128: 646 Nov '65
MEDALS, OLYMPIC--GOLD
MEDAL
Life 57: front cover, 80-1
(col) Oct 30 '64
MEDALS, SAMUEL F. B.
MORSE (given by American
Geographical Society)
Nat Geog 130: 480 (col) Oct
'66
MEDICINE GLASS. See GLASS,
MEDICINE
MEDITERRANEAN SEA
Nat Geog 127: 398-9 (col)
Mar '65
MEHARRY MEDICAL COLLEGE
--NASHVILLE, TENN.
Ebony 18: 168 Sept '63
MEKONG DELTA--VIETNAM
(Republic)
Nat Geog 129: 284-5 (col)
Feb '66
MEKONG RIVER
Nat Geog 134: 738-787 (col)
Dec '68
MELBOURNE, AUSTRALIA

Nat Geog 124: 310-11 (col)
Sept '63
MEMENTOS. See Names of
Persons with Subdivision
Mementos, e. g. WASHING-
TON, GEORGE--MEMEN-
TOS; etc.
MEMORIALS. See Names of
Deceased Persons with Sub-
division Memorial, e. g.
MACARTHUR, DOUGLAS--
MEMORIAL; etc.
MENHIRS--BRITTANY
Nat Geog 127: 490-1 (col)
Apr '65
MENNONITES
Nat Geog 124: 76 (col) July
'63
Nat Geog 126: 566-7 (col)
Oct '64
Nat Geog 128: 226-53 (col)
Aug '65
MERCED RIVER
America's Wonderlands, p.
10-11 (col)
MERCURY PROJECT. See
ASTRONAUTS--PROJECT
MERCURY; SPACE VEHICLES
--U. S.--PROJECT MERCURY;
etc.
MERMAIDS--DISNEYLAND
Nat Geog 124: 197 (col) Aug
'63
MERRY-GO-ROUNDS
Life 56: 83 Mar 6 '64
Nat Geog 129: 777 (col) June
'66
MESA VERDE NATIONAL PARK
America's Wonderlands, p.
296 (col)
MESA VERDE NATIONAL PARK
--WETHERILL MESA
Nat Geog 125: 156-95 (col)
Feb '64
Nat Geog 128: 882-3 (col) Dec
'65
MESOSCAPHS. See SUBMA-
RINE BOATS--MESOSCAPHS
MESSERSCHMITT AIRPLANES.
See ROCKET PLANES, MILI-
TARY--GERMANY--MESSER-
SCHMITT

METEORITES
Nat Geog 129: 35 (col) Jan '66
METROPOLITAN MUSEUM OF
ART--NEW YORK (interior)
Nat Geog 126: 96-7 (col) July
'64
METROPOLITAN OPERA HOUSE
--NEW YORK (interior)
Nat Geog 126: 88-9 (col) July
'64
Life 61: 32-5 (col) Sept 30
'66
METROPOLITAN OPERA HOUSE
(under construction)--NEW
YORK CITY
Ebony 21: 89 Jan '66
MEXICAN WAR 1846-48
Am Heritage 17: 20-27 (paint-
ings, col) June '66
MEXICAN WAR--CAMPAIGNS
AND BATTLES--BUENA
VISTA, 1847
Nat Geog 127: 108-9 (col)
Jan '65
MEXICO
Holiday 39: 46-51, 54-59
(col) Apr '66
Travel 125: 51-54 (col) June
'66
Holiday 44: 50-55 (col) July
'68
Look 32: 28-43 (col) Sept
3 '68
MEXICO--ANTIQUITIES
Nat Geog 134: 492-521 (col)
Oct '68
MEXICO CITY
Holiday 39: 58-63 (col) June
'66
Holiday 44: 36-41, 46-47
(col) July '68
Nat Geog 134: 145-193 (col)
Aug '68
MIAMI, FLA.--STREETS--
BISCAYNE BOULEVARD
Nat Geog 124: 862 (col) Dec
'63
MIAMI BEACH--BEACHFRONT--
AERIAL VIEW
Ebony 23: 184 June '68
MIAMI BEACH, FLORIDA
Life 59: 54-5 Dec 24 '65

Holiday 43: 36-45 (col) June
'68
MIAMI BEACH, FLORIDA--
HOTELS
Nat Geog 124: 861 (col)
Dec '63
MICKEY MOUSE (by Disney)
Nat Geog 124: 157D, 160,
168-71 (col) Aug '63
MICKLEGATE BAR. See
GATES--MICKLEGATE BAR
MIDGETS
Ebony 20: 104-6, 108-13
Oct '65
MILITARY AIRPLANES. See
AIRPLANES, MILITARY
MILITARY MANEUVERS--BIG
LIFT--SECOND ARMORED
DIVISION FLOWN TO GER-
MANY (Federal Republic)
Life 55: 36-36A Nov 1 '63
MILLS. See also WINDMILLS
MILLS, GRIST--PENNSYLVANIA
Nat Geog 128: 241 (col) Aug
'65
MINARETS
Nat Geog 126: 832 (col) Dec
'64
Nat Geog 130: 749 (col) Dec
'66
MINE THROWERS, GERMAN
(used in World War I)
Life 56: 55 (col) Mar 13 '64
MINERS. See also COAL
MINERS
MINERS, GOLD--"FORTY-
NINERS" (engravings and
paintings)
Nat Geog 127: 104-5 (col)
Jan '65
Nat Geog 128: 658-9 (col)
Nov '65
MINES. See COPPER MINES;
SULPHUR MINES; URANI-
UM MINES
MICRONESIA
Holiday 42: 70-75 (col) July
'67
MICRONESIANS (Ifalik atoll)--
PACIFIC
Nat Geog 131: 702-744 (col)
May '67

MINNEAPOLIS--ST. PAUL,
MINNESOTA--AERIAL VIEW
Life 59: 72-73 (col) Dec 24
'65
Ebony 20: 120 Mar '65
MINUTEMAN (guided missile).
See GUIDED MISSILES--
U. S. --MINUTEMAN
MIRROR LAKE
America's Wonderlands,
front cover (col)
MISS AMERICA CONTESTS.
See BEAUTY CONTESTS--
MISS AMERICA CONTESTS
MISS TEEN-AGE AMERICA
CONTESTS. See BEAUTY
CONTESTS--MISS TEEN-AGE
AMERICA CONTEST
MISS UNIVERSE CONTESTS.
See BEAUTY CONTESTS--
MISS UNIVERSE CONTESTS
MISSILES, ANTIAIRCRAFT.
See GUIDED MISSILES
MISSILES, GUIDED. See
GUIDED MISSILES
MISSIONS--NEW MEXICO
Travel 123: 38-41 Feb '65
MISSIONS--NOMBRE DE DIOS--
ST. AUGUSTINE, FLA.
Nat Geog 129: 216 (col) Feb
'66
MISSIONS--SAN XAVIER DEL
BAC--TUCSON, ARIZ.
Nat Geog 125: 548 (col) Apr
'64
Nat Geog 126: 582-3 (col)
Oct '64
MISSIONS--SANTA BARBARA--
CALIFORNIA
Nat Geog 129: 634-5 (col)
May '66
MISSISSIPPI RIVER--SOUTH-
WEST PASS (gateway for
vessels entering delta to New
Orleans)
Nat Geog 129: 386-7 (col)
Mar '66
MISSOURI RIVER--CONFLUENCE
WITH MISSISSIPPI RIVER
(near St. Louis)
Nat Geog 128: 640 (col) Nov
'65

MOBILE, ALABAMA
Nat Geog 133: 368-397 (col)
Mar '68
MOCCASIN MAKERS--TRISTAN
DA CUNHA (island)
Nat Geog 125: 78 (col) Jan
'64
MODERN ARCHITECTURE.
See ARCHITECTURE, MOD-
ERN
MODERN DANCE
Life 59: 96-106 Nov 12 '65
MODS (youth). See YOUTH--
ENGLAND--MODS
MOLNIYA (artificial satellite).
See ARTIFICIAL SATELLITES
--RUSSIA--MOLNIYA
MONACO--HARBOR
Nat Geog 129: 536-7 (col)
Apr '66
MONASTERIES. See also
ABBEYS
MONASTERIES--CAPUCHIN
Life 58: 38A May 28 '65
MONASTERIES--MONTSERRAT--
SPAIN
Nat Geog 127: 302-3 (col) Mar
'65
MONASTERIES--MOUNT ATHOS
--AEGEAN ISLANDS
Holiday 40: 68, 70-77 (col)
Dec '66
MONASTERIES--ST. CATHER-
INE'S (near Mount Sinai)--
EGYPT
Nat Geog 125: 82-127 (col)
Jan '64
MONKEYS, SPACE. See
CHIMPANZEES--PROJECT
MERCURY
MONKS, BUDDHIST
Nat Geog 126: 550 (col) Oct
'64
Nat Geog 128: 586-9 (col)
Oct '65
MONOPRINTING
Sch Arts 64: 14-16 Nov '64
MONORAIL--DISNEYLAND
Nat Geog 124: 196-7 (col)
Aug '63
MONT BLANC
Nat Geog 128: 354-7 (col)

Sept '65

MONT BLANC TUNNEL. See
TUNNELS--MONT BLANC

MONT SAINT MICHEL, FRANCE
(night scene)
Nat Geog 130: 220 (col) Aug
'66

MONTENEGRO
Holiday 36: 54-57 (col) Aug
'64

MONTICELLO (home of Thomas
Jefferson)--CHARLOTTES-
VILLE, VA.
Nat Geog 126: 668-9 (col)
Nov '64
Nat Geog 130: 427-44 (col)
Sept '66

MONTPELIER (home of James
Madison)--ORANGE COUNTY,
VA.
Nat Geog 126: 676-7 (col)
Nov '64

MONTSERRAT (island). See
LEEWARD ISLANDS

MONUMENT VALLEY, UTAH
Nat Geog 128: 874-5, 878-81
(col) Dec '65

MONUMENTS. See Names of
Monuments; Names of Cities
with Subdivision Monuments,
e.g. BALTIMORE--MONU-
MENTS; etc.

MOON
Nat Geog 135: 206-245 (col)
Feb '69

MOON PHOTOGRAPHS (by
Gemini V)
Life 59: front cover, 30-9
(col) Sept 24 '65

MOON PHOTOGRAPHS (by
Ranger 7, 1964)
Life 57: 32-4 Aug 14 '64
Nat Geog 126: 690-1, 696-
702, 705-6 Nov '64

MOON PHOTOGRAPHS (by
Ranger 9, 1965)
Hist of Rocketry and Space
Travel, p. 194

MOON PHOTOGRAPHS (by
Russian Lunik III, 1959)
Life 60: 26-30 Feb 11 '66

MOON PHOTOGRAPHS (by Sur-

veyor, 1966)
Life 60: 39 June 10 '66
Nat Geog 130: 578-90 Oct
'66

MOON PHOTOGRAPHS--PRO-
JECT APOLLO, 1969
Life 67: 24, 25 (col), 26-7
July 18 '69
Life 67: 28-29 (col) Aug 22
'69

MOON PHOTOGRAPHS (taken in
Studios of Modern Publicity
Co.)
Look 27: 68-74 (col), 76 Nov
5 '63

MOON PROBES. See LUNAR
PROBES

MORATORIUM, VIETNAM
Life 67: 52-55 (col), 56, 58-
60 Nov 28 '69

MORMON HAND CART MONU-
MENT--SALT LAKE CITY
Nat Geog 125: 569 (col) Apr
'64

MORMON TEMPLES. See
CHURCHES--MORMON
TEMPLE--SALT LAKE CITY;
etc.

MORNING GLORY POOL
America's Wonderlands, p.
71 (col)

MOROCCO
Life 58: 64-73 (col) Mar 19
'65
Nat Geog 139: 834-865 (col)
June '71

MOROS
Nat Geog 130: 335 (col) Sept
'66

MORTARS. See PESTLES AND
MORTARS

MOSAICS
Sch Arts 64: 10-14 June '65

MOSAICS, CERAMIC TILE
Sch Arts 70: 14-15 Jan '71

MOSAICS, FELT
Instr 77: 59 (col) Jan '68

MOSCOW
Nat Geog 129: 298-351 (col)
Mar '66

MOSCOW--EXHIBITIONS--EX-
HIBITION OF ECONOMIC

ACHIEVEMENTS (permanent
exhibition)
Nat Geog 129: 326-7 (col)
Mar '66
MOSCOW--KOMSOMOL SQUARE
Nat Geog 129: 342-3 (col)
Mar '66
MOSCOW--KREMLIN
Nat Geog 129: 298-9, 308-11
(col) Mar '66
MOSCOW--KREMLIN--PALACE
OF CONGRESSES
Nat Geog 129: 334-5 (col)
Mar '66
MOSCOW--PARADES--MAY DAY
Life 55: 26-7 (col) Sept 13
'63
Nat Geog 129: 302-3, 350-1
(col) Mar '66
MOSCOW--SUBWAYS--METRO
Nat Geog 129: 316-17 (col)
Mar '66
MOSCOW CIRCUS. See CIR-
CUS, MOSCOW
MOSCOW UNIVERSITY--MOS-
COW
Nat Geog 129: 322-3 (col)
Mar '66
MOSQUES (interiors)
Nat Geog 129: 53 (col) Jan
'66
MOSQUES--BRUNEI
Nat Geog 124: 775 (col) Nov
'63
MOSQUES--DOME OF THE
ROCK--JERUSALEM
Nat Geog 126: 791, 828, 831-
3 (col) Dec '64
Nat Geog 130: 785-7 (col)
Dec '66
MOSQUES--GREAT MOSQUE--
AMMAN, JORDAN
Nat Geog 126: 792-3 (col)
Dec '64
MOSQUES--HARAM--MAKKAH,
SAUDI ARABIA
Nat Geog 129: 2-4 (col) Jan
'66
MOSQUES--ISLAMIC CENTER--
WASHINGTON, D.C. (interior)
Nat Geog 126: 759 (col) Dec
'64

MOSQUES--KONYA, TURKEY
Nat Geog 124: 806-7 (col)
Dec '63
MOSQUES--SAN'A, YEMEN
Nat Geog 125: 410, 412-13,
438-9 (col) Mar '64
MOSQUES, MUD--MALI (Re-
public)
Nat Geog 130: 186-7 (col)
Aug '66
MOTELS--U.S. (1960's)
Life 55: 71-5 (col) July 26
'63
MOTORCYCLES
Life 58: 111-113 (col) Apr
23 '65
Ebony 22: 64-5, 68, 70-1
Dec '66
MOTORCYCLES--MINIBIKES
Life 70: 58-61 (col) Jan
22 '71
MOUNT ETNA. See ETNA,
MOUNT
MOUNT EVEREST. See
EVEREST, MOUNT
MOUNT KENNEDY. See KEN-
NEDY, MOUNT
MOUNT RUSHMORE MEMORI-
AL--BLACK HILLS, S.D.
Am Heritage 15: 2 Oct '64
Grade Teach 82: 52 May-
June '65
America's Wonderlands, p.
150, 153-4 (col)
MOUNT SHASTA. See SHASTA,
MOUNT
MOUNT SINAI. See SINAI,
MOUNT
MOUNT TABOR. See TABOR,
MOUNT
MOUNT VERNON (home of
George Washington)--MOUNT
VERNON, VA.
Nat Geog 126: 650-1 (col) Nov
'64
MOUNTAIN CLIMBERS
Ebony 19: 125-8 Nov '63
Travel 133: 29, 31, 33 (col)
Feb '70
MOUNTAIN CLIMBERS--ALPS
Nat Geog 128: 351, 377,
394-5 (col) Sept '65

MOUNTAIN CLIMBERS--EL
CAPITAN
Life 65: 35 (col) Oct 4 '68
Life 69: 46-48 (col) Nov 20
70
MOUNTAIN CLIMBERS--MOUNT
EVEREST (American expedi-
tion, 1963)
Life 55: front cover, 68-72
(col) Sept 20 '63
Nat Geog 124: 461, 468, 473-
4, 479-81, 483-6, 488-9,
492-3, 495-7, 500-2, 511
(col) Oct '63
MOUNTAIN CLIMBERS--MOUNT
KENNEDY
Nat Geog 128: 4, 7, 10-11, 14,
19, 22, 24-5, 27-8, 32-3
(col) July '65
MOUNTAIN CLIMBERS--MOUNT
KILIMANJARO
Ebony 24: 44-6 (col) June '69
MOUNTAIN CLIMBERS--MOUNT
RAINIER
America's Wonderlands, p.
403 (col), 404-7
MOUNTAIN CLIMBERS--MOUNT
TYREE
Nat Geog 131: 836-863 (col)
June '67
MOUNTAIN CLIMBING--
YOSEMITE VALLEY
Look 30: 70-72 (col) June 28
'66
MOUNTAINS. See Names of
Mountains, e.g. ALPS;
DOLOMITES; MATTERHORN;
ROCKY MOUNTAINS; TETON
MOUNTAINS; etc.
MOVING PICTURES--ANIMATED
CARTOONS--"SNOW WHITE
AND THE SEVEN DWARFS"
(by Disney)
Nat Geog 124: 165 (col) Aug
'63
MOZAMBIQUE
Nat Geog 126: 196-231 (col)
Aug '64
Holiday 48: 46-51 (col) Sept-
Oct '70
MUD SLIDES--SOUTHERN CALI-
FORNIA

Nat Geog 136: 552-573 (col)
Oct '69
MUGS, SHAVING
Am Heritage 19: 16-17 (col)
Apr '68
MUIR WOODS--CALIFORNIA
America's Wonderlands, p.
354-55 (col)
MULE TEAMS--MISSISSIPPI
Life 55: 46B Aug 2 '63
MUMMIES--EGYPT
Life 55: 65-8 Nov 15 '63
MUNICH FOUR POWER AGREE-
MENT, 1938
Nat Geog 128: 183 Aug '65
MUSEUM--"HERMITAGE"--
LENINGRAD
Life 58: 54-63, 66-67 (col)
Mar 26 '65
MUSEUM, METROPOLITAN.
See METROPOLITAN MUSE-
UM OF ART--NEW YORK
MUSIC BOXES, ANTIQUE
Life 70: 62-65 (col) Mar 19
'71
MUSIC FESTIVALS. See also
FESTIVALS
MUSIC FESTIVALS--POWDER
RIDGE
Life 69: 34-7 Aug 14 '70
MUSIC FESTIVALS--WOOD-
STOCK
Life 67: 14B, 15-23 (col)
Aug 29 '69
MUSICAL INSTRUMENTS. See
also Names of Instruments,
e.g. ACCORDIONS; ORGANS;
etc.
MUSICAL INSTRUMENTS--
CAMBODIA--GARES
Nat Geog 126: 526 (col)
Oct '64
MUSICAL INSTRUMENTS--
CHINA--ERH HU (fiddle)
Nat Geog 126: 593 (col)
Nov '64
MUSICAL INSTRUMENTS--
EGYPT--MIZMAAR
Nat Geog 127: 594 (col) May
'65
MUSICAL INSTRUMENTS--
ETHIOPIA--KRAR

Nat Geog 127: 564 (col) Apr
'65
MUSICAL INSTRUMENTS--IN-
DIANS, S. AMERICAN--
BAMBOO TRUMPETS
Nat Geog 125: 754-5 (col)
May '64
MUSICAL INSTRUMENTS--
KOREA--KAYACUMS
Nat Geog 124: 932 (col) Dec
'63
MUSICAL INSTRUMENTS--
PHILIPPINES--BANDURRIA
Nat Geog 130: 308 (col)
Sept '66
MUSKETS, FLINTLOCK (used
by voyageurs)
Nat Geog 124: 416 (col)
Sept '63
MUSLIMS AT PRAYER
Nat Geog 125: 438-9 (col)
Mar '64
MYLAI, SOUTH VIETNAM
Life 67: 36-41 (col), 42-45
Dec 5 '69
MYSTIC SEAPORT
Nat Geog 134: 220-239 (col)
Aug '68

N

NAILS, ANCIENT (reproduced
in plaster)
Nat Geog 124: 142 (col) July
'63
NANTUCKET ISLAND
Holiday 36: 62-67 (col) Aug
'64
Holiday 43: 56-61 (col) May
'68
Nat Geog 137: 810-839 (col)
June '70
NATCHEZ, MISSISSIPPI
Nat Geog 134: 640-667 (col)
Nov '68
Holiday 50: 41-43 (col) Sept/
Oct '71
NATIONAL MONUMENTS. See
Names of National Monuments,
e.g. CASTILLO DE SAN MAR-
COS NATIONAL MONUMENT;
etc.

NATURAL BRIDGE OF VIR-
GINIA (drawing)
Am Heritage 15: 62 (col)
Feb '64
NAURU ISLAND
Ebony 23: 114-5 (col), 116,
118, 120 May '68
NAVAHO (guided missile). See
GUIDED MISSILES--U. S. --
NAVAHO
NAVAHO INDIANS. See INDI-
ANS OF NORTH AMERICA--
NAVAHO
NAVAJO NATIONAL MONU-
MENT--ARIZONA
America's Wonderlands, p.
316-19 (col)
NAVIGATION AIDS
Sports Illus 26: 20-24 (col)
Jan 2 '67
NAZARETH, ISRAEL
Nat Geog 127: 422-3 (col)
Mar '65
Nat Geog 128: 835-7 (col)
Dec '65
NEGRO ARTISTS
Ebony 18: 131-2 (col), 134,
136, 138, 140 Sept '63
NEGRO ASTRONAUTS
Ebony 29-32, 36 June '65
NEGRO TEACHERS
Ebony 18: 38, 40, 42 Oct '63
NEGROES IN THE UNITED
STATES--CIVIL RIGHTS.
See CIVIL RIGHTS DEMON-
STRATIONS
NEGROES IN THE UNITED
STATES--HISTORY (ten most
dramatic events)
Ebony 18: 28-34, 36-8 Sept
'63
NEHRU, JAWAHARLAL--FUN-
ERAL RITES
Life 56: front cover, 33-40
(col) June 5 '64
NELSON, ADMIRAL LORD--
STATUE--TRAFALGAR
SQUARE--LONDON
Nat Geog 129: 768-9 (col)
June '66
NEPAL
Life 63: 38-51 (col) Aug 11
'67

Holiday 42: 84 (col) Sept '67
Holiday 48: 56-57 (col) Sept-
    Oct '70
Nat Geog 140: 656-689 (col)
    Nov '71
NEPAL--MUSTANG KINGDOM
    Nat Geog 128: 578-604 (col)
    Oct '65
NETHERLANDS
    Travel 128: 51-54 (col) July
    '67
    Nat Geog 137: 114-145 (col)
    Jan '70
NEUTROGRAPH
    Life 65: 58A-58B Nov 29 '68
NEVADA CITY, CALIF. (near
    site of Comstock lode)
    Life 55: 56-7 July 5 '63
NEVIS (island). See LEEWARD
    ISLANDS
NEW BRITAIN (island)
    Nat Geog 129: 792-817 (col)
    June '66
NEW BRITAIN (island)--NATIVE
    RACES--KAULONG
    Nat Geog 129: 792-817 (col)
    June '66
NEW BRITAIN (island)--NATIVE
    RACES--SENGSENG
    Nat Geog 129: 792-817 (col)
    June '66
NEW GUINEA
    Travel 121: 36-41 Feb '64
NEW GUINEA--NATIVE RACES--
    BIAMI
    Nat Geog 135: 568-591 (col)
    Apr '69
NEW MEXICO
    Nat Geog 138: 300-345 (col)
    Sept '70
NEW ORLEANS
    Nat Geog 139: 152-187 (col)
    Feb '71
NEW ORLEANS--18TH CENT.
    (sketches of A. R. Waud)
    Am Heritage 15: 34-48
    Dec '63
NEW SOUTH WALES
    Nat Geog 132: 591-635 (col)
    Nov '67
NEW TOWNS--COLUMBIA, MD.
    Life 70: 76-83 (col) Jan 8 '71

NEW TOWNS--RESTON, VA.
    Look 29: 52-7 (col) Nov 30
    '65
    Ebony 22: 90-2, 94-6 Dec '66
NEW YEAR, CHINESE--CAM-
    BODIA
    Nat Geog 126: 544-5 (col)
    Oct '64
NEW YORK (city)
    Nat Geog 126: 52-107 (col)
    July '64
    Travel 122: 57-60 (col) Nov
    '64
    Life 59: cover, 24-35 (col),
    58-61 Dec 24 '65
NEW YORK (city) (aerial view)
    Life 56: 60-7 (col) May 1
    '64
    Ebony 23: 184 June '68
NEW YORK (city)--GUGGEN-
    HEIM MUSEUM
    Holiday 36: 36-7 (col) July
    '64
NEW YORK (city)--GUGGEN-
    HEIM MUSEUM (interior)
    Nat Geog 126: 99 (col) July
    '64
NEW YORK (city)--HARBOR
    Nat Geog 126: 80-1 (col)
    July '64
NEW YORK (city)--HUNTING-
    TON HARTFORD'S GALLERY
    OF MODERN ART
    Nat Geog 126: 99 (col) July
    '64
NEW YORK (city)--MANHAT-
    TAN
    Life 59: 55 Dec 24 '65
NEW YORK (city)--PARADES--
    THANKSGIVING DAY (Macy's)
    Nat Geog 126: 72-3 (col) July
    '64
NEW YORK (city)--WHITNEY
    MUSEUM
    Life 61: 95, 96-9 (col) Oct
    7 '66
NEW YORK (city)--WORLD'S
    FAIR, 1964-1965
    Look 28: 17-21, 23 (col), 84-
    5 Feb 11 '64
    Ebony 19: 166-8, 170, 172,
    174, 176, 178 June '64

Look 29: front cover, 31-3
(col) Apr 20 '65
Look 27: 52-4 (col) Nov 19
'63
Life 56: front cover, 26-34
(col) May 1 '64
Nat Geog 127: 504-29 (col)
Apr '65
NEW YORK (city)--WORLD'S
FAIR, 1964-1965 (layout)
Holiday 36: 46-7 (col) July
'64
NEW YORK (city)--WORLD'S
FAIR, 1964-1965--UNI-
SPHERE
Life 56: front cover, 34 (col)
May 1 '64
Nat Geog 127: 504-5 (col)
Apr '65
NEW YORK (city)--WORLD'S
FAIR, 1964-1965--U. S.
PAVILION
Nat Geog 127: 522-3 (col)
Apr '65
NEW ZEALAND
Travel 122: 26-29 Sept '64
Travel 122: 45-49 Oct '64
Travel 124: 51-54 (col) Dec
'65
NEW ZEALAND (Cook Islands)
Nat Geog 132: 202-231 (col)
Aug '67
NEWSPAPER ROCK--PETRI-
FIED FOREST, ARIZONA
America's Wonderlands, p.
39, 226 (col)
NIAGARA FALLS
Am Heritage 15: 62 (drawing,
col) Feb '64
Am Heritage 15: 32-49 (paint-
ings, col) June '64
NICAEA
Nat Geog 124: 800-1, 803
(col) Dec '63
NIKE-CAJUN (rocket). See
ROCKETS, SOUNDING--
U. S. --NIKE-CAJUN
NIKE UNTYING HER SANDAL
Nat Geog 124: 118 (col) July
'63
NIKE-ZEUS (guided missile).
See GUIDED MISSILES--U. S. --

NIKE-ZEUS
NILE RIVER
Nat Geog 127: 583-633 (col)
May '65
NILE RIVER--BLUE NILE
Nat Geog 127: 556, 560-1
(col) Apr '65
NORAD. See NORTH AMERI-
CAN AIR DEFENSE COM-
MAND
NORFOLK, VA.
Nat Geog 126: 378-9 (col)
Sept '64
NORMAN CONQUEST. See
GREAT BRITAIN--NORMAN
CONQUEST
NORMANDY INVASION. See
WORLD WAR II--CAMPAIGNS
AND BATTLES--NORMANDY
INVASION
NORTH AMERICAN AIR DE-
FENSE COMMAND--OBSER-
VATION ROOM--COLORADO
SPRINGS, COLO.
Nat Geog 128: 324-6 (col)
Sept '65
NORTH POLE--DISCOVERY BY
ROBERT E. PERRY, 1909
Nat Geog 128: 539 Oct '65
NORTHERN IRELAND
Nat Geog 126: 232-67 (col)
Aug '64
(The) NORTHWEST
Holiday 45: 48-51 (col) May
'69
NORTHWEST PASSAGE--VOY-
AGE OF S. S. MANHATTAN
Nat Geog 137: 375-391 (col)
Mar '70
NORWAY
Holiday 40: 52-61 (col) Nov
'66
Nat Geog 140: 2-43 (col)
July '71
NOTRE DAME DE FRANCE--
STATUE--LE PUY, FRANCE
Nat Geog 129: 836 (col)
June '66
NOVA SCOTIA
Nat Geog 125: 852-79 (col)
June '64

NUBIA
    Nat Geog 127: 620-1, 626-7
    (col) May '65
NUBIA--ANTIQUITIES
    Nat Geog 124: 586-621 (col)
    Oct '63
NUBIAN DESERT--SUDAN
    Nat Geog 128: 254-5 (col)
    Aug '65
NURSERY SCHOOLS--UGANDA
    Nat Geog 124: 922-3 (col)
    Dec '63

                    O

OAK HILL (home of James
    Monroe)--LOUDON COUNTY,
    VA.
    Nat Geog 126: 681 (col) Nov
    '64
OASES--SAUDI ARABIA
    Nat Geog 129: 37 (col) Jan
    '66
OCEAN LINERS--AMERICA
    Life 56: 63 (col) May 1 '64
OCEANAUTS. See AQUANAUTS
OCEANOGRAPHIC RESEARCH
    --EQUIPMENT. See UNDER-
    WATER STRUCTURES
ODOMETER (used by Thomas
    Jefferson)
    Nat Geog 130: 435 (col)
    Sept '66
OIL DRILLING--SAUDI ARABIA
    Nat Geog 129: 27 (col) Jan
    '66
OIL DRILLING, UNDERSEA
    (offshore)
    Nat Geog 125: 788 (col) June
    '64
    Nat Geog 127: 810 (col) June
    '65
    Nat Geog 129: 29 (col) Jan
    '66; 361 (col) Mar '66
OIL DRILLING AND PROCESSING
    Life 66: 20-27 (col) Feb 14
    '69
OIL REFINERIES--SAUDI ARABIA
    Nat Geog 129: 28-9 (col) Jan
    '66
OIL SLICK--SOUTHERN CALI-

FORNIA COAST
    Life 58-63 (col) Feb 21 '69
OIL SLICK--WEST COAST
    Life 66: 22-27 (col) June 13
    '69
OIL SLICKS
    Life 62: 26-33 (col), 34-35
    Apr 14 '67
    Life 68: 28-35 (col) Mar 6
    '70
    Life 70: 36-43 (col) Feb 5
    '71
    Nat Geog 139: 866-881 (col)
    June '71
OIL TENDERS. See SHIPS--
    OIL TENDERS
OKLAHOMA
    Nat Geog 140: 149-189 (col)
    Aug '71
OKLAHOMA CITY--1889
    Life 59: 55 Dec 24 '65
OKLAHOMA LAND RUSH (paint-
    ing)
    Nat Geog 127: 706-7 (col)
    May '65
OLANA (home of Frederic
    Church)
    Life 60: 64-77 (col) May 13
    '66
OLD NORTH BRIDGE--CON-
    CORD, MASS.
    Nat Geog 130: 820-1 (col)
    Dec '66
OLD SALEM--WINSTON-SALEM,
    N. C.
    Nat Geog 138: 818-837 (col)
    Nov '70
OLDUVAI GORGE--TANZANIA
    Nat Geog 127: 194, 204-5,
    210, 212-14 (col) Feb '65
    Nat Geog 130: 700-9 (col)
    Nov '66
OLYMPIC GAMES, 1896--
    ATHENS, GREECE--100
    METER DASH (Tom Burke)
    Nat Geog 126: 500 Oct '64
OLYMPIC GAMES, 1932--LOS
    ANGELES--80 METER
    HURDLE (Babe Didrikson)
    Nat Geog 126: 509 Oct '64
OLYMPIC GAMES, 1948--
    LONDON--DECATHLON

(Bob Mathias)
Nat Geog 126: 500 Oct '64
OLYMPIC GAMES, 1960--ROME
--BROAD JUMP (Ralph Boston)
Nat Geog 126: 491 (col) Oct
'64
OLYMPIC GAMES, 1960--ROME
--100 METER DASH (Wilma
Rudolph)
Nat Geog 126: 508 (col) Oct
'64
OLYMPIC GAMES, 1964--INNS-
BRUCK, AUSTRIA
Life 56: front cover, 30-38A
(col) Feb 14 '64
OLYMPIC GAMES, 1964--INNS-
BRUCK, AUSTRIA--SKI-
JUMPING
Life 56: front cover, 31-3
(col) Feb 14 '64
Nat Geog 128: 390 (col) Sept
'65
OLYMPIC GAMES, 1964--
TOKYO--U.S. CONTESTANTS
Life 57: 74B-84 (col) Oct 30
'64
OLYMPIC GAMES--SCENES OF
VARIOUS GAMES FROM AN-
CIENT TIMES TO 1964
Nat Geog 126: 491-513 (col)
Oct '64
OLYMPIC GAMES FOR THE
DEAF
Ebony 20: 76-80 Oct '65
OLYMPIC NATIONAL PARK
America's Wonderlands, p.
43 (col)
America's Wonderlands, p.
378-89, 391-5 (col)
OLYMPIC STARS--KENYA
Life 65: 34-41 (col) Nov 22
'68
ONTARIO
Nat Geog 124: 58-97 (col)
July '63
OPAL
Nat Geog 124: 339 (col)
Sept '63
OPERA HOUSE, DEATH VALLEY
Life 68: 42-43 (col) Apr 17
'70
OPERA HOUSE--LA SCALA--

INTERIOR--MILAN
Holiday 45: 56-57 (col) Jan
'69
OPERA HOUSE--SYDNEY,
AUSTRALIA (model)
Nat Geog 124: 355 (col)
Sept '63
OPERA HOUSE--VIENNA
Life 66: 48-49 (col) Feb 28
'69
OPIUM FACTORY
Life 70: 4-6A June 25 '71
OPPORTUNITIES INDUSTRI-
ALIZATION CENTER--PHILA.
Ebony 19: 27-30, 34-6 May
'64
ORBITAL RENDEZVOUS (space
flight)--GEMINI 6 AND
GEMINI 7, DEC. 1965
Hist of Rocketry and Space
Travel, bet. p. 196-7 (col)
Nat Geog 129: 538-49 (col)
Apr '66
ORBITING SOLAR OBSERVA-
TORY. See ARTIFICIAL
SATELLITES--ASTRONOM-
ICAL APPLICATIONS--
ORBITING SOLAR OBSERVA-
TORY
ORBS, ENGLISH--SOVEREIGN'S
ORB
Life 56: 95 Mar 6 '64
ORE CARRIERS--EDWARD L.
RYERSON
Nat Geog 126: 568 (col) Oct
'64
OREGON
Nat Geog 135: 74-115 (col)
Jan '69
OREGON TRAIL--AT INDE-
PENDENCE ROCK--WYOMING
(painting)
Nat Geog 127: 100-1 (col)
Jan '65
Nat Geog 128: 660-1 (col)
Nov '65
ORGAN TRANSPLANTS. See
also specific organs, e.g.,
HEART TRANSPLANTS
ORGAN TRANSPLANTS
Life 59: 66-83 (col) Sept 24
'65

ORGANS--MORMON TABER-
NACLE--SALT LAKE CITY
Nat Geog 125: 567 (col) Apr
'64
ORISSA--INDIA
Nat Geog 138: 546-577 (col)
Oct '70
OROVILLE DAM
Nat Geog 129: 658-9 (col)
May '66
OX TEAMS--CAMBODIA
Nat Geog 126: 538 (col) Oct
'64
OX TEAMS--COSTA RICA
Nat Geog 128: 124, 140-1 (col)
July '65
OX TEAMS--MASSACHUSETTS
Nat Geog 130: 838-9 (col)
Dec '66
OX TEAMS--PORTUGAL
Nat Geog 128: 475 (col) Oct
'65
OX YOKES--MASSACHUSETTS
Nat Geog 130: 838-9 (col)
Dec '66
OX YOKES--PORTUGAL
Nat Geog 128: 475 (col) Oct
'65
OXCARTS (with painted wheels)
--COSTA RICA
Nat Geog 128: 124, 139-41
(col) July '65
OXYGEN MASKS, MOUNTAIN
CLIMBERS'--MOUNT EVER-
EST
Nat Geog 124: 479, 500-2
(col) Oct '63
OZARK MOUNTAINS
Nat Geog 138: 659-689 (col)
Nov '70

P

PACIFIC CREST TRAIL
Nat Geog 139: 742-779 (col)
June '71
PACIFIC OCEAN
Nat Geog 136: 496-499 (col)
Oct '69
PACKET SHIP--"NEPTUNE"
Am Heritage 19: 70-71

painting, col) Dec '67
PACKET SHIP--"RESOLUTE"
Am Heritage 19: 68-69 (paint-
ing, col) Dec '67
PAINTING, FLUORESCENT
Life 69: 68-71 (col) Nov 6
'70
PAINTING--OUTDOOR MURALS
Life 69: 60-63 (col) July
17 '70
PAINTING ON GLASS BOTTLES
Ebony 19: 44, 46 Aug '64
PAKISTAN
Nat Geog 131: 1-47 (col) Jan
'67
Life 69: 26-35 (col) Dec 4
'70
PALACE--FERDINAND CHEVAL
--HAUTEVILLES, FRANCE
Life 70: 70-73 (col) Mar 12
'71
PALACE OF DALAI LAMA--
LHASA, TIBET
Nat Geog 130: 462-3 Oct '66
PALACE OF HEAVENLY
PURITY--PEKING--FORBID-
DEN CITY
Nat Geog 126: 598-9 (col)
Nov '64
PALACES--BLENHEIM--ENG-
LAND
Nat Geog 128: 160-2 (col)
Aug '65
PALACES--BUCKINGHAM--
ENGLAND
Life 56: 79 (col) Mar 6 '64
PALACES--MATEUS--PORTU-
GAL
Nat Geog 128: 492-3 (col)
Oct '65
PALACES--PALAIS DE L'ELY-
SEE--PARIS (interior of
home--President of France)
Life 56: 18-19 (col) Feb 14
'64
PALACH, JAN--FUNERAL
RITES
Life 66: 24-27 (col) Feb 7
'69
PALEONTOLOGY. See FOS-
SILS; MAN, PREHISTORIC
PALM BEACH REGION--

FLORIDA
Holiday 45: 38-40, 42-43, 45
(col) Feb '69
PALM SPRINGS, CALIF.
Nat Geog 129: 616-17 (col)
May '66
PAMPLONA, SPAIN--RUNNING
OF THE BULLS
Nat Geog 127: 324-5 (col)
Mar '65
PAN AMERICAN BUILDING--
NEW YORK
Nat Geog 126: 59 (col) July
'64
PANAMA
Nat Geog 137: 422-439 (col)
Mar '70
PANAMA CANAL
Nat Geog 137: 402-413 (col)
Mar '70
Am Heritage 22: 64 (col),
65-71 June '71
PANAMA (city)
Nat Geog 137: 414-421 (col)
Mar '70
PANTHEON--ROME
Life 60: 72-73 (col) Mar 4
'66
PAPERWEIGHTS, ANTIQUE
Hobbies 68: 53, 66 Sept '63
PAPERWEIGHTS, GLASS
Hobbies 69: 82-83 Mar '64
Hobbies 71: 98L-98N Nov '66
PAPIER-MACHE
Sch Arts 63: 18-19 Mar '64
Grade Teach 82: 34-35 Dec
'64
Grade Teach 83: 60-62 Apr
'66
Sch Arts 70: 14-15 Oct '70
Sch Arts 70: 12-13 June '71
Sch Arts 71: 26-27 Nov '71
PAPIER-MACHE FIGURES
Sch Arts 63: 16-17 Mar '64
Sch Arts 65: 5-9 Mar '66
PAPOOSE BOARDS (cradleboards)
Nat Geog 124: 60 (col) July
'63
Nat Geog 125: 202-3 (col) Feb
'64
PARACHUTE JUMPING. See
PARACHUTING

PARACHUTES
Nat Geog 128: 731 (col) Nov
'65
Life 68: 62-65 (col) May 29
'70
PARACHUTING
Ebony 18: 47-8 (col), 50-1
Oct '63
Ebony 19: 92-4 Nov '63
Nat Geog 125: 266 (col) Feb
'64
Nat Geog 126: 268, 275-7
(col) Aug '64
Ebony 22: 40-2 (col) May
'67
PARADES. See Names of
Cities with Subdivision Pa-
rades; NEW YORK (city)--
PARADES; etc.
PARADISE ICE CAVES
America's Wonderlands, p.
400-1 (col)
PARAGLIDERS. See GLIDERS
(aeronautics)--PARAGLIDERS;
SPACE VEHICLES--LANDING
SYSTEMS--PARAGLIDERS
PARAMOUNT STUDIOS--HOLLY-
WOOD
Life 68: 38-45 (col), 46 Feb
27 '70
PARKS. See AMUSEMENT
PARKS; Names of Cities with
Subdivision Parks, e.g. BOS-
TON--PARKS; Names of
National Parks, e.g. BRYCE
CANYON NATIONAL PARK;
etc.
PARLIAMENT BUILDINGS--
BUDAPEST
Nat Geog 128: 54-5 (col)
July '65
PARLIAMENT BUILDINGS--
LONDON
Nat Geog 129: 770-1 (col)
June '66
PARLIAMENT BUILDINGS--
LONDON--HOUSE OF LORDS
(interior)
Nat Geog 129: 753-5 (col)
June '66
PARLIAMENT BUILDINGS--
OTTAWA, ONTARIO

Nat Geog 124: 96-7 (col)
July '63
PARTHENON
Nat Geog 124: 101-2, 105,
115 (col) July '63; 916-
17 (col) Dec '63
PASADENA, CALIF. --PARADES
--TOURNAMENT OF ROSES
Nat Geog 129: 613 (col) May
'66
PATE DE VERRE
Hobbies 73: front cover, 98K-
98O Oct '68
PAUL VI, POPE--CORONATION,
1963
Life 55: 55-7 (col) July 12
'63
PAUL VI, POPE--ELECTION--
VATICAN--SISTINE CHAPEL,
1963
Life 55: front cover, 22, 24-
5 (col) July 5 '63
PEACE CORPS. See UNITED
STATES--PEACE CORPS
PEARL FISHERIES (pearl farms)
--PHILIPPINES
Nat Geog 130: 342-3 (col)
Sept '66
PEARL HARBOR, ATTACK ON,
1941
Nat Geog 129: 79 (col) Jan
'66
PEDICABS--CAMBODIA
Nat Geog 126: 516-17 (col)
Oct '64
PEDICABS--CHINA (People's
Republic)
Nat Geog 126: 601 (col) Nov
'64
PEDICABS--PHILIPPINES
Nat Geog 130: 334-5 (col)
Sept '66
PEGASUS (artificial satellite).
See ARTIFICIAL SATELLITES
--U. S. --PEGASUS
PEKING--FORBIDDEN CITY
Life 57: 97 (col) July 17 '64
Nat Geog 124: 574 Oct '63
Nat Geog 126: 596-9 (col)
Nov '64
PENITENTES--SPAIN
Nat Geog 127: 331 (col) Mar
'65

PENNSYLVANIA DUTCH
Am Heritage 15: 56-57 (paint-
ing, col), 59 (sketches,
col), 60-63 (col) Apr '64
PENTECOST ISLANDERS
Nat Geog 138: 796-817 (col)
Nov '70
PENTHOUSES--U. S.
Life 57: 82-6 (col) Nov 20
'64
PERRY, COMMODORE MAT-
THEW C. --LANDING IN
JAPAN, 1854
Nat Geog 127: 112-13 (col)
Jan '65
PERU
Nat Geog 125: 212-66 (col)
Feb '64
Travel 126: 51-54 (col) Oct
'66
Life 62: 64-65 (col) Apr 14
'67
PERU--ANTIQUITIES
Nat Geog 125: 244-5 (col)
Feb '64
PERUVIAN ART--ANCIENT
Life 65: 57-58 (col) Oct 18
'68
PESTLES AND MORTARS,
16TH CENT.
Nat Geog 125: 617 (col) May
'64
PETRA, JORDAN
Nat Geog 126: 812-13 (col)
Dec '64
Nat Geog 128: 274 (col)
Aug '65
PETRIFIED FOREST--ARIZONA
America's Wonderlands, p.
276-81 (col)
PETROGLYPHS (rock inscrip-
tions)
America's Wonderlands, p.
233 (col)
PETROGLYPHS (rock inscrip-
tions)--PETRIFIED FOREST,
ARIZONA
America's Wonderlands, p.
39, 226 (col)
PETROGLYPHS--SPIRIT ISLAND
IN NETT LAKE, MINN.
Nat Geog 124: 427 (col) Sept
'63

506 (col) Oct '63
PORTLAND, OREGON--AERIAL
VIEW
Ebony 20: 122 Mar '65
PORTOFINO, ITALY
Nat Geog 127: 232-53 (col)
Feb '65
PORTUGAL
Look 28: 72-85 (col) May 19
'64
Nat Geog 128: 453-500 (col)
Oct '65
Travel 127: 51-54 (col) June
'67
Holiday 49: 47 (map), 48-
55 (col) Feb '71
POSTAGE STAMPS (designed by
Afewerk depicting 1896 Battle
of Adua)
Ebony 20: 92 June '65
POSTAGE STAMPS (of and by
Blacks)
Ebony 25: 142-4, 146, 148
(col) Dec '69
POSTAGE STAMPS, COMMEM-
ORATIVE--JOHN F. KENNEDY
Look 28: 32 June 16 '64
Look 30: 52-4 (col) Nov 29
'66
POSTAGE STAMPS, COMMEM-
ORATIVE--MARTIN LUTHER
KING, JR.
Ebony 24: 33 (col) Apr '69
POSTAGE STAMPS--LIECHTEN-
STEIN
Life 55: 45, 47-9 (col) Aug
30 '63
POSTAGE STAMPS--NORTH
VIETNAM
Life 58: cover (col) Feb 26
'65
POSTAGE STAMPS--STEINS
AND OTHER DRINKING
VESSELS
Hobbies 76: 89-91 July '71
POSTAGE STAMPS--TONGA
Life 55: 44 (col) Oct 11 '63
POSTAGE STAMPS--U.S.--24
CENT STAMPS, 1869
Life 55: 50 Nov 29 '63
POSTAGE STAMPS--U.S.--24
CENT STAMPS, 1918 (inverted

airplanes)
Life 55: 50 Nov 29 '63
POSTAL CARDS (picture cards)
Hobbies 68: 118 Sept '63
Am Heritage 19: 18-21 (col)
Dec '67
POSTAL CARDS (picture cards)
--ADVERTISING
Hobbies 68: 120 Aug '63
POSTAL CARDS (picture cards)
--BULLFIGHT
Hobbies 69: 120 Sept '64
POSTAL CARDS (picture cards)
--CHRISTMAS GREETINGS
OF THE PAST
Hobbies 68: 116 Dec '63
POSTAL CARDS (picture cards)
--COLONIAL FIREARMS,
18TH CENT.
Hobbies 69: 126 Mar '64
POSTAL CARDS (picture cards)
--CUSTER'S LAST BATTLE
Hobbies 73: 124-125 Apr '68
POSTAL CARDS (picture cards)
--EGYPT
Hobbies 69: 120 Aug '64
POSTAL CARDS (picture cards)
--GUNFIGHTERS OF THE OLD
WEST
Hobbies 69: 120-121 July '64
POSTAL CARDS (picture cards)
--INDIANA, 20TH CENT.
Hobbies 71: 120-121 Oct '66
POSTAL CARDS (picture cards)
--JAMESTOWN EXPOSITION,
1907
Hobbies 72: 114-115 Apr '67
POSTAL CARDS (picture cards)
--LIGHTHOUSES
Hobbies 71: 118-119 Jan '67
POSTAL CARDS (picture cards)
--LUCKY LINDY
Hobbies 72: 120-121 Oct '67
POSTAL CARDS (picture cards)
--MILITARY LEADERS OF
W.W.I.
Hobbies 70: 124-125 Feb '66
POSTAL CARDS (picture cards)
--MOUNT VESUVIUS
Hobbies 69: 116 Oct '64
POSTAL CARDS (picture cards)
--NAPOLEON

Hobbies 72: 120-121 Jan '68
POSTAL CARDS (picture cards)
--1906 SAN FRANCISCO DIS-
ASTER
Hobbies 71: 120-121 Apr '66
POSTAL CARDS (picture cards)
--OLD NEW YORK
Hobbies 71: 120-121 May '66
POSTAL CARDS (picture cards)
--PHILADELPHIA
Hobbies 68: 120 July '63
POSTAL CARDS (picture cards)
--SIGNED BY THE AUTHORS
Hobbies 74: 124-125 May '69
POSTAL CARDS (picture cards)
--3-DIMENSIONAL
Hobbies 72: 114-115 May '67
POSTAL CARDS (picture cards)
--UNCLE TOM MONUMENT
AND HOME
Hobbies 68: 124 Sept '63
POSTAL CARDS (picture cards)
--WASHINGTON, D.C.
Hobbies 72: 115-116 June '67
POSTAL CARDS (picture cards)
--WINDMILLS
Hobbies 71: 118-119 Feb '67
POSTAL CARDS (picture cards)
--WORLD WAR I
Hobbies 70: 124-125 Jan '66
POSTERS--BUFFALO BILL'S
WILD WEST SHOW
Nat Geog 129: 581 (col) Apr
'66
POSTERS--MILITARY ENLIST-
MENT. See POSTERS, WAR
POSTERS, POLITICAL--PRESI-
DENTIAL CANDIDATE
ABRAHAM LINCOLN, 1860
Nat Geog 127: 667, 669 (col)
May '65
POSTERS, POLITICAL--PRESI-
DENTIAL CANDIDATE
FRANKLIN PIERCE, 1852
Nat Geog 127: 115 (col) Jan
'65
POSTERS, WAR--CIVIL WAR--
U.S.
Nat Geog 127: 672 (col) May
'65
POSTERS, WAR--WORLD WAR I
(U.S.)

Am Heritage 19: 49-64 (col)
Oct '68
POT RESTS, INDIAN (N. Ameri-
can)--MESA VERDE NATION-
AL PARK
Nat Geog 125: 201 (col) Feb
'64
POT RESTS, INDIAN (N. Ameri-
can)--PUEBLOS, 20TH CENT.
Nat Geog 125: 200 (col) Feb
'64
POTSDAM CONFERENCE, 1945.
See BERLIN CONFERENCE,
1945
POTTERY, CHINESE--PORCE-
LAINS
Am Heritage 2 (col) June '65
POTTERY--FAIENCE, 20TH
CENT.--FRANCE
Nat Geog 129: 853 (col)
June '66
POTTERY, INDIAN (N. Ameri-
can)--MESA VERDE NATION-
AL PARK
Nat Geog 125: 156, 160-1,
169, 172, 185, 190, 196-
7, 204, 210 (col) Feb '64
POTTERY, INDIAN (N. Ameri-
can)--PUEBLOS, 20TH CENT.
Nat Geog 125: 197, 200, 204
(col) Feb '64
POTTERY, SPANISH
Nat Geog 127: 305 (col) Mar
'65
POTTERY--STONEWARE
Sch Arts 63: 23-27 Sept '63
Sch Arts 63: 30 Nov '63
POTTERY CRAFT
Sch Arts 65: 11-12, 28-30
Sept '65
POTTERY FIRING, INDIAN
(N. American)--PUEBLOS,
20TH CENT.
Nat Geog 125: 204-5 (col)
Feb '64
POWELL, LAKE--ARIZONA
Nat Geog 125: 560-1 (col)
Apr '64
Holiday 39: 64-65, 67 (col)
May '66
Nat Geog 132: 45-81 (col)
July '67

Travel 131: 27 (col), 28, 29
(col), 31 Apr '69
PUGET SOUND (at sunset)
Life 59: 89 (col) Dec 24 '65
PUPPETS
Grade Teach 82: 36-37 Dec
'64
Sch Arts 66: 5-7, 9 Nov '66
Sch Arts 70: 28-29 Nov '70
PUPPETS (how to make)
Sch Arts 63: 11-13 Oct '63
Sch Arts 64: 25-32 Apr '65
Sch Arts 69: 8-9, 18-19
June '70
Sch Arts 70: 34-38 June '71
PUPPETS--GREECE
Nat Geog 124: 125 (col) July
'63
PUPPETS, HAND
Sch Arts 65: 5-9 Nov '65
PUPPETS--SALZBURG MARIO-
NETTE THEATER
Nat Geog 128: 389 (col) Sept
'65
PYGMIES. See DWARFS--
PYGMIES
PYRAMIDS--GIZA
Nat Geog 127: 590-1 (col)
May '65
Nat Geog 128: 280-1 (col)
Aug '65

Q

Q-SHIPS. See SUBMARINE
WARFARE--Q-SHIPS
QUEBEC
Nat Geog 139: 416-441 (col)
Mar '71
QUECHUA INDIANS. See IN-
DIANS OF SOUTH AMERICA
--BOLIVIA--QUECHUA
QUEENSLAND (state) AUSTRA-
LIA--COASTLINE (Gold
Coast)
Nat Geog 124: 372 (col) Sept
'63

R

RACE HORSES. See HORSES,

RACE
RACE TRACK--GLORIOUS
GOODWOOD--W. SUSSEX
DOWNS, ENGLAND
Sports Illus 25: 27-30 (col)
July 25 '66
RACE TRACK--INDIANAPOLIS
Holiday 45: 80-81 (col) May
'69
RADAR DEFENSE NETWORK--
DEW LINE STATION (near
Barrow)--ALASKA
Nat Geog 128: 682-3 (col)
Nov '65
RADAR STATIONS--U. S. --
BERING STRAIT (Air Force
Air Control and Warning
System)
Nat Geog 128: 331 (col) Sept
'65
RADIO RECEIVING APPARATUS
--ONE-TUBE SET, 1923
Nat Geog 128: 575 Oct '65
RADIO TELESCOPE (near
Arecibo)--PUERTO RICO
Life 55: 119-21 Nov 8 '63
RADIO TELESCOPE (near
Parkes)--NEW SOUTH WALES
(state) AUSTRALIA
Nat Geog 124: 368-9 (col)
Sept '63
RADIO TELESCOPE, STAN-
FORD UNIVERSITY'S--
CALIFORNIA
Life 55: 18-19 Aug 2 '63
RAFTS, BALSA LOG
Nat Geog 126: 294-5 (col)
Aug '64
Life 65: 22-25 (col) Oct 4
'68
RAFTS--PROJECT APOLLO
Life 55: 34-5 (col) Sept 27
'63
RAFTS, RUBBER
Nat Geog 128: 889 (col) Dec
'65
RAILROAD CONSTRUCTION.
See RAILROAD ENGINEERING
RAILROAD ENGINEERING--
BUILDING UNION PACIFIC
RAILROAD IN NEBRASKA,
19TH CENT.
Nat Geog 128: 664 Nov '65

489 (col) Apr '67
RHODE ISLAND
Nat Geog 134: 370-401 (col)
Sept '68
RHODESIA
Life 59: 45 (col), 46A-46B
Dec 10 '65
RICE FIELDS--LOUISIANA
Nat Geog 129: 370 (col) Mar
'66
RICE PADDIES--JAPAN
Life 57: 17 (col) Sept 11 '64
RICE TERRACES--BALI
Nat Geog 124: 452-3 (col)
Sept '63
RICE TERRACES--PHILIP-
PINES
Nat Geog 130: 302-3 (col)
Sept '66
RICE TRANSPLANTING--CAM-
BODIA
Nat Geog 126: 539 (col) Oct
'64
RICE, WILD--HARVESTING BY
INDIANS--BIG RICE LAKE,
MINN.
Nat Geog 124: 428 (col) Sept
'63
RICHMOND, VA.--CONQUEST
BY U.S.--CIVIL WAR, 1865
(painting)
Nat Geog 127: 438-9 (col)
Apr '65
RICKSHAS, MOTORIZED--SAN
FRANCISCO
Nat Geog 129: 644 (col) May
'66
RICKSHAS--MOZAMBIQUE IS-
LAND
Nat Geog 126: 210-11 (col)
Aug '64
RIFLES
Look 29: 80, 82 Feb 23 '65
RIFLES--CARBINES--M-1--
U.S., 1944
Nat Geog 128: 156 Aug '65
RIFLES--M-16--U.S. (used
during Vietnamese War)
Nat Geog 128: 332 (col)
Sept '65
RIOTS--KENT STATE UNIVER-
SITY

Life 68: 30-37 May 15 '70
RIOTS--NEW YORK (city)--
HARLEM, 1964
Life 57: 14-19 (col) July 31
'64
RIOTS, RACE--DETROIT
Life 63: 16-23 (col) Aug 4
'67
RIOTS, RACE--NEWARK, NEW
JERSEY
Life 63: 16-29 (col) July 28
'67
RIOTS, RACE--YALE UNIVER-
SITY
Life 68: 38-39 (col) May 15
'70
RITES AND CEREMONIES--
BAHA'I
Ebony 20: 48-9 (col), 50, 52-
6 Apr '65
Ebony 23: 124-5 (col), 126
Apr '68
RITES AND CEREMONIES--
COBRA FESTIVAL--INDIA
Nat Geog 128: 392-409 (col)
Sept '70
RIVERS. See Names of Rivers,
e.g. NILE RIVER; SNAKE
RIVER; ZAMBEZI RIVER;
etc.
RIVERS OF IDAHO
Nat Geog 137: 212-239 (col)
Feb '70
RIYADH, SAUDI ARABIA
Nat Geog 129: 12-13 (col)
Jan '66
ROAD BUILDING--ETHIOPIA
Nat Geog 127: 564-5 (col)
Apr '65
ROBOTS
Ebony 25: 64-5 June '70
ROCK OF CASHEL--IRELAND
Look 35: 44-45 (col) Mar 23
'71
ROCK-CLIMBING
Holiday 45: 62-63 (col) May
'69
ROCKERS (youth). See YOUTH
--ENGLAND--ROCKERS
ROCKET LAUNCHERS--U.S.--
CIVIL WAR
Hist of Rocketry and Space

Nat Geog 125: 378-9 (col)
Mar '64
ROCKETS--CARRIERS--U. S. --
SATURN 1 B
Hist of Rocketry and Space
Travel, p. 171
ROCKETS--CARRIERS--U. S. --
SATURN 5 (cutaway drawings)
Hist of Rocketry and Space
Travel, p. 173
Life 57: 94-5 Sept 25 '64
ROCKETS--CARRIERS--U. S. --
SATURN 5 (models)
Life 57: 82-3 (col) Sept 25
'64
Nat Geog 125: 362, 374-5,
395-7 (col) Mar '64
ROCKETS--CARRIERS--U. S. --
THOR-DELTA, 1962
Hist of Rocketry and Space
Travel, p. 161
ROCKETS--CARRIERS--U. S. --
TITAN 3C, 1965
Hist of Rocketry and Space
Travel, p. 169-70
ROCKETS--CARRIERS--U. S. --
TITAN-GEMINI
Hist of Rocketry and Space
Travel, p. 163, 165
ROCKETS, SOUNDING--AUS-
TRALIA--AEOLUS
Hist of Rocketry and Space
Travel, p. 154
ROCKETS, SOUNDING--ENG-
LAND--SKYLARK
Hist of Rocketry and Space
Travel, p. 158
ROCKETS, SOUNDING--FRANCE
--TACTITE
Hist of Rocketry and Space
Travel, p. 155
ROCKETS, SOUNDING--JAPAN
--KAPPA 150
Hist of Rocketry and Space
Travel, p. 158
ROCKETS, SOUNDING--U. S. --
AEROBEE
Hist of Rocketry and Space
Travel, p. 152
Nat Geog 128: 721 (col) Nov
'65
ROCKETS, SOUNDING--U. S. --
ASTROBEE, 1964

Hist of Rocketry and Space
Travel, p. 160
ROCKETS, SOUNDING--U. S. --
NIKE-CAJUN, 1962
Hist of Rocketry and Space
Travel, p. 154
ROCKETS, SOUNDING--U. S. --
VIKING 4, 1950
Hist of Rocketry and Space
Travel, p. 152
ROCKY MOUNTAIN NATIONAL
PARK
America's Wonderlands, p.
138-47 (col)
ROCKY MOUNTAIN REGION
Holiday 34: 29, 36-39, 52-
53, 60-61, 64-65, 68-73
(col) Aug '63
ROCKY MOUNTAINS--CANADI-
AN ROCKIES
Holiday 34: 30-31, 97, 100
(col) Aug '63
Nat Geog 130: 352-93 (col)
Sept '66
RODEO SCHOOL
Ebony 19: 122-4, 126, 128,
130, 132 June '64
RODEOS.   See also BRONC
RIDING; CALF RIDING
RODEOS
Nat Geog 125: 556 (col) Apr
'64
Life 59: 50-59 (col) Aug 20
'65
Sports Illus 29: 35-39 (col)
July 1 '68
Travel 134: 31 (col), 32, 33
(col) July '70
Ebony 25: 116-18 Oct '70
RODEOS--RODEO CLOWNS
Life 55: 37-44 July 19 '63
ROMAN RUINS--ETCHINGS
Life 60: 38-39 Mar 11 '66
ROME
Nat Geog 137: 744-777 (col)
June '70
ROME, ANCIENT (painting by
Pannini)
Life 60: 36-37 (col) Mar 11
'66
ROOSEVELT, FRANKLIN D. --
FIRESIDE CHATS

Nat Geog 129: 75 Jan '66
ROOSEVELT, FRANKLIN D. --
FUNERAL RITES
Am Heritage 21: 8 (col), 78-
79, 81-83 (col) 85 Aug '70
ROOSEVELT, FRANKLIN D. --
SIGNING DECLARATION OF
WAR AGAINST JAPAN, DE-
CEMBER 1941
Nat Geog 130: 616 Nov '66
ROPE WORKS--BELFAST
Nat Geog 126: 244 (col) Aug
'64
ROUNDUPS--SADDLE HORSES--
WYOMING
Nat Geog 129: 570-1 (col)
Apr '66
ROUNDUPS--WILD HORSES--
MONTANA
Nat Geog 125: 578-9 (col)
Apr '64
ROYAL NAVAL COLLEGE--
ENGLAND. See BRITAN-
NIA ROYAL NAVAL COL-
LEGE
RUBBER TREES
Nat Geog 124: 748-9 (col)
Nov '63
Nat Geog 126: 541 (col) Oct
'64
RUG FACTORIES--COUNTY
DOWN, NORTHERN IRELAND
Nat Geog 126: 244-5 (col)
Aug '64
RUGBY FOOTBALL
Sports Illus 24: 31-33 (col)
Apr 4 '66
RUGS, HANDMADE--PORTUGAL
Nat Geog 128: 485 (col) Oct
'65
RUGS, ORIENTAL
Hobbies 71: 36-37 June '66
RUMANIA
Nat Geog 135: 810-845 (col)
June '69
RUNNEMEYDE MEADOW (near
Windsor)
Life 58: 75-77 (col), 80 (en-
graving) May 28 '65
RUSSELL CAVE--ALABAMA
(painting)
America's Wonderlands,

p. 494-6, 497-9 (col)
RUSSIA
Life 55: entire issue (col)
Sept 13 '63
Holiday 34: 60-61, 66-67,
74-75, 96-97 (col) Oct '63

S

SAAB (guided missile). See
GUIDED MISSILES--SWEDEN
--SAAB
SABANEROS. See COWBOYS--
COSTA RICA
SABLE (island)
Nat Geog 128: 398-431 (col)
Sept '65
SACRAMENTO, CALIFORNIA--
AERIAL VIEW
Ebony 20: 116 Mar '65
SADDLE, ULYSSES S. GRANT'S
Nat Geog 127: 437 (col) Apr
'65
SADDLES, WESTERN
Nat Geog 129: 871, 877, 888
(col) June '66
SAGAMORE HILL (home of
Theodore Roosevelt)--OY-
STER BAY, N.Y.
Nat Geog 128: 545 (col) Oct
'65
SAGUARO NATIONAL MONU-
MENT--ARIZONA
America's Wonderlands, p.
58-9 (col)
SAHARA DESERT
Nat Geog 132: 696-725 (col)
Nov '67
Holiday 44: 62-5 (col) Dec
'68
SAIGON
Nat Geog 127: 834-71 (col)
June '65
SAILBOAT RACING--CANADIAN
NATIONAL EXHIBITION RE-
GATTA
Nat Geog 124: 68-9 (col)
July '63
SAILBOATS
Look 27: 42 (col) July 16
'63

Holiday 36: 97 (col), 99 Aug
'64
Holiday 39: 39-45 (col) July
'66
Life 63: 60-63 (col), 65
July 28 '67
Life 63: 119-120, 122 Sept
15 '67
Sports Illus 30: 41, 50-51,
54-55 (col) June 2 '69
Sports Illus 34: 39-42 (col)
June 21 '71
Sports Illus 35: 14-16 (col)
Aug 16 '71
SAILBOATS--CARINITA-CLASS
Nat Geog 129: 646-7 (col)
May '66
SAILBOATS--DINGHIES
Nat Geog 124: 521 (col) Oct
'63
Nat Geog 125: 879 (col) June
'64
SAILBOATS--DREDGES (dredging
for oysters in Chesapeake
Bay)
Nat Geog 126: 387 (col) Sept
'64
SAILBOATS--FELUCCAS (nag-
gars)--EGYPT
Nat Geog 127: 584-5, 600 (col)
May '65
SAILBOATS--GYPSY MOTH IV
(Sir Francis Chichester's
voyage)
Life 62: 28-37, 88 (col), 89,
101-102 June 9 '67
SAILBOATS--JUNK BOAT
Ebony 22: 129-30 Dec '66
SAILBOATS--KETCHES
Nat Geog 124: 208-9 (col)
Aug '63
Nat Geog 126: 159, 162, 169,
171, 174, 179, 184, 190-
1, 195 (col) Aug '64; 383,
(col) Sept '64; Nat Geog
127: 583, 586, 593, 596,
619, 622, 630, 634 (col)
May '65
SAILBOATS, LIGHTNING-CLASS
Nat Geog 126: 395 (col) Sept
'64
SAILBOATS--NILE RIVER

Nat Geog 124: 603 (col) Oct
'63
SAILBOATS--SUNFISH
Holiday 62-63 (col) June '69
SAILBOATS--TURNABOUTS
Nat Geog 125: 854 (col) June
'64
SAILING CARDS FOR CLIPPER
SHIPS (during Calif. gold
rush)
Nat Geog 127: 105 (col) Jan
'65
SAILING SHIP--"THE RA"
Life 66: 89-90 June 6 '69
SAILING SHIP--"RA II" (voyage
of Thor Heyerdahl)
Nat Geog 139: 44-71 (col)
Jan '71
SAILING VESSELS--BRIGAN-
TINES
Nat Geog 129: 262-9 (col)
Feb '66
SAILING VESSELS--PORTUGAL
Life 57: 60-1 (col) July 24
'64
Nat Geog 128: 500 (col) Oct
'65
SAILING VESSELS--WINDJAM-
MERS, 1964
Life 57: 54-66 (col) July 24
'64
SAILING VESSELS--WINDJAM-
MERS--FINLAND, 1930
Nat Geog 130: 474-5 Oct '66
SAILPLANES. See GLIDERS
(aeronautics)--SAILPLANES
ST. AUGUSTINE, FLA.
Nat Geog 129: 196-229 (col)
Feb '66
ST. AUGUSTINE, FLA.--
DEDICATION BY SPANIARDS,
1565 (painting)
Nat Geog 129: 198-9 (col)
Feb '66
ST. AUGUSTINE, FLA.--
STREETS--ST. GEORGE
Nat Geog 129: 208-9 (col)
Feb '66
ST. GEORGE'S, GRENADA
Nat Geog 128: 756-8 (col)
Dec '65
ST. KITTS (island). See LEE-

WARD ISLANDS
ST. LAWRENCE SEAWAY--
SNELL LOCK
Nat Geog 129: 97 (col) Jan
'66
ST. LOUIS
Nat Geog 128: 605-41 (col)
Nov '65
ST. LOUIS--AERIAL VIEW
Life 59: 84 (col) Dec 24 '65
ST. LOUIS, 1846 (painting)
Nat Geog 128: 642-3 (col)
Nov '65
ST. LOUIS--CITY PLANNING--
MEMORIAL PLAZA
Nat Geog 128: 608-9 (col)
Nov '65
ST. LOUIS--MONUMENTS--
GATEWAY ARCH (designed
by Eero Saarinen)
Nat Geog 128: 614-19 (col)
Nov '65
ST. LUCIA (island). See
WINDWARD ISLANDS
ST. MALO, FRANCE
Nat Geog 127: 496-7 (col)
Apr '65
ST. MARY LAKE--GLACIER
NATIONAL PARK
America's Wonderlands, p.
26-7 (col)
ST. PATRICK--STATUE--
COUNTY DOWN, NORTHERN
IRELAND
Nat Geog 126: 260 (col) Aug
'64
ST. PAUL'S CATHEDRAL
Life 71: 60 (col) Aug 21 '71
ST. PETER'S CATHEDRAL--
ROME. See CATHEDRALS--
ST. PETER'S--ROME
ST. PETER'S SQUARE--ROME
Look 29: 25 Jan 12 '65
Life 59: cover, 22-23 (col),
Dec 17 '65
Nat Geog 137: 778-780 (col)
June '70
ST. VINCENT (island). See
WINDWARD ISLANDS
SALK INSTITUTE FOR BIO-
LOGICAL STUDIES--LA
JOLLA, CALIF.

Look 31: 52-53 Jan 10 '67
SALT CARAVANS--SAHARA
DESERT
Nat Geog 128: 694-711 (col)
Nov '65
SALT-EVAPORATION BEDS--
PHILIPPINES
Nat Geog 130: 324-5 (col)
Sept '66
SALT LAKE CITY--AERIAL
VIEW
Life 59: 86 (col) Dec 24 '65
SALVAGE, UNDERWATER
Holiday 37: 70-75, 77-79
(col) June '65
SALVATION ARMY BAND
Life 56: 30 Jan 31 '64
SALZBURG, AUSTRIA
Look 29: 44-45 (col) June
29 '65
SAMOA, AMERICAN
Travel 125: 35-38 (col) Mar
'66
Holiday 42: 54-55 (col) July
'67
SAMPANS--VIETNAM (Republic)
Nat Geog 127: 850-1 (col)
June '65
Nat Geog 129: 280 (col) Feb
'66
SAN ANTONIO, TEX.--AERIAL
VIEW
Ebony 23: 184 June '68
SAN DIEGO, CALIF.
Nat Geog 136: 114-147 (col)
July '69
SAN DIEGO, CALIF.--HARBOR
Nat Geog 129: 624-5 (col)
May '66
SAN FRANCISCO
Life 59: 74, 86 (col) Dec 24
'65
Holiday 47: 40-47, 62-67 Mar
'70
SAN FRANCISCO, 1906
Life 59: 51 Dec 24 '65
SAN FRANCISCO--CHINATOWN
Nat Geog 129: 644 (col) May
'66
SAN FRANCISCO--STREETS--
MARKET STREET (night
scene)

Nat Geog 129: 642-3 (col)
  May '66
SAN FRANCISCO BAY
  Nat Geog 136: 594-637 (col)
    Nov '69
SAN FRANCISCO BAY--1850
  Life 59: 54 Dec 24 '65
SAN FRANCISCO NATIONAL
  BANK
  Ebony 20: 121 June '65
SAN JOSE, COSTA RICA
  Nat Geog 128: 126-7 (col)
    July '65
SAN JUAN MOUNTAINS--
  COLORADO
  Life 70: 32-33 (col) Jan 8
    '71
SAN MARCO (artificial satellite).
  See ARTIFICIAL SATELLITES
  --ITALY--SAN MARCO
SAN MARINO, ITALY
  Nat Geog 132: 232-251 (col)
    Aug '67
SAN SIMEON, CALIF. (home of
  William Randolph Hearst)
  Nat Geog 129: 639 (col) May
    '66
SAND CASTING
  Sch Arts 69: 16-17 Oct '69
SANDSTONES, INDIAN (N.
  American)--MESA VERDE
  NATIONAL PARK
  Nat Geog 125: 163 (col) Feb
    '64
SANTA CRUZ ISLAND
  Life 68: 53-55, 58-59 (col)
    May 8 '70
SANTA FE TRAIL CARAVAN
  (painting)
  Nat Geog 128: 654-5 (col)
    Nov '65
SANTA MARTA, COLOMBIA
  Holiday 45: 94-95 (col) Apr '69
SAPPHIRES--STAR OF INDIA
  Life 57: 77 (col) Nov 13 '64
SARATOGA SPRINGS, N. Y.
  (1860's to early 20th cent.)
  Life 55: 52B-61 July 26 '63
SARCEE INDIANS. See INDIANS
  OF NORTH AMERICA--CANADA
  --SARCEE
SARDANA--DANCE--SPAIN
  Nat Geog 127: 300 (col) Mar '65

SATURN (rocket). See ROCK-
  ETS--CARRIERS--U. S. --
  SATURN 1; SATURN 1B;
  SATURN 5
SAUDI ARABIA
  Nat Geog 129: 2-53 (col) Jan
    '66
SCARECROW
  Instr 77: 138 (col) Oct '67
  Am Heritage 21: 74-77 (col)
    Apr '70
SCHOOL BUILDINGS, AMISH--
  PENNSYLVANIA
  Nat Geog 128: 251 (col) Aug
    '65
SCHOOL BUILDINGS--GABON
  Nat Geog 126: 328-9 (col)
    Sept '64
SCHOOL BUILDINGS, MODERN
  Life 71: 72-74 (col) Oct 22
    '71
SCHOOL BUILDINGS, "STACK-
  ABLE LEARNING SPACES"
  Life 69: 32-3 (col) Nov 6 '70
SCHOOL HOUSES. See SCHOOL
  BUILDINGS
SCHOOL INTEGRATION
  Ebony 20: 34-6, 38, 40, 42,
    44, May '65
  Ebony 21: 29-32, 34-7 May
    '66
SCHOOL OF FINE ARTS--HAR-
  LEM
  Ebony 21: 80-2, 84-6 May
    '66
SCHOOL WITHOUT WALLS--
  PHILADELPHIA
  Life 66: 40-41 (col) May 16
    '69
SCHOOLROOMS. See CLASS-
  ROOMS
SCHOONERS. See also SHIPS
SCHOONERS
  Nat Geog 125: 852, 861, 866
    (col) June '64
  Nat Geog 128: 774 (col) Dec
    '65
SCOTLAND--HIGHLANDS
  Holiday 37: 82-83 (col) Mar
    '65
  Nat Geog 133: 398-435 (col)
    Mar '68

SEALS 136

UNDERWATER LABORA-
TORIES
SEALS--PRESIDENT OF U. S.
See UNITED STATES--
SEALS--PRESIDENT OF U. S.
SEAPLANES--LOCKHEED SIRI-
US (piloted by Charles A.
Lindbergh, 1933)
Nat Geog 124: 562 Oct '63
SEAPLANES, MILITARY--
ENGLAND--SHORT BOMBER
(used in World War I)
Life 56: 72 Mar 20 '64
SEAS. See Names of Seas,
e.g. BLACK SEA; GALILEE;
SEA OF; etc.
SEATTLE--1910
Life 59: 54 Dec 24 '65
SEDGWICK, MAJOR GENERAL
JOHN--STATUE--GETTYS-
BURG
Nat Geog 124: 11 (col) July
'63
SEGOVIA, SPAIN
Nat Geog 127: 322-3 (col)
Mar '65
SEMINOLE INDIANS. See INDI-
ANS OF NORTH AMERICA--
SEMINOLES
SEQUOIA NATIONAL PARK
America's Wonderlands, p.
32-3 (col)
America's Wonderlands, p.
358-9, 361-9 (col)
Nat Geog 129: 628-9 (col)
May '66
SEVILLE, SPAIN--PLAZA DE
ESPAÑA
Nat Geog 127: 292-3 (col)
Mar '65
SEWING BEES
Life 69: 58-62 (col) July 31
'70
SEXTANT
Nat Geog 127: 270 (col) Feb
'65
SEYCHELLES (islands in the
Indian Ocean)
Holiday 44: 20-25 (col) Aug
'68
Life 71: 44-51 (col) Oct 29
'71

SHAKER REVIVAL--PLEASANT
HILL, KY.
Look 28: 56-63 (col) Dec 1
'64
SHAKERS
Life 62: 58-67 Mar 17 '67
SHAKESPEARE, WILLIAM--
TOMB--STRATFORD-ON-
AVON
Nat Geog 125: 620 (col) May
'64
SHAKESPEAREAN COSTUME.
See COSTUME, SHAKESPEAR-
EAN
SHAKESPEARE'S ENGLAND
Nat Geog 125: 614-65 (col)
May '64
SHANGHAI--STREETS--BUND
Nat Geog 126: 618-19 (col)
Nov '64
SHANGHAI--STREETS--
NANKING ROAD
Nat Geog 126: 628-9 (col)
Nov '64
SHASTA, MOUNT
Nat Geog 129: 678-9 (col)
May '66
SHEEP HERDING. See also
SHEPHERDS
SHEEP HERDING--BASQUES--
NEVADA
Nat Geog 129: 870-88 (col)
June '66
SHEIKS
Nat Geog 125: 444 (col) Mar
'64
Nat Geog 126: 804, 816-17,
824, 835 (col) Dec '64
SHELLS
Hobbies 71: 130 Mar '66
Holiday 39: 99-104 (col) July
'66
Nat Geog 135: 386-429 (col)
Mar '69
SHENANDOAH VALLEY--VIR-
GINIA
Travel 121: 30-35 May '64
America's Wonderlands, p.
466-9 (col)
Nat Geog 137: 554-587 (col)
Apr '70
SHEPHERDS (near Sea of

Galilee)
Nat Geog 128: 832-3 (col) Dec
'65
SHEPHERDS--RUMANIA
Nat Geog 128: 70 (col) July
'65
SHERPAS--MOUNT EVEREST
Nat Geog 124: 473, 483, 485,
492-3, 495, 500, 507 (col)
Oct '63
SHERPAS--NEPAL
Nat Geog 130: 544-77 (col)
Oct '66
SHIELDS. See also ARMOR
SHIELDS, VIKING
Nat Geog 126: 714, 733 (col)
Nov '64
SHINTO PALANQUINS--JAPAN
Nat Geog 126: 484 (col) Oct
'64
SHIPBUILDING--FRANCE
Nat Geog 130: 230 (col) Aug
'66
SHIPS. See also AIRCRAFT
CARRIERS; ICE BREAKING
VESSELS; OCEAN LINERS;
ORE CARRIERS; SAILING
VESSELS; SCHOONERS;
STEAMBOATS; STEAMSHIPS;
SUBMARINE BOATS; WAR-
SHIPS
SHIPS--"BEAGLE" (Darwin's
expedition ship)
Nat Geog 136: 450, 458-459
(col) Oct '69
SHIPS, CLIPPER--"YOUNG
AMERICA"
Am Heritage 19: 72-73 (paint-
ing, col) Dec '67
SHIPS--"CONSTITUTION" ("Old
Ironsides") (painting)
Am Heritage 16: 4-5, 8-11
(col) Dec '64
Am Heritage 21: 24-25 (col),
26-27 Feb '70
SHIPS--GALLEONS--FRANCE,
1565 (painting)
Nat Geog 129: 206 (col) Feb
'66
SHIPS--GALLEONS--SPAIN,
1565 (painting)
Nat Geog 129: 206-7 (col) Feb
'66

SHIPS--GALLEONS--SPAIN,
1715 (paintings)
Nat Geog 127: 6-8 (col) Jan
'65
SHIPS--GENOA, 1097 (painting)
Nat Geog 124: 816-17 (col)
Dec '63
SHIPS, IRONCLAD (U. S. Civil
War) "CAIRO" (salvage)
Life 58: 41-42 Feb 12 '65
SHIPS--"LUSITANIA." See
SUBMARINE WARFARE--
SINKING OF "LUSITANIA"
SHIPS--"MAYFLOWER." See
"MAYFLOWER" (ship)
SHIPS--NELSON'S FLAGSHIP,
"H. M. S. VICTORY"
Nat Geog 124: 258 (col) Aug
'63
SHIPS--OIL TENDERS
Nat Geog 129: 359 (col) Mar
'66
SHIPS--"U. S. S. MANHATTAN"
Life 67: 42-45 (col) Sept 26
'69
SHIPS, VIKING
Nat Geog 126: 711-13, 718,
725 (col) Nov '64
SHIPS, WHALING (model)
Nat Geog 130: 830 (col) Dec
'66
SHOES
Look 29: 70-72 Feb 9 '65
Ebony 22: 122 Apr '67
Ebony 23: 111 (col), 112
Feb '68
Life 71: 54-56 (col) Nov 5 '71
SHOES, ANKLE-STRAP
Life 59: 57-58, 62 Sept 24
'65
SHOES (modern)
Look 28: 35 (col), 37 Feb
11 '64
SHOSHONI INDIANS. See INDI-
ANS OF NORTH AMERICA--
SHOSHONI
SHOULDER POLES (used for
carrying bundles, baskets,
etc. at both ends)
Nat Geog 124: 449, 451 (col)
Sept '63; 742, 768 (col)
Nov '63

SHOVELS, STEAM, 1906 (used in
building Panama Canal)
Nat Geog 128: 546 Oct '65
SHRINES--INDIAN RIVER, MICHI-
GAN
Nat Geog 126: 562 (col) Oct
'64
SHRINES--IZUMO--JAPAN
Life 57: 50-1 (col) Sept 11
'64
SHRINES--MEIJI--TOKYO
Nat Geog 126: 468-9 (col)
Oct '64
SHUFFLEBOARD COURT--
FLORIDA
Nat Geog 124: 891 (col) Dec
'63
SHYSTER (guided missile).
See GUIDED MISSILES--
RUSSIA--SHYSTER
SIAMESE TWINS
Life 58: 41-42 June 25 '65
SIBERIA
Life 58: 80-83 Jan 22 '65
Nat Geog 131: 297-347 (col)
Mar '67
SIERRA NEVADA MOUNTAINS
Holiday 38: 64 (col) Oct '65
SIGNS--ADVERTISING
Life 69: 26-33 (col) July 24
'70
SIGNS, SHOP--MALAYSIA
Nat Geog 124: 742-3 (col)
Nov '63
SIKKIM
Life 58: 36-38 (col) Apr 23
'65
Nat Geog 138: 698-713 (col)
Nov '70
SILK SCREEN PROCESS
Sch Arts 64: 35-38 Oct '64
Sch Arts 64: 17-19 Feb '65
Instr 74: 42 May '65
Sch Arts 65: 16-19 Oct '65
Grade Teach 85: 155 (col),
156-158 Jan '68
SILKWORM INDUSTRY--CHINA
(People's Republic)
Nat Geog 126: 634-5 (col)
Nov '64
SILVERWARE--TEAPOT (by
Paul Revere)

Nat Geog 130: 804 (col) Dec
'66
SINAI, MOUNT
Nat Geog 125: 82, 103-6 (col)
Jan '64
SINGAPORE
Nat Geog 130: 268-99 (col)
Aug '66
Holiday 42: 32-41 (col) Aug
'67
SIOUX INDIANS. See INDIANS
OF NORTH AMERICA--SIOUX
SISTINE CHAPEL. See VATI-
CAN--SISTINE CHAPEL
SKATEBOARDING
Ebony 20: 112 Apr '65
Life 58: cover, 126C-128,
130, 132, 134 May 14 '65
SKATEBOARDS
Life 56: 89-90 June 5 '64
SKATING, FIGURE
Life 60: 93 Mar 11 '66
Sports Illus 32: 20-24 (col)
Jan 26 '70
SKATING STARS
Sports Illus 32: 18-19 Mar 9
'70
SKEAN (guided missile). See
GUIDED MISSILES--RUSSIA--
SKEAN
SKI JUMPS, SYNTHETIC--
JAPAN
Life 57: 38-9 Sept 11 '64
SKI LIFTS
Sports Illus 32: 28-29 (col)
Feb 9 '70
SKI RESORTS. See Names of
Areas or Resorts, e.g.
JACKSON HOLE SKI AREA;
etc.
SKIERS
Sports Illus 28: 24, 28-30,
32-34 (col), 37, 45, 47
(col) Feb 5 '68
Sports Illus 32: 13-16 (col)
Feb 2 '70
Life 68: cover, 54-55 (col),
59, 63, 64 (col) Mar 6
'70
Ebony 26: 100-1 (col), 102-
5 Jan '71
Look 35: 35-38 Feb 23 '71

Life 70: 62-67 (col) Mar 5 '71

SKIERS--CANADIAN ROCKIES
Nat Geog 130: 354-5 (col) Sept '66

SKIERS--RUSSIA
Nat Geog 129: 324-5 (col) Mar '66

SKIING
Look 29: 79-83, 87-88 (col), 92, 98-100, 102 (col) Dec 14 '65

SKIING--CANADA
Sports Illus 32: 38-45 (col) Mar 30 '70
Sports Illus 35: 48-54 (col) Dec 6 '71

SKIING--CHILEAN ANDES
Holiday 41: 72-77 (col) Feb '67

SKIING--FRANCE
Ebony 20: 148-52 Apr '65

SKIING--GSTAAD
Holiday 47: 60-63 (col) Jan '70

SKIING--NEW ENGLAND
Sports Illus 30: 38-43 Feb 10 '69

SKIING--NEW ZEALAND
Holiday 43: 78-83 (col) Mar '68

SKIING--NORWAY
Holiday 38: 64-67 (col) Dec '65

SKIING--SNOWMASS, COLORADO
Holiday 45: 64-67 (col) Feb '69

SKIING--SUN VALLEY
Holiday 42: 62-67 (col) Nov '67
Look 34: 41-3 (col) Feb 24 '70

SKIING--SWITZERLAND
Holiday 37: 74-77 (col) Jan '65

SKIING--SWITZERLAND
Holiday 45: 46-49 (col) Jan '69
Travel 134: 28, 29 (col), 30, 31 (col), 32, 33 (col) Nov '70
Travel 136: 34-35, 37 (col),

38, 39 (col) Dec '71

SKIING--UTAH
Sports Illus 23: 52-60 (col) Nov 15 '65
Holiday 48: 26-29 (col) Nov '70

SKIING, SLUSH--MT. BAKER, WASHINGTON
Life 59: 62, 65 July 30 '65

SKIING TECHNIQUE BY FALCH (sketches)
Sports Illus 21: 47-50 (col) Nov 23 '64

SKIING TECHNIQUE BY EDDIE MORRIS
Sports Illus 23: 61-65 (drawings) Nov 15 '65

SKIJORING
Life 56: 38 Apr 24 '64

SKIN DIVING
Ebony 22: 66-8, 70 (col) Nov '66

SKYLARK (rocket). See ROCKETS, SOUNDING--ENGLAND--SKYLARK

SKYSCRAPERS--CHICAGO
Holiday 41: 49-51 (col) Mar '67

SKYSCRAPERS--NEW YORK (helicopter view)
Nat Geog 126: 92-3 (col) July '64

SLAG HEAPS (near Sudbury)--ONTARIO
Nat Geog 124: 82-3 (col) July '63

SLAVERY--UNITED STATES--FUGITIVE SLAVES. See UNDERGROUND RAILROAD--FUGITIVE SLAVES ARRIVING AT NEWPORT, IND.

SLED DOG RACING
Sports Illus 26: 54-55, 58-60 (col) Jan 23 '67

SLEDS (sledges)
Nat Geog 127: 257, 270-1 (col) Feb '65

SLEDS, CHILDREN'S--RUSSIA
Nat Geog 129: 324 (col) Mar '66

SLEDS, VALIER'S RS-1, 1929 (rocket powered)

ARTIFICIAL SATELLITES;
GUIDED MISSILES; LUNAR
PROBES; ROCKETS; SPACE
PROBES
SPACE VEHICLES--EGYPT--
KAHER (model)
Nat Geog 127: 594 (col) May
'65
SPACE VEHICLES--EQUIPMENT
--PROJECT APOLLO
Life 65: 16-22 (col) Dec 20
'68
SPACE VEHICLES--GEMINI V
Life 59: 61-67 (col) Sept 3
'65
SPACE VEHICLES--LANDING
SYSTEMS
Life 66: 34-35, 38 May 2
'69
SPACE VEHICLES--LANDING
SYSTEMS--LUNAR EXCUR-
SION MODULE FOR LAND-
ING ON MOON (model)
Hist of Rocketry and Space
Travel, bet. p. 196-7
(col), p. 218-19
Life 57: 85-6 (col) Oct 2 '64
Nat Geog 125: 356, 358, 363,
384, 387, 395-8 (col) Mar
'64
Nat Geog 127: 135-6 (col)
Jan '65
Nat Geog 129: 552-3 (col)
Apr '66
SPACE VEHICLES--LANDING
SYSTEMS--PARACHUTES
Nat Geog 125: 389 (col) Mar
'64
SPACE VEHICLES--LANDING
SYSTEMS--PARAGLIDERS
Nat Geog 125: 370 (col) Mar
'64
SPACE VEHICLES--LANDING
SYSTEMS--PROJECT APOLLO
Life 66: cover, 20-22, 24-25,
26-27 (drawing) (col) Mar
14 '69
SPACE VEHICLES--LAUNCHING
Nat Geog 126: 693 (col) Nov
'64
SPACE VEHICLES--LAUNCHING
PADS--CAPE KENNEDY

Nat Geog 124: 882-3 (col)
Dec '63
SPACE VEHICLES--MAINTEN-
ANCE AND REPAIR--TOOLS
FOR USE DURING FLIGHT
Life 55: 37 Sept 27 '63
SPACE VEHICLES--MANUFAC-
TURE--PROJECT APOLLO
Nat Geog 130: 810-11 (col)
Dec '66
SPACE VEHICLES--RECOVERY
--KORABL SPUTNIK 2--
RECOVERY CAPSULE, 1960
(Russia)
Hist of Rocketry and Space
Travel, p. 181
SPACE VEHICLES--RECOVERY
--PROJECT GEMINI
Nat Geog 127: 132-3 (col)
Jan '65
SPACE VEHICLES--RUSSIA--
VOSTOK 4, 1962
Hist of Rocketry and Space
Travel, p. 206
SPACE VEHICLES--SAFETY
DEVICES AND MEASURES--
BALLUTES
Life 55: 38 (col) Sept 27 '63
SPACE VEHICLES--TESTING--
PROJECT APOLLO--VAC-
UUM CHAMBERS
Nat Geog 127: 135 (col) Jan
'65
SPACE VEHICLES--U. S. --
FERRY, ATOMIC POWERED
(painting of proposed ve-
hicle for travel to the moon)
Life 57: 78-9 (col) Oct 2 '64
SPACE VEHICLES--U. S. --
PROJECT APOLLO
Hist of Rocketry and Space
Travel, p. 218-19
Nat Geog 125: 388-9 (col)
Mar '64
SPACE VEHICLES--U. S. --
PROJECT APOLLO (models)
Hist of Rocketry and Space
Travel, bet. p. 196-7
(col), 216, 218-21
Nat Geog 125: 356, 358, 362-
3, 387, 390, 394-8, 401
(col) Mar '64

SPACE VEHICLES--U. S. --
PROJECT GEMINI
Hist of Rocketry and Space
Travel, bet. p. 196-7
(col), p. 210
Nat Geog 125: 364 (col) Mar
'64
Nat Geog 128: 442-3, 446
(col) Sept '65
Nat Geog 129: 538-49 (col)
Apr '66
SPACE VEHICLES--U. S. --
PROJECT GEMINI (models)
Nat Geog 125: 360-1, 363,
366-70 (col) Mar '64
Nat Geog 128: 318 (col) Sept
'65
SPACE VEHICLES--U. S. --
PROJECT MERCURY
Hist of Rocketry and Space
Travel, bet. p. 196-7
(col), p. 207
SPACE VEHICLES--U. S. --
SPACE FLIGHT TO MARS
(model)
Hist of Rocketry and Space
Travel, bet. p. 196-7
(col)
SPACE WALKS. See SPACE
FLIGHT--MANNED FLIGHTS
--PROJECT GEMINI--SPACE
WALKS
SPAIN
Travel 123: 51-54 (col) Mar
'65
Nat Geog 127: 292-339 (col)
Mar '65
Holiday 37: 53-57 (col), 58-
59, 60-67, 153-160 (col)
Apr '65
SPANISH-AMERICAN WAR--
U. S. See UNITED STATES
--SPANISH-AMERICAN WAR
SPANISH ARMADA (relics)
Nat Geog 135: 746-777 (col)
June '69
SPEARPOINTS, BARBED (used
by voyageurs)
Nat Geog 124: 416 (col) Sept
'63
SPECTACLES. See SUN
GLASSES

SPINDLE WHORLS, NORSE
(probably used by Vikings in
Newfoundland)
Nat Geog 126: 708 (col) Nov
'64
SPINNAKERS, YACHT
Nat Geog 124: 346 (col) Sept
'63
SPINNING, COTTON--INDIANS,
S. AMERICAN--ERIGBAAGTSA
--BRAZIL
Nat Geog 125: 744 (col) May
'64
SPINNING-WHEEL
Nat Geog 130: 439 (col) Sept
'66
SPORTS, UNUSUAL
Life 70: 89-90 May 14 '71
SPORTSWEAR. See COSTUME
SPORTS
SPRAYING AND DUSTING. See
AIRPLANES IN INSECT CON-
TROL; TREE SPRAYING
SPRINT NIKE-X (guided missile).
See GUIDED MISSILES--U. S.
--SPRING NIKE-X
SPURS, COWBOYS'
Nat Geog 129: 366 (col) Mar
'66
SPURS, GEORGE WASHINGTON'S
Nat Geog 126: 652 Nov '64
SPUTNIK (artificial satellite).
See ARTIFICIAL SATELLITES
--RUSSIA--SPUTNIK
STADIUM, WORKERS'--PEKING,
CHINA
Life 60: 72-74, 76 (col) Mar
11 '66
STADIUMS
Sports Illus 27: 31-37 (col)
July 10 '67
STADIUMS--ASTRODOME--
HOUSTON, TEXAS
Life 58: 86-8 (col) Apr 9 '65
Look 29: 96-7 (col) Apr 20
'65
Life 58: 76A-78 Apr 23 '65
Ebony 23: 190 June '68
STADIUMS--ASTRODOME--
HOUSTON, TEX. (interior)
Life 61: 47 (col) July 8 '66
STADIUMS--MEMORIAL

COLISEUM--LOS ANGELES
Life 55: 26-7 Aug 30 '63
STADIUMS--OLYMPIC STADIUM
--INNSBRUCK, AUSTRIA
Life 56: 30-1 (col) Feb 14
'64
STADIUMS--OLYMPIC STADIUM
--TOKYO
Nat Geog 126: 512-13 (col)
Oct '64
STADIUMS--YANKEE STADIUM
--NEW YORK
Life 56: 66 (col) May 1 '64
STAGE SETTINGS--"AFTER THE
FALL"
Life 56: 64A-65 Feb 7 '64
STAGE SETTINGS--"AIDA"
Nat Geog 126: 88-9 (col)
July '64
STAGE SETTINGS--"BAREFOOT
IN THE PARK"
Life 55: 32-3 Nov 22 '63
STAGE SETTINGS--"HAMLET"
Life 56: 84-5, 91-2, 96, 98
Apr 24 '64
STAGE SETTINGS--"HAMLET"
(movie)
Life 56: 78B-81, 95, 99 Apr
24 '64
STAGE SETTINGS--"HELLO,
DOLLY"
Life 56: front cover, 107-9
(col) Apr 3 '64
STAGE SETTINGS--"WINTER'S
TALE"
Nat Geog 126: 70-1 (col)
July '64
STAGECOACH, AMERICAN--
"TRENTON DILIGENCE"
Am Heritage 15: 52-53
(painting, col) Feb '64
STAGECOACHES--ATTACK BY
APACHE INDIANS (painting
by Frederic Remington)
Nat Geog 128: 662-3 (col)
Nov '65
STAINED GLASS MURAL--
PAINTING BY ETHIOPIAN
ARTIST
Ebony 20: 90-91 (col) June
'65
STAINED GLASS WINDOWS

Sch Arts 63: 35-7 Dec '63
Ebony 19: 146 May '64
Nat Geog 125: 628 (col) May
'64; 884 (col) June '64
STAMPS, POSTAGE. See
POSTAGE STAMPS
STANFORD UNIVERSITY--
HOOVER INSTITUTION ON
WAR, REVOLUTION, AND
PEACE--STANFORD, CALIF.
Nat Geog 128: 577 Oct '65
STATE HOUSES. See CAPI-
TOLS
STATE PARKS (parks in vari-
ous states)
Nat Geog 124: 648-707 (col)
Nov '63
STATE PARKS--CALIFORNIA--
HUMBOLDT REDWOODS
STATE PARK
Nat Geog 126: 21, 24-5 (col)
July '64
STATE PARKS--INDIANA--
INDIANA DUNES
Nat Geog 124: 684-5 (col)
Nov '63
STATE PARKS--LOUISIANA--
EVANGELINE MEMORIAL
STATE PARK
Nat Geog 129: 352-3 (col)
Mar '66
STATEN ISLAND (lithograph)
Am Heritage 17: 24-25 (col)
Aug '66
STATUE OF LIBERTY
Ebony 25: 103 June '70
STATUE OF LIBERTY (aerial
view, 1930)
Nat Geog 124: 564 (col) Oct
'63
STATUE OF LIBERTY (large
illus. of the head)
Nat Geog 126: 74-5 (col)
July '64
STATUES. See Name of De-
ceased or Commemorative
Event with Subdivision Statue,
e.g. LINCOLN ABRAHAM--
STATUE; IWO JIMA--
STATUE; etc.
STEAM SHOVELS. See
SHOVELS, STEAM

CALHOUN
Life 55: 34 July 5 '63
SUBMARINE BOATS, ATOMIC
POWERED--U. S. --SHARK
Nat Geog 127: 173 (col) Feb
'65
SUBMARINE BOATS, ATOMIC
POWERED--U. S. --SKATE
Nat Geog 127: 185 (col) Feb
'65
SUBMARINE BOATS, ATOMIC
POWERED--U. S. --TECUM-
SEH
Life 55: 34 July 5 '63
SUBMARINE BOATS, ATOMIC
POWERED--U. S. --THRESHER
Nat Geog 125: 759 June '64
SUBMARINE BOATS--MESO-
SCAPHS
Nat Geog 128: 370-1 (col)
Sept '65
SUBMARINE DISASTERS--
THRESHER (atomic powered
submarine sunk off New
England coast, 1963)
Nat Geog 125: 759-77 (col)
June '64
SUBMARINE WARFARE. See
also GUIDED MISSILES--
U. S. --LAUNCHING FROM
SUBMARINE BOATS
SUBMARINE WARFARE--Q-
SHIPS--ENGLAND (used
against German U-boats in
World War I)
Life 56: 74 Apr 17 '64
SUBMARINE WARFARE--SINK-
ING OF LUSITANIA BY
GERMAN U-BOAT, 1915
(painting)
Life 56: 58-9 (col) Apr 17
'64
SUBMARINE WARFARE--U-
BOATS--GERMANY (used in
World War I)
Life 56: 60-3 (col) Apr 17
'64
SUBMERSIBLE DECOMPRESSION
CHAMBERS. See DECOM-
PRESSION CHAMBERS, SUB-
MERSIBLE--SDC
SUBMERSIBLE PORTABLE IN-

FLATABLE DWELLINGS.
See UNDERWATER STRUC-
TURES--SUBMERSIBLE
PORTABLE INFLATABLE
DWELLINGS (SPID)
SUBROC (guided missile). See
GUIDED MISSILES--U. S. --
LAUNCHING FROM SUBMA-
RINE BOATS--SUBROC
SUBWAYS. See Names of
Cities with Subdivision Sub-
ways, e. g. MOSCOW--SUB-
WAYS; etc.
SUDAN--NATIVE RACES--NUBA
Nat Geog 130: 672-99 (col)
Nov '66
SUEZ CANAL
Nat Geog 128: 284-5 (col)
Aug '65
SUFFRAGETTES--PROTEST
MARCH, 1913
Nat Geog 128: 108-9 July '65
SULPHUR MINES, UNDERSEA
(offshore)
Nat Geog 129: 384-5 (col)
Mar '66
SUN. See also ECLIPSES,
SOLAR
SUN
Nat Geog 128: 712-43 (col)
Nov '65
SUN, PHOTOGRAPHY OF. See
ASTRONOMICAL PHOTOG-
RAPHY
SUN GLASSES (used by Thomas
Jefferson)
Nat Geog 130: 435 (col) Sept
'66
SUN GLASSES, MODERN
Life 58: 59-60, 63 June 4
'65
SUNDIALS, SLATE
Nat Geog 127: 491 (col) Apr
'65
SUNKEN TREASURE. See
BURIED TREASURE
SUPERHIGHWAYS. See EX-
PRESS HIGHWAYS
SUPERMARKETS. See also
FOOD STORES
SUPERMARKETS--PHILIPPINES
Nat Geog 130: 305 (col) Sept
'66

SUPERMARKETS--ROCKVILLE,
M.D.--SUPER GIANT
Life 57: 36 (col) Oct 16 '64
SUPERSONIC TRANSPORT
Look 28: 93-95 May 5 '64
SURF RIDING
Life 57: 68-70 July 3 '64
Nat Geog 124: 356-7 (col)
Sept '63
Look 28: 54-57 (col) June 30
'64
Ebony 20: 109-11 Apr '65
Life 61: 141-142, 144 Oct
14 '66
Holiday 42: 62-67 (col) Sept
'67
Life 68: 48-49 (col) Mar 6
'70
Travel 134: 50, 52-3 (col)
July '70
Life 71: 72-5 (col) Oct 1 '71
SURGICAL INSTRUMENTS
Life 58: 98B Apr 2 '65
SURINAM. See DUTCH GUIANA
(Surinam)
SURTSEY (island)
Nat Geog 127: 712-25 (col)
May '65
SURVEYOR (space probe). See
LUNAR PROBES--U.S.--
SURVEYOR
SWAZILAND--SOUTH AFRICA
Nat Geog 136: 266-293 (col)
Aug '69
SWEDEN
Look 29: 49-57 (col) Feb 9
'65
Holiday 40: 46-51 (col) Nov
'66
SWIMMING POOLS--DECORATED
Life 69: 76-80 (col) Oct 9 '70
SWINGS, GARLANDED
Nat Geog 126: 571 (col) Oct
'64
SWITZERLAND
Travel 127: 55-58 (col) Feb
'67
Nat Geog 136: 72-113 (col)
July '69
SWORD, ROBERT E. LEE'S
Nat Geog 127: 467 (col) Apr
'65

SWORDS--BROADSWORDS
Nat Geog 127: 730 (col) June
'65
SWORDS, MEDIEVAL
Nat Geog 130: 250 Aug '66
SWORDS, TOLEDO (with deco-
rated cup hilt)--SPAIN
Nat Geog 127: 328 (col) Mar
'65
SYDNEY, AUSTRALIA
Nat Geog 124: 348-9 (col)
Sept '63
SYMBOLS
Look 34: 42-43 (col) Jan 13
'70
SYMBOLS, OLYMPIC
Nat Geog 126: 506 (col) Oct
'64
SYMPHONY OF THE NEW
WORLD--MANHATTAN, N.Y.
Ebony 22: 39-40, 42-4, 46
Nov '66
SYNCOM (artificial satellite).
See COMMUNICATIONS
SATELLITES--U.S.--SYN-
COM

T

TABOR, MOUNT
Nat Geog 128: 839 (col)
Dec '65
TACTITE (rocket). See
ROCKETS, SOUNDING--
FRANCE--TACTITE
TAHITI
Holiday 41: 46-53, 55-59, 61-
63 (col) Feb '67
TAHOE, LAKE
Holiday 38: 76-77, 84-85
(col) Dec '65
TAIWAN
Nat Geog 135: 1-45 (col)
Jan '69
TAJ MAHAL--AGRA, INDIA
Nat Geog 129: 95 (col) Jan
'66
Life 63: 44-59 (col) Nov 3
'67
Holiday 47: 65 (col) Apr '70
TALOS (guided missile). See

GUIDED MISSILES--U. S. --
LAUNCHING FROM SHIPS--
TALOS
TANKS, MILITARY--FRANCE,
1918
Life 56: 58-9 (col) Mar 13
'64
TANKS, MILITARY--U. S., 1963
Life 55: 36A Nov 1 '63
TANZANIA--ANTIQUITIES
Nat Geog 130: 700-9 (col)
Nov '66
TARTANS--BALMORAL
Life 56: 81 (col) Mar 6 '64
TARTANS--CAMERON HIGH-
LANDERS
Life 56: 80 (col) Mar 6 '64
TARTANS--MACDONALD DRESS
Nat Geog 125: 863 (col) June
'64
TARTANS--MCLEOD DRESS
Nat Geog 126: 236 (col) Aug
'64
TARTANS--ROYAL STUART
Nat Geog 128: 89 (col) July
'65
TASMANIA
Travel 131: 44, 46 (col), 47,
48 (col), 49, 50 (col), 51
May '69
TATTOOS--MAKONDE TRIBE--
MOZAMBIQUE
Nat Geog 126: 214-15 (col)
Aug '64
TATTOOS, NUBA--SUDAN
Nat Geog 130: 672-3, 689-91
(col) Nov '66
TAXICABS, HORSE-DRAWN--
SARATOGA SPRINGS, N. Y.
Life 55: 54-5 July 26 '63
TCHIKAO INDIANS. See INDI-
ANS OF SOUTH AMERICA--
TCHIKAO
TEA FIELDS--CEYLON
Nat Geog 129: 462-3, 466-7
(col) Apr '66
TEA PICKERS, MECHANIZED--
RUSSIA
Life 55: 56 (col) Sept 13 '63
TEA PICKERS--MOZAMBIQUE
Nat Geog 126: 334-5 (col)
Aug '64

TEA TASTERS
Nat Geog 126: 401 (col) Sept
'64
TEACHER OF THE YEAR
Look 32: 35-36, 38-40 May
14 '68
Look 35: 51-54 May 4 '71
TEACHERS, NEGRO. See
NEGRO TEACHERS
TEACHING METHODS--GREAT
BRITAIN
Life 66: 50-52, 56 Apr 11
'69
TEL AVIV, ISRAEL
Nat Geog 127: 398-9 (col)
Mar '65
TELEPHONE CALLS, PRESI-
DENT'S FIRST--RUTHER-
FORD B. HAYES TALKING
WITH A. G. BELL, 1877
Nat Geog 127: 663 May '65
TELEPHONE WITH TV RE-
CEIVER. See PICTURE-
PHONE
TELEVISION IN EDUCATION
Life 70: 42-45 (col) Apr 2
'71
TEMPLE, EGYPTIAN (Abu
Simbel)
Life 61: 32-37 (col) Dec 2
'66
TEMPLE, EGYPTIAN
(Akhenaten)
Nat Geog 138: 634-655 (col)
Nov '70
TEMPLE OF APOLLO--BAS-
SAE, GREECE
Holiday 47: 78-79 (col) Apr
'70
TEMPLE OF ATHENA NIKE--
ATHENS, GREECE
Nat Geog 124: 116 (col) July
'63
TEMPLE OF DANDARA--
EGYPT
Nat Geog 127: 603 (col) May
'65
TEMPLE OF HEAVEN--PE-
KING
Nat Geog 126: 598 (col) Nov
'64
TEMPLE OF LUXOR--COLON-

NADE--EGYPT
Nat Geog 127: 608 (col) May
'65
TEMPLE OF POSEIDON--
GREECE
Nat Geog 124: 134 (col) July
'63
TEMPLE OF QUEEN HATSHEP-
SUT (near Thebes)--EGYPT
Nat Geog 127: 607 (col) May
'65
TEMPLE OF RAMSES II
Life 59: cover, 28-33 (col)
Oct 29 '65
TEMPLE OF SETHOS I--GAL-
LERY OF KINGS--EGYPT
Nat Geog 127: 602 (col) May
'65
TEMPLES, CHINESE--VIETNAM
(Republic)
Nat Geog 127: 852-3 (col)
June '65
TEMPLES, HINDU--BALI
Nat Geog 124: 457 (col) Sept
'63
TEMPLES--INDIA
Holiday 45: 49 Feb '69
TEMPLES, ROMAN
Life 60: 56-57 (col) Mar 4
'66
TEMPLES (ziggurats)--UR
(painting)
Nat Geog 130: 742-3 (col)
Dec '66
TENNESSEE VALLEY AUTHORI-
TY--FONTANA DAM
Nat Geog 129: 74-5 (col) Jan
'66
TENNIS--HISTORY
Am Heritage 22: 48-49, 50
(col), 51-59 June '71
TENNIS CHAMPIONS
Ebony 18: 120 Sept '63
Ebony 18: 151-2, 154 Oct '63
Look 30: 110-114 Apr 19 '66
Life 59: 61-62, 64, 66 Oct
15 '65
Sports Illus 29: 27-28 (col)
Sept 16 '68
Life 65: 30-31 (col), 32-35
Sept 20 '68
Life 67: 77-80 Sept 12 '69

Sports Illus 32: 14-17 Feb 9
'70
TENNIS COURTS
Nat Geog 130: 794-5 (col) Dec
'66
TENNIS COURTS--FOREST
HILLS, LONG ISLAND, NEW
YORK
Sports Illus 25: 41-44 (col)
Aug 29 '66
TENTS, MODERN (for vacation
camping)
Nat Geog 125: 573 (col) Apr
'64
Nat Geog 126: 23 (col) July
'64
TENTS--MOUNTAIN CLIMBERS
--MOUNT EVEREST
Nat Geog 124: 467, 473, 484-
5 (col) Oct '63
TEPEES, INDIAN (illus. by
George Catlin)
Nat Geog 128: 648-9 (col)
Nov '65
TEST SITES--ROCKETS. See
ROCKETS--TESTING--TEST
SITES
TETON MOUNTAINS
Nat Geog 128: 886-91 (col)
Dec '65
Nat Geog 129: 560-2, 590
(col) Apr '66
Travel 132: 48 (col) July '69
Life 67: 48-49 (col) Dec 19
'69
America's Wonderlands, p.
100-2 (col)
TEXAS TOWERS. See ARTI-
FICIAL ISLANDS--TEXAS
TOWERS
TEXTILE DESIGN--BEDOUINS
Nat Geog 129: 30-3 (col)
Jan '66
TEXTILE DESIGN--PERU
(ancient)
Nat Geog 125: 230-1 (col)
Feb '64
TEXTILE WORKERS--U.S.--
CHILDREN
Nat Geog 128: 538 Oct '65
THAILAND
Travel 124: 51-54 (col)

Aug '65
Nat Geog 132: 82-125 (col)
July '67
THAMES RIVER--ENGLAND
Nat Geog 125: 648-51 (col)
May '64
THATCHERS (near Widecombe)
--ENGLAND
Nat Geog 124: 232 (col) Aug
'63
THATCHERS--TRISTAN DA
CUNHA (island)
Nat Geog 125: 64-5 (col)
Jan '64
THEATER BUILDINGS--DALLAS
THEATER CENTER--DALLAS
Life 56: 69 Jan 31 '64
THEATER BUILDINGS--FORD'S
THEATER--WASHINGTON,
D. C.
Life 64: 76-78 (col) Mar 1
'68
Nat Geog 137: 392-401 (col)
Mar '70
THEATER BUILDINGS--GLOBE
--LONDON (painting)
Nat Geog 125: 654-6 (col)
May '64
THEATER BUILDINGS--ROYAL
SHAKESPEARE THEATRE--
STRATFORD-ON-AVON
(interior)
Nat Geog 125: 657-8 (col)
May '64
THEATER BUILDINGS--SHAKE-
SPEARE THEATRE--STRAT-
FORD-ON-AVON. See
THEATER BUILDINGS--
ROYAL SHAKESPEARE
THEATRE--STRATFORD-
ON-AVON
THEATRICAL COSTUME. See
COSTUME, THEATRICAL--
(name of theatrical produc-
tion, e.g., "APPLAUSE")
THEODOLITE (used by Thomas
Jefferson)
Nat Geog 130: 435 (col) Sept
'66
THOR-DELTA (rocket). See
ROCKETS--CARRIERS--U. S.
--THOR-DELTA

THRESHING MACHINES, 1878
(drawing)
Nat Geog 127: 662-3 May '65
THRONES--PAPAL THRONE--
VATICAN--SISTINE CHAPEL
Life 55: front cover (col)
July 5 '63
THUNDERBIRD (guided missile).
See GUIDED MISSILES--
ENGLAND--THUNDERBIRD
TIBET
Life 59: 36-43 (col) Oct 8
'65
TIE DYEING
Sch Arts 68: 18-19 Apr '69
TIMBUKTU. See TOMBOUC-
TOU, MALI (Republic)
TIMES SQUARE--NEW YORK
(New Year's Eve)
Nat Geog 126: 62-3 (col)
July '64
TINY TIM (rocket). See
ROCKETS--U. S. --TINY TIM
TIROS (artificial satellite).
See ARTIFICIAL SATELLITES
--U. S. --TIROS
TITAN (guided missile). See
GUIDED MISSILES--U. S. --
TITAN
TITAN (rocket). See ROCK-
ETS--CARRIERS--U. S. --
TITAN 3C
TITAN-GEMINI (rocket). See
ROCKETS--CARRIERS--U. S.
--TITAN-GEMINI
TITICACA, LAKE
Nat Geog 139: 272-293 (col)
Feb '71
TIVOLI GARDENS--COPEN-
HAGEN. See AMUSEMENT
PARKS--TIVOLI GARDENS--
COPENHAGEN
TLINGIT INDIANS. See INDI-
ANS OF NORTH AMERICA--
ALASKA--TLINGIT
TOBACCO FIELDS--ONTARIO
Nat Geog 124: 77 (col) July
'63
TOBACCO PIPES. See PIPES,
TOBACCO
TOBOGGANING
Nat Geog 125: 722 (col) May
'64

TOKAIDO--JAPAN
  Holiday 41: 34-45 (col) June
    '67
TOKYO
  Nat Geog 126: 447-87 (col)
    Oct '64
  Holiday 46: 52-55 (col) Sept
    '69
TOLEDO, SPAIN
  Nat Geog 127: 328-9 (col)
    Mar '65
TOMAHAWKS
  Nat Geog 128: 655 (col) Nov
    '65
TOMBOUCTOU, MALI (Re-
  public)
  Nat Geog 130: 182-3 (col)
    Aug '66
TOMBS. See Names of De-
  ceased with Subdivision
  Grave; Mausoleum; Tomb,
  e.g. KENNEDY, JOHN F.
  --GRAVE; etc.
TOMBSTONES--NEW ENGLAND,
  17TH AND 18TH CENT.
  Am Heritage 21: 19-26 Aug
    '70
TONGA
  Life 63: 58-65 (col) July 21
    '67
TOOLS. See Names of Tools,
  e.g. AXE BLADE; ICE
  CHISEL; etc.
TOOLS, SPACE. See SPACE
  VEHICLES--MAINTENANCE
  AND REPAIR--TOOLS FOR
  USE DURING FLIGHT
TOOLS, VOYAGEURS'
  Nat Geog 124: 415-16 (col)
    Sept '63
TOPAZE (guided missile). See
  GUIDED MISSILES--FRANCE
  --TOPAZE
TOPRIDGE--SUMMER HOME OF
  MARJORIE MERRIWEATHER
  POST
  Life 59: 66-71 (col) Nov 5
    '65
TOROWEAP OVERLOOK--GRAND
  CANYON
  America's Wonderlands, p.
    174 (col)

TOTEM POLES--ALASKA
  Nat Geog 127: 798-9, 804
    (col) June '65
TOURNAMENT OF ROSES.
  See PASADENA, CALIF.--
  PARADES--TOURNAMENT
  OF ROSES
TOWER BRIDGE--LONDON
  Life 55: 89 Aug 16 '63
TOWER BRIDGE--LONDON
  (night scene)
  Nat Geog 129: 744-5, 782-3
    (col) June '66
TOWER OF LONDON
  Nat Geog 125: 651-3 (col)
    May '64
  Nat Geog 128: 220-1 (col)
    Aug '65
  Nat Geog 129: 782-3 (col)
    June '66
  Nat Geog 134: 670-671 (col)
    Nov '68
TOWER OF THE WINDS--
  GREECE (drawings)
  Nat Geog 131: 586-595 (col)
    Apr '67
TOWERS--PEACE TOWER--
  OTTAWA, ONTARIO
  Nat Geog 124: 97 (col) July
    '63
TOWERS--SPANISH-COLONIAL
  CALIFORNIA TOWER--BAL-
  BOA PARK--SAN DIEGO,
  CALIF.
  Nat Geog 129: 622 (col) May
    '66
TOWN CRIERS--ENGLAND
  Nat Geog 124: 241 (col) Aug
    '63
TOWN HALLS. See Names of
  Cities with Subdivision Town
  Hall, e.g. STOCKHOLM--
  TOWN HALL; etc.
TOYS
  Ebony 23: 122-4, 126-9 Nov
    '67
  Ebony 25: 75-7, 79-80 Nov
    '69
  Ebony 25: 84-6, 88, 90-1
    Dec '69
  Ebony 27: 135-6, 138, 140,
    142 Nov '71

Life 71: 79-82 (col) Nov 12
  '71
TOYS, "DISCOVERY"
  Life 55: 121-4 Nov 22 '63
TRACK. See also JUMPING,
  POLE VAULTING, SHOT
  PUTTING, HURDLING
TRACK MEET--UNITED STATES
  VS RUSSIA--LENINGRAD
  Sports Illus 33: 9-12 (col)
    Aug 3 '70
TRACK STARS--AFRICAN
  Ebony 21: 100-2, 104, 106,
    108 May '66
TRACK STARS--TAIWANESE
  Life 69: 34-35 (col) July 10
    '70
TRACK STARS--U.S.
  Ebony 21: 69-70, 72, 74,
    76 July '66
  Sports Illus 33: 10-12 (col)
    July 6 '70
  Sports Illus 34: 10-11 (col)
    Feb 1 '71
TRACTORS, KEROSENE DRIVEN
  --1903
  Life 59: 92 (col) Nov 19 '65
TRADING POSTS
  Nat Geog 124: 421 Sept '63
TRAFALGAR SQUARE--LON-
  DON. See LONDON--TRA-
  FALGAR SQUARE
TRAINS. See RAILROADS--
  TRAINS
TRAMS
  Look 29: 91-93 Feb 23 '65
TRANSBAY BRIDGE--SAN
  FRANCISCO (night scene)
  Nat Geog 129: 640-1 (col)
    May '66
TRANS-BAY FEDERAL SAV-
  INGS BANK (largest Negro
  savings and loan institution)
  Ebony 20: 124 June '65
TRANSPLANTATION OF OR-
  GANS, TISSUES, etc. See
  ORGAN TRANSPLANTS
TRAPS, BEAVER. See
  BEAVER TRAPS
TREATIES--SIGNING OF NU-
  CLEAR TEST BAN TREATY
  BY JOHN F. KENNEDY,

OCTOBER 1963
  Life 55: 44B Oct 18 '63
  Nat Geog 129: 109 (col) Jan
    '66
TREATIES--SIGNING OF TREATY
  OF 1783 ACKNOWLEDGING
  U.S. INDEPENDENCE FROM
  ENGLAND (Peace of Paris)
  Nat Geog 126: 662 (col) Nov
    '64
TREATIES--SIGNING OF
  TREATY OF VERSAILLES
  FOLLOWING END OF WORLD
  WAR I, 1919
  Life 56: 86B June 5 '64
TREE, GENERAL SHERMAN--
  SEQUOIA NATIONAL PARK,
  CALIFORNIA
  America's Wonderlands, p.
    31, 363-6 (col)
TREE, NATIONAL GEOGRAPHIC
  SOCIETY (World's third tallest
  tree)
  America's Wonderlands, p.
    8-9 (col)
TREE, WORLD'S TALLEST--
  REDWOOD CREEK AREA--
  HUMBOLDT COUNTY,
  CALIF.
  Nat Geog 126: 3-7, 10-11
    (col) July '64
  Nat Geog 129: 674 (col) May
    '66
TREE HOUSE--ARCADIA,
  CALIFORNIA
  Look 28: M5-M7 Aug 11 '64
TREE SPRAYING--CITRUS
  GROVE
  Nat Geog 130: 344-5 (col)
    Sept '66
TREES. See also RUBBER
  TREES
TRINIDAD
  Nat Geog 140: 690-701 (col)
    Nov '71
TRISTAN DA CUNHA (island)
  Life 55: 72-8 July 12 '63
  Nat Geog 125: 60-81 (col)
    Jan '64
TROLLS
  Life 56: 107-8 (col) Apr 24
    '64

UNDERWATER SALVAGE. See
SALVAGE, UNDERWATER
UNDERWATER STRUCTURES.
See also UNDERWATER
LABORATORIES
UNDERWATER STRUCTURES--
MINIATURE SUBMARINES;
OIL DRILLING EQUIPMENT;
SEA IGLOOS; NUCLEAR
POWER PLANTS; PRESSURE
CHAMBERS (paintings and
photographs of proposed
devices)
Nat Geog 125: 778-801 (col)
June '64
UNDERWATER STRUCTURES--
SUBMERSIBLE PORTABLE
INFLATABLE DWELLINGS
(SPID)
Nat Geog 127: 530-47 (col)
Apr '65
UNDERWEAR, WOMEN'S (1960's)
Life 55: 83-5 (col) Aug 9 '63
UNIFORMS, MILITARY. See
COSTUME, MILITARY
UNIFORMS, SPORTS. See
BASEBALL CLUBS; FOOT-
BALL; etc.
UNITED NATIONS--CHARTER
SIGNING BY U.S., JUNE
1945
Nat Geog 129: 89 Jan '66
UNITED NATIONS--GENERAL
ASSEMBLY (Lyndon B. John-
son addressing, Dec. 1963)
Nat Geog 129: 118-19 (col)
Jan '66
UNITED NATIONS--HEAD-
QUARTERS
Nat Geog 126: 77 (col) July
'64
Nat Geog 129: 68 (col) Jan
'66
UNITED NATIONS CHILDREN'S
CHOIR OF LOS ANGELES
Ebony 18: 63-4, 66, 68, 70
July '63
UNITED NATIONS GUIDES
Ebony 18: 34-8 Aug '63
UNITED STATES--ARMED
FORCES--SPECIAL FORCES
Ebony 19: 47-8, 50, 52, 54

Apr '64
Ebony 21: 68-70, 72-3 Sept
'66
UNITED STATES--CIVIL WAR--
CAMPAIGNS AND BATTLES--
APPOMATTOX, 1865
Nat Geog 127: 435-69 (col)
Apr '65
UNITED STATES--CIVIL WAR--
CAMPAIGNS AND BATTLES--
VICKSBURG, 1863 (Currier
and Ives print)
Nat Geog 124: 38-9 (col)
July '63
UNITED STATES--CIVIL WAR--
GENERAL LEE SIGNING SUR-
RENDER TO GENERAL GRANT
AT APPOMATTOX COURT
HOUSE, APRIL 1865
Nat Geog 127: 464-5 (col)
Apr '65
UNITED STATES--CIVIL WAR--
NAVAL OPERATIONS--BAT-
TLE OF HAMPTON ROADS,
1862 (ships Monitor and
Merrimac)
Nat Geog 126: 380-1 (col)
Sept '64
UNITED STATES--CIVILIAN
CONSERVATION CORPS
(1930's)
Nat Geog 129: 73 Jan '66
UNITED STATES--COAST
GUARD
Life 63: 26-41 (col) July 7
'67
Life 63: 38-49 (col) July 14
'67
UNITED STATES--CONGRESS
(joint session, Jan. 14, 1963)
Nat Geog 125: 29-31 (col)
Jan '64
UNITED STATES--CONGRESS--
SENATE (first official por-
trait Sept. 24, 1963)
Nat Geog 125: 40-1 (col)
Jan '64
UNITED STATES--JOB CORPS
--PENNSYLVANIA
Nat Geog 129: 116 (col) Jan
'66
UNITED STATES--LIBRARY OF

CONGRESS (interior)
Nat Geog 126: 748-9 (col)
Dec '64
UNITED STATES--NASA--
MANNED SPACECRAFT
CENTER
Nat Geog 127: 139 (col)
Jan '65
Travel 132: 56-7 July '69
UNITED STATES--NAVY--
AIRCRAFT CARRIERS;
AIRPLANES; HELICOPTERS;
SHIPS; SUBMARINE BOATS
Nat Geog 127: 146-87 (col)
Feb '65
UNITED STATES--NAVY--
BLUE ANGELS (precision
flying team)
Nat Geog 124: 895 (col) Dec
'63
UNITED STATES PEACE CORPS
Look 28: 70-73 June 16 '64
UNITED STATES--PEACE CORPS
(activities in various coun-
tries)
Nat Geog 126: 297-345 (col)
Sept '64
UNITED STATES--PEACE
CORPS--BOLIVIA
Nat Geog 129: 106 (col) Jan
'66
UNITED STATES--SEALS--
PRESIDENT OF U.S.
Life 57: 25 Aug 14 '64
UNITED STATES--SPANISH-
AMERICAN WAR--CAM-
PAIGNS AND BATTLES--
SAN JUAN HILL (Frederic
Remington painting)
Nat Geog 128: 542-3 (col)
Oct '65
UNITED STATES AIR FORCE
ACADEMY--COLORADO
SPRINGS
Nat Geog 136: 180-181 (col)
Aug '69
UNITED STATES AIR FORCE
ACADEMY--CHAPEL--
COLORADO SPRINGS
Sch Arts 65: 38-40 Jan '66
UNITED STATES CENTENNIAL
EXHIBITION--PHILADELPHIA,

MAY 10, 1876 (watercolors)
Am Heritage 23: 17-32 (col)
Dec '71
UNIVERSITIES. See Name of
University, e.g. MADRID
UNIVERSITY; MOSCOW UNI-
VERSITY; etc.
UNIVERSITY OF CALIFORNIA,
BERKELEY, CALIF.
Nat Geog 129: 670-1 (col)
May '66
UR
Nat Geog 130: 739-89 (col)
Dec '66
URANIUM MINES--WYOMING
Nat Geog 129: 568 (col) Apr
'66
URBAN REDEVELOPMENT.
See Names of Cities with
Subdivision City Planning,
e.g. ST. LOUIS--CITY
PLANNING
URN, COFFEE (designed by
Thomas Jefferson)
Nat Geog 130: 435 (col) Sept
'66

V

V-E DAY
Life 58: 40-43 (col) May 21
'65
V-2 (rocket). See ROCKETS--
GERMANY--V-2; ROCKETS--
U.S.--V-2
VAIL, COLORADO
Holiday 36: 98-103 (col) Dec
'64
VALENTINES
Instr 77: 138-139 (col) Feb
'68
VALLEY FORGE
Nat Geog 126: 652 Nov '64
VANCOUVER, BRITISH COLUM-
BIA
Nat Geog 130: 394-5 (col)
Sept '66
VANGUARD (artificial satellite).
See ARTIFICIAL SATELLITES
--U.S.--VANGUARD
VAQUEROS. See COWBOYS--

157 VILCABAMBA

VILCABAMBA, CORDILLERA
Nat Geog 126: 268-96 (col)
Aug '64
VILLAGES--NEW ENGLAND
Nat Geog 130: 816-17 (col)
Dec '66
VINEYARDS. See GRAPES--
VINEYARDS
VINLAND
Am Heritage 16: 6-7 (map)
Oct '65
VIRGIN ISLANDS
Holiday 40: 60-67 (col) Dec
'66
Travel 128: 51-54 (col) Dec
'67
Nat Geog 133: 66-103 (col)
Jan '68
VIRGIN ISLANDS--BUCK ISLAND
Nat Geog 139: 674-683 (col)
May '71
VIRGIN ISLANDS, BRITISH.
See LEEWARD ISLANDS
VIRGIN ISLANDS NATIONAL
PARK
America's Wonderlands, p.
546-9 (col)
VIRGIN RIVER
America's Wonderlands, p.
194 (col)
VIRGINIA, UNIVERSITY--
CHARLOTTESVILLE, VA.
Nat Geog 126: 670-1 (col)
Nov '64
VISTA
Ebony 20: 88-90, 92-4 Sept
'65
VOLCANOES--GUNUNG AGUNG--
BALI
Nat Geog 124: 436-8 (col)
Sept '63
VOLCANOES--PHILIPPINES--
VOLCANO ISLAND
Life 59: 108-116 (col) Oct
15 '65
VOLCANOES--TRISTAN DA
CUNHA (island)
Nat Geog 125: 70-1 (col)
Jan '64
VOLCANOES--VESUVIUS--ITALY
Holiday 39: 44-45 (col) Jan
'66

VOLCANOES IN ERUPTION (near
Iceland), 1963
Life 55: 36-36A (col) Dec 13
'63
VOLCANOES IN ERUPTION--
IRAZU--COSTA RICA
Nat Geog 128: 122-4, 134-7,
(col) July '65
VOLCANOES IN ERUPTION--
KILAUEA IKI--HAWAII
America's Wonderlands, 48-
9 (col)
America's Wonderlands, p.
536-9 (col)
VOLCANOES IN ERUPTION--
MOUNT MAZAMA--OREGON
(painting and diagrams)
America's Wonderlands, p.
411 (col)
VOLCANOES IN ERUPTION--
TAAL--PHILIPPINES
Nat Geog 130: 307 Sept '66
VOLLEY BALL (in action)
Ebony 20: 112 Apr '65
VOLTA RIVER DAM--GHANA
Ebony 19: 154 May '64
VOSTOK (space vehicle). See
SPACE VEHICLES--RUSSIA
--VOSTOK
VOTING BOOTHS--CHILE
Life 57: 49 Sept 18 '64
VOYAGE ACROSS THE ATLAN-
TIC "TINKERBELLE" ROBERT
MANRY
Life 59: 30-39 (col) Sept 17
'65
VULCAN RAPIDS--GRAND CAN-
YON
America's Wonderlands, p.
175 (col)

W

WALDEN POND--MASSACHU-
SETTS
Nat Geog 130: 823 (col) Dec
'66
WALES
Nat Geog 127: 727-69 (col)
June '65
Look 33: 68-74 (col) June 24
'69

WALL--BYBLOS (built by Cru-
saders between 1103 and
1187)
  Nat Geog 124: 828-9 (col)
    Dec '63
WALL--CHINA. See GREAT
  WALL OF CHINA
WALT DISNEY WORLD--OR-
  LANDO, FLORIDA
  Life 71: 44-50 (col) Oct 15
    '71
WAR GAMES--U. S. --MARINE
  CORPS AND NAVY--AMPHI-
  BIOUS LANDINGS
  Nat Geog 127: 157 (col) Feb
    '65
WARSHIPS. See also BATTLES,
  NAVAL
WARSHIPS--ENGLAND--EREBUS
  (used as rocket ship in War
  of 1812)
  Hist of Rocketry and Space
    Travel, p. 32
WARSHIPS--GERMANY--
  CRUISERS (surface raiders
  used in World War I)
  Life 56: 78A Apr 17 '64
WARSHIPS--U. S. --CRUISERS--
  LONG BEACH
  Nat Geog 127: 153-4 (col)
    Feb '65
WARSHIPS--U. S. --CRUISERS,
  GUIDED-MISSILE--BOSTON
  Nat Geog 127: 168 (col) Feb
    '65
WARSHIPS--U. S. --DESTROY-
  ERS--C. TURNER JOY
  Life 57: 21 Aug 14 '64
WARSHIPS--U. S. --DESTROY-
  ERS--CHARLES S. PERRY
  Nat Geog 127: 171 (col) Feb
    '65
WARSHIPS--U. S. --DESTROY-
  ERS--MADDOX
  Life 57: 21 Aug 14 '64
WARSHIPS--U. S. --DESTROY-
  ERS--SAMUEL B. ROBERTS
  Nat Geog 127: 170 (col) Feb
    '65
WARSHIPS--U. S. --FRIGATES
  --BAINBRIDGE
  Nat Geog 127: 153-4 (col)

    Feb '65
WARSHIPS--U. S. --GUNBOATS
  --CIVIL WAR
  Nat Geog 124: 38-9 July '63
WARSHIPS--U. S. --MAINE
  (exploding in Havana harbor,
  1898)
  Nat Geog 127: 709 (col) May
    '65
WARSHIPS--U. S. --OLYMPIA--
  SPANISH-AMERICAN WAR,
  1898 (painting)
  Nat Geog 128: 536 Oct '65
WARSHIPS--U. S. --SACRAMENTO
  (shown refueling other ships)
  Nat Geog 127: 178 (col) Feb
    '65
WARSHIPS--"USS TAUSSIG"
  Ebony 21: 25-7 (col) July
    '66
WASHINGTON, BOOKER T. --
  BIRTHPLACE--ROCKY
  MOUNT, VA.
  Ebony 18: 109 Sept '63
WASHINGTON, D. C.
  Nat Geog 126: 736-81 (col)
    Dec '64
  Look 29: cover, 21-25, 28-
    29, 40-41 (col) Apr 6 '65
  Nat Geog 131: 500-539 (col)
    Apr '67
WASHINGTON, D. C. --AERIAL
  VIEW
  Ebony 20: 116 Mar '65
WASHINGTON, D. C. --NATION-
  AL CULTURAL CENTER.
  See JOHN F. KENNEDY
  CENTER FOR THE PER-
  FORMING ARTS--WASHING-
  TON, D. C.
WASHINGTON, D. C. --STREETS
  --PENNSYLVANIA AVENUE
  Nat Geog 126: 745 (col) Dec
    '64
WASHINGTON, D. C. --STREETS
  --PENNSYLVANIA AVENUE
  PROJECT (sketches of pro-
  posed new plan)
  Nat Geog 126: 744-7 (col)
    Dec '64
WASHINGTON, DINAH--FUN-
  ERAL RITES

Ebony 19: 146-7 Mar '64
WASHINGTON, GEORGE (at
Dorchester Heights) (painting
by Leutze)
Am Heritage 19: 12 (col) Dec
'67
WASHINGTON, GEORGE--
CROSSING THE DELAWARE
(painting)
Ebony 19: 94 Apr '64
WASHINGTON, GEORGE--
MEMENTOS
Nat Geog 126: 652 Nov '64
WASHINGTON, GEORGE--
SWEARING IN CEREMONY,
APRIL 30, 1789 (painting)
Nat Geog 129: 410 (col) Mar
'66
WASHINGTON, GEORGE--
TOMB--MT. VERNON, VA.
Am Heritage 15: 58 (draw-
ing, col) Feb '64
Nat Geog 127: 120 (col) Jan
'65
WASHINGTON (state)--NORTH
CASCADES
Nat Geog 133: 642-667 (col)
May '68
WATCH CHAINS
Nat Geog 127: 680 (col) May
'65
WATER FRONTS--HELSINKI
Nat Geog 125: 280-1 (col)
Feb '64
WATER FRONTS--NORFOLK,
VA.
Nat Geog 126: 378-9 (col)
Sept '64
WATERBEDS
Life 70: 52-4 (col) Mar 12
'71
WATERCOLORS
Instr 73: 38-39 Mar '64
WATERFALLS--ROCKY MOUN-
TAIN NATIONAL PARK
America's Wonderlands, p.
147 (col)
WATERTON-GLACIER INTER-
NATIONAL PEACE PARK--
CANADA-U.S.
Nat Geog 130: 356-7 (col)
Sept '66

WATERTON LAKE
America's Wonderlands, p.
130-1 (col)
WAURA INDIANS. See INDIANS
OF SOUTH AMERICA--
BRAZIL--WAURA
WEAPONS. See ARQUEBUSES;
AXES, BATTLE; CANNON;
MINE THROWERS; MUSKETS;
RIFLES
WEAVING
Sch Arts 63: 19 Sept '63
Sch Arts 64: 33 Mar '65
Sch Arts 64: 16-18 June '65
Sch Arts 66: 6-10, 38-40
Apr '67
Sch Arts 67: 4-9, 18-30 Dec
'67
Grade Teach 85: 106-111 Dec
'67
Sch Arts 68: 13-17 Apr '69
Sch Arts 70: 19-23 Jan '71
WEAVING, BELT--INDIAN
(N. American)--PUEBLOS,
20TH CENT.
Nat Geog 125: 209 (col) Feb
'64
WEAVING, CHAIR (wicker
chairs)--FRANCE
Nat Geog 129: 852 (col) June
'66
WEDDING CEREMONIES
Look 35: 44-47 (col) June
29 '71
WEDDING CEREMONIES--
AFRICA
Ebony 20: 25-7 (col), 28, 30,
32 Oct '65
WEDDINGS--GREECE--KING
CONSTANTINE AND PRIN-
CESS ANNE-MARIE
Life 57: 48-50 (col) Oct 9
'64
WEDDINGS--GREECE--PRINCE
JUAN CARLOS AND PRIN-
CESS SOPHIA
Nat Geog 124: 113 (col) July
'63
WEDDINGS, HINDU--SINGAPORE
Nat Geog 130: 292-3 (col)
Aug '66
WEDDINGS--INDIA--MAHARAJA

OF RAJPIPLA AND PRIN-
CESS OF JAISALMER
Nat Geog 127: 66-79 (col)
Jan '65
WEDDINGS--ISRAEL
Nat Geog 127: 407 (col) Mar
'65
WEDDINGS--ITALY
Life 55: 56-7 Aug 23 '63
WEDDINGS--JAPAN
Life 57: 110 Sept 11 '64
WEDDINGS--PORTUGAL
Nat Geog 128: 466-7 (col)
Oct '65
WEDDINGS--RUSSIA--ASTRO-
NAUTS VALENTINA TERESH-
KOVA AND ANDRIAN NIKO-
LAYEV
Life 55: 49 Nov 15 '63
WEDDINGS--SIKKIM--CROWN
PRINCE OF SIKKIM AND
HOPE COOKE
Nat Geog 124: 708-27 (col)
Nov '63
WEDDINGS--U. S. --GROVER
CLEVELAND AND FRANCES
FOLSOM, JUNE 2, 1886
Nat Geog 130: 634 Nov '66
WEDDINGS--U. S. --LUCI JOHN-
SON AND PATRICK NUGENT
Nat Geog 130: 636-7 (col)
Nov '66
WEDDINGS--U. S. --ALICE
ROOSEVELT AND NICHOLAS
LONGWORTH
Nat Geog 130: 637 Nov '66
WEIGHTLESSNESS
Nat Geog 127: 131 (col) Jan
'65
WELL, JACOB'S--NABLUS,
JORDAN
Nat Geog 126: 818 (col) Dec
'64
WELL, MARY'S--NAZARETH,
ISRAEL
Nat Geog 128: 834 (col) Dec
'65
WELLS, VILLAGE--BODRUM,
TURKEY
Nat Geog 124: 148 (col) July
'63
WEST GERMANY. See GER-
MANY

WESTMINSTER ABBEY
Nat Geog 130: 227 (col) Aug
'66
WESTMINSTER ABBEY (night
scene)
Nat Geog 128: 201-2 (col)
Aug '65
WESTMINSTER BRIDGE--LON-
DON
Nat Geog 129: 770-1 (col)
June '66
WHEAT--HARVESTING BY
ETHIOPIANS (winnowing with
wooden fork)
Nat Geog 127: 557 (col) Apr
'65
WHEEL, SPINNING. See
SPINNING-WHEEL
WHEELBARROWS, WOODEN,
1855
Nat Geog 127: 80 (col) Jan
'65
WHITE CLIFFS OF DOVER.
See DOVER, ENGLAND--
WHITE CLIFFS
WHITE HOUSE, 18TH AND 19TH
CENT.
Am Heritage 15: 33-39 Aug
'64
WHITE HOUSE, 1814 (after pil-
lage by British)
Nat Geog 126: 674 (col) Nov
'64
WHITE HOUSE, 1814 (burning
by British army)
Nat Geog 130: 602-3 (col)
Nov '66
WHITE HOUSE, 1829 (lithograph)
Nat Geog 127: 87 Jan '65
WHITE HOUSE--EAST ROOM
Nat Geog 130: 610, 624-5,
632-3 (col) Nov '66
WHITE HOUSE--EASTER-EGG
ROLL, 1963
Nat Geog 130: 640 (col) Nov
'66
WHITE HOUSE--INTERIOR
(diagram)
Life 65: 8-10 (col) July 5
'68
WHITE HOUSE--JACQUELINE
KENNEDY GARDEN

Nat Geog 130: 630 (col) Nov
'66
WHITE HOUSE--PRESIDENT KEN-
NEDY'S OFFICE
Nat Geog 125: 1A (col) Jan
'64; 313 (col) Mar '64
WHITE HOUSE--RED ROOM
Nat Geog 125: 352-3 (col)
Mar '64
WHITE HOUSE--STATE DINING
ROOM
Nat Geog 130: 626-7 (col)
Nov '66
WHITE HOUSE--VIEWS FROM
GEORGE WASHINGTON'S
ADMINISTRATION TO PRES-
ENT (1960's)
Nat Geog 130: 593-643 (col)
Nov '66
WHITE HOUSE--YELLOW OVAL
ROOM
Nat Geog 130: 630-1 (col)
Nov '66
WHITE SANDS OF NEW MEXICO
America's Wonderlands, p.
264-73 (col)
WILLIAM I, THE CONQUEROR,
KING OF ENGLAND--TOMB
--CAEN, FRANCE
Nat Geog 130: 214 (col) Aug
'66
WILLIAMSBURG, VIRGINIA
Nat Geog 134: 790-823 (col)
Dec '68
WILSON, WOODROW--ADDRESS-
ING JOINT SESSION OF CON-
GRESS
Nat Geog 128: 560-1 Oct '65
WINDJAMMERS. See SAILING
VESSELS
WINDMILLS, DUTCH
Travel 133: 35 (col) Mar '70
WINDMILLS (with sails)--
PORTUGAL
Nat Geog 128: 486 (col) Oct
'65
WINDMILLS--SPAIN
Nat Geog 127: 326-7 (col)
Mar '65
WINDOWS, STAINED-GLASS.
See STAINED-GLASS WIN-
DOWS

WINDWARD ISLANDS
Nat Geog 128: 755-801 (col)
Dec '65
WINDWARD ISLANDS--DOMINICA
(island)
Life 59: 46-59 (col) Aug 6 '65
WINTER HAVEN, FLA.
Nat Geog 124: 877 (col) Dec
'63
WINTER SCENES
Life 55: 94B-95 Oct 11 '63
WITCHES
Look 35: 40-44 (col) Aug 24
'71
WOMEN--RUSSIA
Nat Geog 129: 336-7 (col)
Mar '66
WOMEN AS ASTRONAUTS--
RUSSIA
Life 55: 42-3 Sept 13 '63
WOMEN CARRYING BASKETS
ON HEADS--BALI
Nat Geog 124: 436, 444-5
(col) Sept '63
WOMEN CARRYING BASKETS
ON HEADS--PORTUGAL
Nat Geog 128: 454 (col) Oct
'65
WOMEN CARRYING WATER
JUGS ON HEADS--CEYLON
Nat Geog 129: 497 (col) Apr
'66
WOMEN'S LIBERATION
Life 71: 40-42 (col), 43-51
Aug 21 '71
WOOD CARVINGS. See
CARVINGS, WOOD
WOODWORKING
Life 68: 74-78 June 12 '70
WORKSHOPS, COMMUNITY
SCIENCE--LOS ANGELES
Ebony 18: 66-8, 70-1, 72
Aug '63
WORLD WAR I--CAMPAIGNS
AND BATTLES
Life 56: 42-60B (col) Mar
13 '64
WORLD WAR I--CAMPAIGNS
AND BATTLES--MARNE,
FIRST BATTLE OF, 1914
Life 56: 47 Mar 13 '64
WORLD WAR I--CAMPAIGNS

AND BATTLES--MARNE,
SECOND BATTLE OF, 1918
Life 56: 58-9 (col) Mar 13
'64
WORLD WAR I--CAMPAIGNS
AND BATTLES--SOMME,
1916
Life 56: 48-9 Mar 13 '64
WORLD WAR I--CAMPAIGNS
AND BATTLES--VERDUN,
1916
Life 56: 54-5 (col) Mar 13
'64
WORLD WAR I--NAVAL OPERA-
TIONS. See also SUBMA-
RINE WARFARE
WORLD WAR I--NAVAL OPERA-
TIONS
Life 56: 58-80 Apr 17 '64
WORLD WAR I--NAVAL OPERA-
TIONS--JUTLAND, 1916
Life 56: 66-73 (col) Apr 17
'64
WORLD WAR II--CAMPAIGNS
AND BATTLES--NORMANDY
INVASION (D-Day, June 6,
1944)
Nat Geog 128: 188-9 Aug '65
Nat Geog 129: 68-9 Jan '66
WORLD WAR II--JAPANESE
SURRENDER SIGNED A-
BOARD U.S.S. MISSOURI,
SEPTEMBER 2, 1945
Life 57: 95 July 17 '64
Nat Geog 129: 85 (col) Jan
'66
WORLD'S FAIR, 1964-1965.
See NEW YORK (city)--
WORLD'S FAIR, 1964-1965
WORLD'S FAIR HOUSE
Look 28: 42 (col), 44 Feb 11
'64
WORLD'S FAIRS. See also
EXPO (e.g., EXPO '67--
MONTREAL)
WRESTLING
Ebony 20: 100-2, 104 June
'65
WRESTLING, SUMO--JAPAN
Life 57: 36-7 Sept 11 '64
Nat Geog 126: 481 (col) Oct
'64

WUPATKI NATIONAL MONU-
MENT--ARIZONA
America's Wonderlands, p.
330-1 (col)
WYOMING
Nat Geog 129: 554-93 (col)
Apr '66

X

X-RAYS
Look 28: 30-32, 35-37 June
30 '64

Y

YACHT RACING--AMERICA'S
CUP RACES
Life 68: 56-58 (col) May 15
'70
Sports Illus 32: 18-19 June
22 '70
Sports Illus 33: 16-20 (col)
Aug 17 '70
Life 69: 26-31 (col) Sept 4
'70
Sports Illus 33: 13-14 (col)
Sept 7 '70
Sports Illus 33: 13-15 (col)
Oct 5 '70
YACHT RACING--"BLOCK IS-
LAND"
Life 71: 38-43 (col) July 23
'71
YACHTS
Nat Geog 125: 855, 858-9,
864-70, 872-3, 877-9 (col)
June '64
Nat Geog 127: 234-5, 242-3
(col) Feb '65
Nat Geog 130: 482-3 (col)
Oct '66
Life 69: 70-73 (col) Sept 11
'70
YACHTS--"CHRISTINA" (owned
by Onassis)
Life 66: 74-75 (col) Jan 10
'69
YACHTS--"CONSTELLATION"
Life 56: 68-9 (col) June 12
'64

163 YACHTS

YACHTS--"FINISTERRE"
Nat Geog 128: 758-61, 770-1,
774, 777, 788-9 (col) Dec
'65
Nat Geog 130: 489, 491, 498-9,
507-8, 511, 533, 536 (col)
Oct '66
YACHTS--"GUINEVERE"
Nat Geog 126: 180-1 (col) Aug
'64
YALE UNIVERSITY
Holiday 37: 76-81 (col) May
'65
YALE UNIVERSITY--LIBRARIES
--BEINECKE RARE BOOK AND
MANUSCRIPT LIBRARY
Life 55: 97, 100 Nov 15 '63
YALTA--"BIG THREE" (Churchill,
Roosevelt, Stalin)
Nat Geog 128: 192 (col) Aug
'65
YAWLS. See YACHTS
YELLOWSTONE FALLS--YEL-
LOWSTONE NATIONAL PARK
Nat Geog 128: 894 (col) Dec
'65
YELLOWSTONE LAKE
America's Wonderlands, p.
86-7 (col)
YELLOWSTONE NATIONAL
PARK
Nat Geog 132: 636-661 (col)
Nov '67
America's Wonderlands, p.
16-17 (col)
America's Wonderlands, p.
68-9, 78-9 (col)
YEMEN
Nat Geog 125: 402-44 (col)
Mar '64
YOHO NATIONAL PARK--
BRITISH COLUMBIA
Nat Geog 130: 380-1 (col)
Sept '66
YORK, ENGLAND--STREETS--
SHAMBLES
Nat Geog 125: 638-9 (col)
May '64
YORKSHIRE, ENGLAND
Holiday 37: 84-91 (col) May
'65
YOSEMITE FALLS

America's Wonderlands, p.
338 (col)
YOSEMITE NATIONAL PARK
America's Wonderlands, p.
36-7 (col)
America's Wonderlands, p.
339-41, 346-51 (col)
Am Heritage 15: 19 (col) Oct
'64
Nat Geog 129: 662-3 (col)
May '66
YOSEMITE VALLEY
America's Wonderlands, p.
10-11 (col)
America's Wonderlands, p.
340-1 (col)
YOSEMITE VALLEY (paintings)
America's Wonderlands, p.
342-45 (col)
YOUNG, WHITNEY M.--FUN-
ERAL RITES
Ebony 26: 31 (col), 32-4, 36
May '71
YOUTH--ENGLAND--MODS
Life 57: 62, 64 Sept 18 '64
YOUTH--ENGLAND--ROCKERS
Life 57: 62, 64 Sept 18 '64
YUGOSLAVIA
Life 60: 52-61 (col) May 27
'66
Nat Geog 137: 590-633 (col)
May '70
YUKON RIVER
Life 70: 34-35 (col) Jan 8
'71

Z

ZAMBEZI RIVER--CAHORA-
BASSA GORGE--MOZAM-
BIQUE
Nat Geog 126: 222 (col) Aug
'64
ZAMBIA
Ebony 20: 27-9 (col), 30,
32, 34 Feb '65
Holiday 39: 39-47 (col) June
'66
ZEPPELINS. See AIRSHIPS
ZERMATT, SWITZERLAND
Nat Geog 128: 374-5 (col)

Sept '65
ZIGGURATS.   See TEMPLES
  (ziggurats)
ZION NATIONAL PARK
  America's Wonderlands, p.
    184, 186-7, 190, 196
    (col)